THE FABRICATION OF LOUIS XIV

The Fabrication of Louis XIV

PETER BURKE

YALE UNIVERSITY PRESS
NEW HAVEN AND LONDON · 1992

First published in paperback 1994.
Reprinted 1999, 2003

Set in Linotron Garamond by Best-set Typesetter Ltd., Hong Kong
Printed and bound in Great Britain by The Bath Press, Bath

Library of Congress Cataloging-in-Publication Data

Burke, Peter.
The fabrication of Louis XIV / by Peter Burke.
p. cm.
Includes bibliographical references and index.
ISBN 0-300-05153-0 (hbk.)
ISBN 0-300-05943-4 (pbk.)
1. Louis XIV, King of France, 1638-1715—Public opinion.
2. France—Kings and rulers—Public opinion. 3. Government publicity—France—History—17th century. 4. Public opinion—France—History—17th century. I. Title.
DC126.5.B87 1992
944'.033—dc20 91-11899
CIP

A catalogue record for this book is available from the British Library.

PARA MARIA LÚCIA

You see at once, that majesty is made out of the wig, the high-heeled shoes, and cloak . . . Thus do barbers and cobblers make the gods that we worship.

William Thackeray

CONTENTS

LIST OF ILLUSTRATIONS

PREFACE TO THE PAPERBACK EDITION

The opportunity has been taken to make a small number of minor corrections to the original text. In addition the following volumes, published since the book first appeared, should be noted: Ahrens, K. (1990) *H. Rigauds Staatsporträt Ludwigs XIV*, Worms; Couvreur, M. (1992) *J.-B. Lully: musique et dramaturgie au service du Prince*, Brussels; Holm, B. (1991) *Solkonge og Månekejser*, Copenhagen; Reckow, F. (ed.) (1992) *Die Inszenierung des Absolutismus*, Erlangen.

ACKNOWLEDGEMENTS

Over the years in which I have been working on Louis XIV I have received help and advice from many people. In particular, I should like to thank Derek Beales, Antonia Benedek, Robin Briggs, Ivan Gaskell, Serge Grozinski, Mark Jones, Margaret McGowan, Maj Nodermann, Betsy Rosasco, Allan Ellenius and the European Science Foundation group working on 'Iconography, Propaganda and Legitimation'. The Wissenschaftskolleg at Berlin offered me an ideal environment in which to draft the book in 1989–90, while another old regime was in the process of demolition. I should also like to thank the audiences who commented on various parts of this study in lecture form in Amsterdam, Berlin, Cambridge, Campinas, Ithaca, Jerusalem, London, Lund, Munich, New York, Oxford, Providence, Tokyo, Uppsala and York. For improvements to the penultimate version of the book I am most grateful to my wife, Maria Lúcia, to my Emmanuel colleague, Henry Phillips, and to Peter France, with whom I taught a course on 'Literature and Society in the Age of Louis XIV' at the University of Sussex in 1972. I should also like to thank the staff of Yale University Press, especially Sheila Lee, for their help and their attention to verbal and pictorial detail.

1. 'The most famous image of Louis'. *Portrait of Louis XIV* by Hyacinthe Rigaud, oil on canvas, *c.* 1700. Louvre, Paris.

I

INTRODUCING LOUIS XIV

Ces cordes qui attachent le respect à tel ou tel en particulier, sont des cordes de l'imagination.

Pascal, *Pensées*

LOUIS XIV, king of France, succeeded to the throne in 1643 at the age of four and reigned for seventy-two years, until his death in 1715. He is the protagonist of this book. Its purpose, however, is not to provide yet another biography of the sun-king. There are many such, some of them excellent.[1] This study, on the other hand, is concerned not so much with the man or the king as with his image. Not with his self-image, although this has been reconstructed.[2] Not with his image in the eyes of posterity, which has been the subject of other studies.[3] It is the public image of the king on which the book will focus, the place of Louis XIV in the collective imagination.

This study, like others by the author, is intended as a contribution to the history of communication, the history of the production, circulation and reception of symbolic forms.[4] It is concerned with contemporary representations of Louis XIV, with his image as it was portrayed in stone, bronze, paint and even wax. It also deals with his 'image' in the metaphorical sense of the view of the king projected by texts (poems, plays, histories), and by other media, such as ballets, operas, court rituals and other forms of spectacle.

The public image of Louis has been the subject of a substantial number of studies by specialists in art, literature, numismatics, and so on, not only in France but in the United States, Germany and elsewhere. Monographs have been written about the iconography of his portraits, about his equestrian statues, and about the medals representing the major events of his reign.[5] The theatrical décor of Versailles, which needs to be viewed as 'message' as well as 'setting', has been the subject of a large number of studies.[6] There is a general survey of the representations of Louis XIV in the French literature of his time, as well as a close analysis of particular literary portraits and the strategies of the writers.[7] There are monographs on the official historians of the reign, and on government propaganda during the War of the Spanish Succession.[8] Ballets, operas and other spectacles have been the object of many studies.[9] The idea of a sun-king has been traced back to the ancient world.[10] The relation between art and politics in this period, virtually passed over by Voltaire in his famous *Siècle de Louis XIV* (1751), has been studied with care in the last hundred years, notably by Augusta Dilke (a lady who had some reason for regarding herself as the model for George Eliot's Dorothea) and by Ernest Lavisse (whose position in the intellectual establishment of his day should have afforded him insights into the situation 300 years earlier).[11]

All the same, there exists no general account, so far as I know, of contemporary representations of Louis XIV. As a historian of royal rituals remarked a few years ago, 'The cult of the Sun King . . . has not yet received the comprehensive study it deserves.'[12] Even the unfavourable views of Louis, at home and abroad, have been examined only piecemeal.[13]

In this book my aim is to see the royal image as a whole. Since Louis himself and his ministers were concerned with the whole system of communication, we should follow their example and join together what has been put asunder by different academic disciplines.[14] My intention is to analyse the individual images of Louis XIV in order to reveal his public image in his time. However, this analysis is not made for its own sake. The book is intended as a case-study of the relations between art and power, and more specifically of the 'making of great men'.[15] Hence the comparisons and contrasts made in Chapter 12 are an essential part of the project.

Louis is an obvious choice for such a case-study for several reasons. The king himself and his advisers were very much concerned with the royal image. Apart from the time taken by rituals of different kinds, the king must have spent many hours sitting for his various portraits. The care with which these portraits were scrutinised is suggested by an annotation on a drawing of the king on campaign in Flanders: 'it is necessary to show the King lifting his cane, instead of leaning on it' [*il faut que le Roi ait la canne haute, au lieu de s'appuyer dessus*].[16] Louis was also extremely fortunate in the quality of the artists, writers and composers in his service. His image-making was a model for other monarchs (below, p. 170). It is also extremely well documented. Hundreds of paintings, medals and engravings of the king have survived. Versailles still exists in a form that allows us to imagine its appearance in the king's day. Most remarkable of all, a number of confidential documents have survived, from private letters to the minutes of committee meetings, allowing us to glimpse the intentions and the methods of the makers of the king's image in different media.[17]

The great value of looking at the media as a whole is that this viewpoint makes change more visible. It would have been strange indeed if representations of Louis had not changed in the course of a reign that lasted for seventy-two years (including fifty-four of so-called 'personal rule'). The earliest portraits show him as a baby in swaddling clothes; the last, as an old man in a wheelchair. Between these dates his profile on medals and coins changed a number of times. Over the years, new institutions were founded to glorify the king, artists and ministers came and went, victories were followed by defeats.

One of the advantages of a strictly chronological approach is to show whether changes in different media take place at the same time (suggesting a high degree of central control) or follow their own rhythm (suggesting that the arts were relatively autonomous). Unfortunately, it is not easy to be rigorously chronological. The king's image was under constant revision. For example, new medals were struck to celebrate, or to reinterpret, events that had taken place earlier in the reign. Thus we have to keep two time-scales in mind, what might be called 'medallic time' as well as the time of events.[18] The Grande Galerie at Versailles needs to be studied both as a representation of earlier events (1661, say, or 1672) and as a cultural event in itself, in the 1680s.

Hence it is scarcely surprising to find that although historians have often identified turning-points in the history of the royal image, they disagree about the dates. Some emphasise 1670 (or thereabouts), when the king stopped dancing in court ballets and comparisons with Alexander the Great became less frequent.[19] Others have made a case for 1674, as a time when the language of festivals began to change, and for 1677, as the apogee of the cult of the king.[20] The significance of 1679, when a mythological programme for the Grande Galerie was replaced by an historical one, has often been noted.[21] Other scholars prefer 1682–3, when the grand fêtes declined and the court settled at Versailles, or 1685–6, when statues of Louis were designed for public squares all over

France.[22] I hope to have assembled enough material in the pages that follow to allow readers to reach their own decisions.

It is clear that a study of this kind is a child of its time. As early as 1912, the 'glory enterprise' of Louis XIV reminded a French scholar of contemporary publicity.[23] The parallel is even more obvious in the late twentieth century, when heads of state from Richard Nixon to Margaret Thatcher have confided their image to advertising agencies.[24] In modern terms, my concern is with 'the selling of Louis XIV', with the packaging of the monarch, with ideology, propaganda and the manipulation of public opinion.

The danger of anachronism is obvious enough. I have no wish to present the panegyrists of Louis XIV as the exact equivalents of Saatchi and Saatchi. In fact, the reference to selling is not such an anachronistic idea as one might have thought, since the duc de Saint-Simon, who knew the king personally, once asserted that no one knew as well as Louis 'how to sell his words, his smile, even his glances'. All the same, seventeenth-century culture was very different from ours, and these differences are necessarily reflected in images of rulers (below, p. 198).

Another modern way of describing this book would be to call it a study of 'propaganda' for Louis XIV, of attempts to mould or manipulate 'public opinion', or a study of 'ideology' (in the sense of 'the ways in which meaning serves to sustain relations of domination').[25] All three concepts – propaganda, public opinion and ideology – were lacking in the seventeenth century. The Roman *Congregatio de propaganda fidei* was a committee for 'the propagation of the faith', not for 'propaganda' in the political sense of the term. The modern concept of propaganda goes back only as far as the late eighteenth century, when the techniques of persuasion used by supporters of the French Revolution were compared to Christian techniques of conversion.[26] Historians are always well advised to look for what is not present in a particular place and time, and these particular absences are surely significant.

However, they do not signify that seventeenth-century viewers and listeners were unaware of attempts at persuasion, or even manipulation. Given the stress on rhetoric in the education of elites at this time, they were probably more conscious of techniques of persuasion than most of us are today.[27] If the term propaganda is defined broadly enough, for example as 'the attempt to transmit social and political values', it is difficult to object to its use about the seventeenth century.[28] Yet there is a danger inherent in calling a study like this one an analysis of propaganda for Louis XIV. The danger is that of encouraging author and readers alike to interpret the poems, paintings and statues representing the king as if they were nothing but attempts to persuade, rather than (say) expressions of the king's power and the devotion of some at least of his subjects. As the ancient historian Paul Veyne recently suggested, some works of art are created to exist rather than to be seen. The reliefs on Trajan's Column, for example, are invisible from the ground.[29]

It might be more exact to say that the representations of Louis were commissioned to add to his glory. The writings of the period leave us in no doubt about the importance of reputation or glory for rulers and nobles alike. In a dictionary of the period, glory was distinguished from praise because 'praise is given by individuals, and glory by the world in general' [*la louange se donne par les particuliers, et la gloire par le général du monde*].[30] *Gloire* was a keyword of the time.[31] Its importance was emphasised in Louis' *Mémoires*.[32] Mademoiselle de Scudéry received a medal from the Académie Française for her essay on the subject.[33] Glory personified appeared in plays, in ballets and on public monuments. There was a Fountain of Glory in the gardens at Versailles.

It was also commonplace in the seventeenth century to observe that magnificence had a political function. It gave the king *éclat*. *Eclat* was another keyword of the time, with meanings ranging from a 'flash' of lightning to a 'clap' of thunder, but always referring to something unexpected and impressive. Magnificence was considered to be impressive, in the literal sense of leaving an 'impression' on the viewers like a stamp on a piece of wax.

Thus Colbert described the palace of the Louvre as impressing respect on the peoples of the world [*toute la structure imprime le respect dans l'esprit des peuples*].[34] The reference is probably to the peoples of Europe rather than to the French alone. As Louis in his turn (or more exactly, one of his secretaries) explained to the Dauphin, festivals please one's subjects and give foreigners 'an extremely useful impression of magnificence, power, wealth and grandeur' [*une impression très avantageuse de magnificence, de puissance, de richesse et de grandeur*].[35] Bossuet used similar language when he remarked in his treatise on politics that the court of a king is 'dazzling and magnificent' [*éclatante et magnifique*] in order 'to make the peoples respect him' [*pour imprimer aux peuples un certain respect*].[36] The social theorist Montesquieu, who grew up during Louis XIV's reign, made a similar point: 'The magnificence and splendour which surround kings form part of their power' [*Le faste et la splendeur qui environnent les rois font une partie de leur puissance*].[37]

Seventeenth-century views of the relation between art and power can be arranged along a spectrum. On one side there were the writers who appear to have taken the royal image at its face value, whether they were poets writing odes to the king, historians narrating his victories or scholars describing the decorations at Versailles. They described statues and other monuments as a means for 'the instruction of the people', encouraging them to love and obey their prince.[38]

On the other side, there were the observers, moralists and satirists who viewed the glorification of the king as essentially a trick played on the public by cynical and time-serving flatterers. A generation earlier, a writer in the service of Cardinal Richelieu had suggested that 'fine words' were a way for the prince to 'seduce' the people, 'to deceive them by appearances', 'to lead them by the nose'.[39] In similar fashion critics of Louis XIV made considerable use of the idea of another keyword of the time, *divertissement*, 'diversion' in the double sense of 'entertainment' and 'distraction'. They argued that festivals and spectacles – like ancient Roman circuses – were staged in order to distract the people from politics, or in La Bruyère's vivid phrase, to put them to sleep [*laisser le peuple s'endormir dans les fêtes, dans les spectacles*].[40]

Seventeenth-century concepts of this kind certainly illuminate the court of Louis XIV. We cannot afford to ignore them. On the other hand, a twentieth-century historian writing for a twentieth-century audience cannot ignore modern concepts either, whether they come from political science, social anthropology or social psychology. What interests me in historical writing is above all the task of mediating between two cultures, the past and the present, of setting up a dialogue between the two systems of concepts, of translating from one language into the other. 'Propaganda' is one useful modern concept, but there are others.

It might, for instance, be helpful to think of this book as a study of the myth of Louis XIV.[41] The phrase seems appropriate in the first instance because Louis was constantly being compared with the gods and heroes of classical mythology, such as Apollo and Hercules. However, the term 'myth' might be employed in a more ambitious – and more controversial – manner. We might define a myth as a story with a symbolic meaning (such as the triumph of good over evil) in which the characters, whether heroes or villains, are portrayed larger than life. A particular story stands at the point of intersection between archetype and conjuncture, in other words, between a heritage of images and specific individuals and events.[42]

A myth of Louis XIV existed in the sense that he was presented as omniscient [*informé de tout*], as invincible, godlike, and so on. He was the perfect prince, associated with the return of the golden age. Poets and historians described the king as a 'hero' and his reign, in the words of Racine, as 'an unbroken series of marvels'.[43] His public image was not simply favourable: it had a sacred quality.

Professional historians often use the term 'myth' to mean 'a story that is not true' (in contrast to their own stories, as they see them). My concern here, however, is not with the 'real' Louis as opposed to the mythical. On the contrary, what I am interested in is precisely the reality of the myth, in the sense of its effects on the world outside the media – on foreigners, on Louis' subjects, and not least on the king himself. The term 'myth' also has the advantage of reminding us that artists and writers did not confine themselves to static images of the king but tried to present a narrative, *l'histoire du roi* as they called it, in paintings, tapestries, medals and engravings as well as in official histories. To combine this sense of movement with the sense of spectacle, we might employ the concept of the 'theatre' of Louis XIV.

It is tempting to go still further and speak of the 'theatre state' of the sun-king. The concept of the 'theatre state' was launched a decade ago by the American anthropologist Clifford Geertz in his influential study of nineteenth-century Bali.[44] The phrase would surely have appealed to the contemporaries of Louis XIV, who were accustomed to see the world as a stage. Louis used the metaphor himself on occasion (below, pp. 8, 45). The duc de Saint-Simon used terms such as *comédie* and *scène* again and again in his descriptions of the court.[45] More than one of the sermons preached on the occasion of the king's death referred to his life as a grand 'spectacle'.[46]

Ritual in particular was viewed as a kind of drama, which had to be staged in order to encourage obedience. A German scholar, J. C. Lünig, who published a general study of public ceremonies in 1719–20, called it the *Theatrum Ceremoniale* and explained that such a theatre was necessary because 'Among common people . . . physical impressions have a greater impact than the language which addresses the intellect and reason.' Louis' memoirs make a similar point.[47] Analyses of the importance of ritual in contemporary politics proceed on similar assumptions.[48]

In the pages that follow, I shall make considerable use of a dramaturgical perspective, drawing in particular on the work of the social anthropologist Erving Goffman, who stressed the importance of performance or what he called the 'presentation of self' in everyday life, the art of 'impression management', the difference between the 'front' and 'back regions', the function of the setting and its 'properties', and so on.[49]

All these modern terms have their uses in the study of Louis XIV. Versailles, for example, was a setting for the king to display his power. Access to the monarch was carefully controlled and came in a series of stages. The visitors passed from outer to inner courtyards, climbed stairs, waited in anterooms, and so on before they were allowed a glimpse of the king.

The language of Goffman would scarcely have surprised such contemporaries of the king as La Rochefoucauld or Saint-Simon. Saint-Simon, for example, frequently uses the term *les derrières* to mean the area 'behind the scenes' at court. Louis is sometimes described as living his whole life in public. In a sense this was true: he was always being observed by someone, if only by his valets. However, some of his activities, political and non-political, were less public than others. His relationships with his mistresses, like his marriage to Madame de Maintenon, took place backstage. There are no references to these relationships in the official media, even if everyone knew about them. They have to be reconstructed from a variety of unofficial sources, including private letters and even the memoirs of one of the royal valets. (Unfortunately, his observations end in 1653, when he was disgraced.)[50]

Another term related to the theatre also has its uses for this study: the term 'representation'.[51] One of its principal meanings was 'performance'. The Jesuit Menestrier, an expert on emblems, spectacles and other symbolic forms, published a book on musical 'representations' in 1681. When he first saw the Duchess of Burgundy, aged eleven, Louis remarked to Madame de Maintenon that when the time came for her to play her part on the stage of the court, she would do it with grace and charm [*Quand il faudra un jour qu'elle représente, elle sera d'un air et d'une grâce à charmer*].[52] Another definition of representation in a dictionary of this period is that of an 'image which brings back absent objects to mind and to memory' [*Image qui nous remet en idée et en la mémoire les objets absents*].[53]

To 'represent' also meant 'to take the place of someone'. In this sense, ambassadors, provincial governors and magistrates all represented Louis. So did the queen, when the king was on campaign in 1672. So, in a somewhat different sense of the term 'representation', did the royal secretaries, who were authorised to imitate not only the king's signature but his handwriting as well.[54] Even Louis' love-letters were written by someone else (the marquis de Dangeau at one point). The royal memoirs contrast the letters written in the king's name with the ones written by the king himself – but ironically enough, this very passage, together with the rest of the famous *Mémoires*, was ghost-written by a secretary.[55]

Inanimate objects also represented the king, notably his coins, which bore his image and sometimes his name (the gold *louis* was worth about 15 livres). So did his coat of arms and his personal device, the sun. So did his bed, or the table laid for his meal, even if the king was absent. It was, for example, forbidden to wear one's hat in the room where the royal table was laid.[56]

Among the most important of the inanimate representations of the king were his portraits. The artist Charles Lebrun was described as representing in a portrait of the king 'all his high qualities, as if in a very clear mirror' [*il y représente comme dans une glace très pure toutes ses hautes qualités*].[57] These paintings were also treated as if they were substitutes for the king. The famous portrait of the king by Rigaud (see Figure 1), for example, took his place in the throne room at Versailles when the king was elsewhere. To turn one's back on the portrait was an offence, like turning one's back on the king.[58] Other portraits presided over festivals in the king's honour in the provinces.[59] They might even be carried in procession like the image of a saint.[60] The comparison is not as far-fetched as it may seem, since the king was sometimes represented as St Louis.

Louis might usefully be viewed as representing himself, in the sense that he consciously played the part of a king. His self-consciousness, and also the difference between front and back regions at court, can be illustrated from the memoirs of an Italian nobleman who visited the court in the 1670s. 'In private' [*en son particulier*], in other words in his chamber, surrounded by a small group of courtiers, Louis let his gravity slip, but if the door opened, 'he immediately changed his attitude and expression, as if he had to appear on stage' [*il compose aussitôt son attitude et prend une autre expression de figure, comme s'il devait paraître sur un théâtre*].[61]

Louis also took the place of God, as the court preacher Jacques-Bénigne Bossuet and other political theorists pointed out. Rulers were 'living images' [*images vivantes*] of God, 'representatives of God's majesty' [*les représentants de la majesté divine*].[62]

We might also say that Louis represented the state. A minor political writer of the time declared that a king was 'he who represents the whole commonwealth' [*celui qui représente toute la république*]. Louis is, of course,

notorious for the epigram attributed to him, 'the state is me' [*l'état c'est moi*]. If he did not say this, at least he allowed his secretaries to write in his name that 'when one has the state in view, one is working for oneself' [*quand on a l'état en vue, on travaille pour soi*].[63] Friends and enemies of the regime agreed with this identification. Bossuet declared that 'the whole state is in him' [*tout l'Etat est en lui*], while a Protestant pamphlet complained that 'the king has taken the place of the state' [*Le roi a pris la place de l'Etat*].[64]

However, to represent the state is not the same as to be identified with it. Bossuet reminded the king that he would die while his state ought to be immortal, and on his deathbed Louis is reported to have remarked, 'I am departing, but the state will remain after me' [*Je m'en vais, mais l'état demeurera après moi*].[65] It will not do to take the notorious epigram too literally.

An advantage of the term 'representation' is that it can refer not only to the visual or literary portraits of the king, the image projected in or by the media, but also to the image received, the image of Louis in the collective imagination or, as French historians and anthropologists say, the 'collective representations' of the time. The disadvantage of the phrase 'collective representations', at least in English, is that they may be taken to imply that everyone had an identical image of the king, or even that there is such a thing as a collective imagination, on the model of Jung's collective unconscious. To avoid these misunderstandings, a different title has been chosen.

I did not entitle this book the 'fabrication' of Louis XIV in order to deconstruct or demolish the king, as the revolutionaries demolished his statues in 1792. I would not deny that the king was actually rather good at his job, *le métier du roi*, as the royal memoirs call it. He did not take all the decisions that were attributed to him at the time, but he did take some of them. Louis was much more than a 'painted king', as some seventeenth-century writers describe a weak monarch. The term 'fabrication' is not intended to imply that Louis was artificial while other people are natural. In a sense, as Goffman shows with great skill, we all construct ourselves. Louis was unusual only in the assistance he received in the work of construction.

The title was chosen for two more positive reasons.[66] In the first place, 'fabrication' is a process-word and I should like to concentrate on the process of image-making, over more than half a century. Today, thanks to hindsight, Versailles and the memoirs of Saint-Simon, the image of the old king almost obliterates those of his younger incarnations. A term like 'fabrication', like the chronological organisation of this essay, may help communicate a sense of development. For the same reason, it may be useful to speak of the gradual 'mythologisation' of actual events, such as the crossing of the Rhine in 1672 or the Revocation of the Edict of Nantes in 1685, in their successive representations in different media. What we might call the 'authorised version' of the story of the king was subject to continual revision.

In the second place, the phrase 'the fabrication of Louis XIV' rather than 'the fabrication of an image' suggests the importance of the effects of the media on the world, the importance of what has been called 'the making of great men' or 'the symbolic construction of authority'.[67] The king was viewed by most of his contemporaries as a sacred figure. He was credited with the power to heal sufferers from skin disease by virtue of his 'royal touch'.[68] He was charismatic in every sense – the original sense of having been anointed with chrism, a symbol of divine grace, as well as the modern sense of a leader surrounded by an aura of authority. However, this charisma required constant renewal. This was the essential aim of the presentation of Louis, on his stage in Versailles, as it was the aim of the re-presentation of the king in the media of communication.

To sum up. The approach adopted in this book is the result of a certain disenchantment with two opposed views of rulers and their images, the 'cynical' and the 'innocent' views as one might call them. The cynical view, which had its supporters in the seventeenth century, as we have seen, would dismiss the image of the king as vanity, megalomania or narcissism, or explain it by the flattery of careerist courtiers, or present it, in the manner of modern communications analysis, as an example of the creation of 'pseudo-events' and the transformation of events which contradict the image into 'non-events' by media specialists who do not believe in what they are doing. According to this view, the official art and literature of the period should be interpreted as a form of 'ideology', defined as a series of tricks intended to manipulate readers, listeners and viewers.[69]

The rival view of image-making suggests that it was and should be taken seriously, in the sense that it responded to psychological needs. The term 'ideology', if it is used at all, is redefined to refer to the power of symbols over everyone, whether they are conscious of this power or not. According to this view, the praises of a king are homage to a role, not the flattery of an individual. A centralised state needs a symbol of centrality. The ruler and his court, often seen as an image of the cosmos, are a sacred or an 'exemplary' centre for the rest of the state.[70]

In his study of nineteenth-century Bali, Clifford Geertz has carried this line of argument still further. In Bali, according to Geertz, the state was not much concerned with government, 'which it pursued indifferently and hesitantly'. On the contrary, it pointed 'toward spectacle, toward ceremony, toward the public dramatization of the ruling obsessions of Balinese culture: social inequality and status pride. It was a theater state in which the kings and princes were the impresarios, the priests the directors, and the peasants the supporting cast, stage crew, and audience.' Hence Geertz criticises the cynical view as reductionist, and argues that royal ritual was not an instrument, still less a fraud, but an end in itself. 'Power served pomp, not pomp power.'[71]

Whether this is an accurate or inaccurate description of nineteenth-century Bali does not concern us here. What does concern us is Geertz's model of the relation between pomp and power. Is it or is it not relevant to early modern Europe, and in particular to France? The most obvious example of a 'theatre state' in seventeenth-century Europe is surely the papacy, which lacked military force (as Stalin once asked, How many divisions has the Pope?), but compensated for this with the splendour of its rituals and their settings.[72] In the case of Louis XIV, too, the model has its uses. Louis was regarded as a sacred ruler, and his court was viewed as a reflection of the cosmos. This was the point of the many comparisons between the king and Jupiter, Apollo and the sun.

From a comparative standpoint, one might say that each of the two rival models emphasises certain insights at the price of excluding others. The cynics are indeed reductionist, and refuse to consider myth, ritual and worship as responses to a psychological need. They assume too easily that ruling classes in the past were as cynical as they themselves are. On the other hand, the rival model assumes too easily that everyone in a given society believed in its myths. It has no place for concrete examples of falsification and manipulation.

In the case of Louis XIV, too, both approaches lead to insights. On one side, I would agree with the cynics that Louis was not as marvellous a monarch as he was painted. The evidence to be presented below makes it quite clear that the government tried to mislead the public on some occasions, from the sacking of Heidelberg (below, pp. 110, 125, 200, 206) to the defeat at Blenheim. It is also likely that some courtiers and some writers sang the praises of Louis for the sake of their own careers, hitching their wagons to the sun.

But it would be a mistake to make the ideas of sincerity and authenticity central to the analysis of the behaviour of either Louis or his courtiers. The modern cult of sincerity did not exist in the seventeenth century. Other values, like decorum, were considered more important.[73] In any case, the system did not run on flattery alone. It is unlikely that all the contributions to the king's glorification were cynical in the sense of being attempts to persuade others of something in which one does not believe oneself. It is possible, to say the least, that Louis himself, the court and the country believed in the idealised image of the king, as in the virtues of the royal touch (cf. Chapter 11). Viewed out of context, the image of Louis XIV as a sacred, invincible monarch may well appear to be a case of megalomania. However, we have to learn to see it in context as a collective creation and – to some extent at least – as a response to demand, even if the public were not completely aware of what they wanted. The processes by which images sustain power are all the more powerful for being partially unconscious.

Both models, then, have their uses. It might be argued that the tension between them is also a fruitful one. If it is possible to resolve the oppositions and achieve a synthesis, it might be along the following lines. The king and his advisers were well aware of the methods by which people can be manipulated by symbols. After all, most of them had been trained in the art of rhetoric. However, the aims in the service of which they manipulated others were of course chosen from the repertoire offered by the culture of their time. The aims as well as the methods are part of history, and part of the story told in this book.

In the following chapters, I attempt to combine a chronological approach with an analytic one. A narrative account of the fabrication of the king over more than seven decades is sandwiched between thematic chapters discussing the media of the period and the reception of the messages at home and abroad. To conclude the analysis, I try to stand back and view Louis from a distance, comparing and contrasting his public image with that of other seventeenth-century monarchs and placing it in the history of images of rulers over the long term.

The goal of this study might be summed up in a formula derived from the analysts of communication in our time, as the attempt to discover who was saying what about Louis to whom, through what channels and codes, in what settings, with what intentions, and with what effects.[74] The next chapter will be concerned with the channels and codes, in other words with the media of persuasion.

2. 'The young Louis'. *Jean Warin Presenting His Medal to the Infant Louis*, anonymous painting, *c.* 1648. Musée de la Monnaie, Paris

II

PERSUASION

C'est un grand art que de savoir bien louer.

Bouhours

THIS CHAPTER offers a brief description, or better, perhaps, a collage of the images of Louis XIV, emphasising recurrent themes, motifs and commonplaces. However – as theorists of communication often remark – it is impossible to separate the message from the medium in which it is presented. Literary critics make a similar point about the impossibility of separating the content from the form and the need for awareness of genres and their conventions. Hence the composite portrait of the king is preceded by a discussion of media and genres.

Media

Since the famous essay on the Laocoön by the German critic Lessing (1766), critics have tended to emphasise the specific characteristics of each artistic medium. In the age of Louis XIV, however, as in that of the Renaissance, there was more stress on parallels between the arts, from poetry to painting.[1] Scenes from the life of the king were presented in similar ways in different media. Equestrian portraits and statues echoed each other, medals were reproduced on bas-reliefs, and eulogies of the king were written in the form of descriptions of paintings, notably Félibien's *Portrait du roi* (1663), which purports to describe a painting by Lebrun.[2]

In this array of media, it is difficult to decide whether the visual images illustrated the texts or the other way round. The important point is surely that they influenced and reinforced one another. The figure of Victory, for example, appears not only on medals, statues and paintings, but in plays such as Corneille's *Toison d'Or* (1660). The temporary triumphal arches erected for royal entries and the arches in stone constructed in Paris and elsewhere mirrored each other. The sculptured reliefs around the statue of Louis on the Place des Victoires imitated some of the medals of the reign, but a medal was also struck to commemorate the inauguration of the statue. Medals and monuments were engraved. There were many representations of representations of the king and his actions.

Visual images of Louis were available in paint, bronze, stone, tapestry (or more rarely in pastel, enamel, wood, terracotta and even wax). They range from childhood (Figure 2), to the dignified old age of the famous portrait by Hyacinthe Rigaud (see Figure 1). The sheer number of statues and painted portraits of the king, of which more than 300 have survived, was remarkable by the standards of the time.[3] So was the number of engravings of the king, of which nearly 700 can still be found in the Bibliothèque Nationale. So was the colossal scale of some of the projects, such as the standing statue of Louis on the Place des Victoires, or the equestrian statue for the Place Louis-le-Grand, so huge that twenty men could sit down to lunch inside the horse – and in fact did so while the statue was being installed.

Images of the king were sometimes grouped to form a narrative. Unusual for the period was the number of representations of Louis in serial form. A famous series of paintings by Lebrun, known as 'the history of the king' [*l'histoire du roi*], represented major events of the reign up to the 1670s. This 'narratio', as rhetoricians would call it, was reproduced in the form of tapestries, and it was engraved. The medals struck to commemorate the events of the reign (over 300 of them, again an unusually high number) were engraved and the engravings published as the 'medallic history' of the king. The so-called 'royal almanacs' had engraved frontispieces representing a different event each year, and these too were described on occasion as 'the history of the king'.

The importance of media that could be reproduced mechanically deserves emphasis. Reproductions magnified the king's visibility. Medals, which were relatively expensive, might be struck in hundreds of copies. 'Prints', on the other hand (woodcuts, etchings, copperplates, steel engravings, and even mezzotints), were cheap. They were reproduced in thousands of copies and could therefore make a major contribution to spreading views of Louis as well as news about him.[4]

The royal image was also constructed out of words, oral and written, in prose and verse, French and Latin. The oral media included sermons and speeches (to the provincial Estates, for example, or by ambassadors abroad). Poems in praise of the king were continually being produced. Histories of the reign were written, circulated and even published in the lifetime of the king. Periodicals, notably the *Gazette de France*, published twice a week, and the *Mercure Galant*, published every month, devoted considerable space to the king's actions.[5] The Latin inscriptions for monuments and medals were composed with care by leading writers, including Racine. They were an art-form in themselves, combining brevity with dignity. These inscriptions made a considerable contribution to the effectiveness of images, since they instructed viewers how to interpret what they saw.

There were also multi-media events in which words, images, actions and music formed a whole. Plays by Molière or Racine were frequently performed as part of an evening's entertainment, which also included a ballet. Indeed, in 1670 the *Gazette* referred to a performance of *Le bourgeois gentilhomme* as a ballet 'accompanied by a comedy'. The *ballet de cour* was not a ballet in the modern sense but something more like a masque, in other words, an episodic form of dramatic entertainment in which poets such as Isaac Benserade, composers, choreographers and artists all collaborated.[6] In the 1670s and 1680s, Jean-Baptiste Lully and Philippe Quinault managed to replace the ballet by a more unified form of musical play, the opera. The lyrics of ballets and operas frequently introduced complimentary references to the actions of the king, especially in the prologues.[7] Plays, ballets and operas were often embedded in a larger festival, which might in turn be planned to glorify a particular event, as the 'diversions' of Versailles in 1674, for example, commemorated the capture of the province of Franche-Comté.[8]

Extraordinary (in other words, non-recurrent) rituals such as the king's anointing in 1654 or his wedding in 1660, and recurrent rituals such as touching the sick in order to cure them or receiving foreign ambassadors, might also be regarded as multi-media events, which presented the 'living image' of the king.[9] So indeed might the everyday actions of the king – getting up, taking meals, going to bed – actions so highly ritualised that they may be regarded as mini-dramas.

The setting for these rituals was usually a palace: the Louvre, Saint-Germain, Fontainebleau and, increasingly, Versailles. Versailles in particular might be regarded as a permanent exhibition of images of the king.[10] Louis saw himself everywhere, even on the ceiling. When the

3. 'The palace of the Sun King'. Cour de marbre, Versailles

clock installed in 1706 struck the hours, a statue of Louis appeared and Fame descended to crown him with laurel.

A palace is more than the sum of its parts. It is a symbol of its owner, an extension of his personality, a means for his self-presentation (Figure 3). As we shall see (p. 67), Colbert criticised designs for the Louvre by the Italian sculptor-architect Gianlorenzo Bernini on the grounds that they were inconvenient and impractical, but even Colbert was concerned to have 'a façade worthy of the prince'.[11] Versailles in particular was an image of the ruler who supervised its construction with such loving care. It was not only the setting for performances, it was itself the subject of performances such as Lully's *Grotte de Versailles* (1668), *Les fontaines de Versailles* (1683) by Lalande and Morel, and *Le canal de Versailles* (1687) by Philidor. Engravings of Versailles were officially published and distributed to increase the glory of the king.

Genres

Images are not as easy to read as they seem, at least when the cultural distance between the maker and the viewer is as great as that which separates us from the seventeenth century. To bridge this gap it is only prudent to pay considerable attention to contemporary descriptions of these images. Some may be found in contemporary guides to Versailles, which like the inscriptions on monuments and medals, were designed to shape the perceptions of the viewers.[12] As we have seen, descriptions of royal portraits were made by poets and historians.

In order not to misinterpret the images of Louis, we need to take into account not only the media, but also the different genres and their functions. Each genre had its own conventions or formulae. The audience, or part of it, were familiar with these conventions, which shaped their expectations and interpretations. Unlike post-romantic viewers and listeners, who reject the cliché as an offence against spontaneity, the seventeenth-century public seems to have had no objection to commonplaces and formulae.[13]

As for the function of the image, it was not, generally speaking, to provide a recognisable copy of the king's features or a cool description of his actions. On the contrary, the aim was to celebrate Louis, to glorify him, in other words to persuade viewers, listeners and readers of his greatness. To do this, artists and writers drew on a long tradition of triumphal forms.

The royal entry into cities, for example, generally followed the model of a Roman triumph, and the account of the entry of Louis into Paris with his queen in 1660 was indeed entitled their *entrée triomphante*[14] (Figure 4). As in other royal entries into cities, the couple passed through a series of temporary triumphal arches, which marked the nature of the occasion. Permanent triumphal arches were also constructed in Paris during the reign of Louis XIV, at the Porte St Denis, the Porte St Antoine and the Porte St Martin, as well as in provincial towns from Lille to Montpellier.

Another triumphal form was the equestrian statue, again an ancient Roman genre, and one that stamped the central spaces of the city with the image of the ruler. The conventions for these equestrian monuments were fairly strict. The horseman was generally represented in Roman armour. The horse generally trotted. Under its feet there might be some figure representing the defeat of the forces of evil or disorder.

A few portraits of Louis showed him in a relatively informal way, in his own clothes, hunting, sitting in an armchair or even playing billiards.[15] It is likely, however, that these portraits were made for private rather than public display. Most paintings of the king conformed to the genre known to art historians as the 'state portrait', constructed

4. *A Temporary Triumphal Arch Set Up in the Marché Neuf*, engraving from *Entrée Triomphante . . .*, 1660. British Library, London

5. 'Louis enthroned'. *Portrait of Louis XIV as Protector of the Academy of Painting and Sculpture* by Henri Testelin, oil on canvas, 1666–8. Château de Versailles

according to the 'rhetoric of the image' developed during the Renaissance for the portrayal of important people. In these state portraits the sitter is generally presented life-size or larger than life, standing or seated on a throne (Figure 5). His eye-level is higher than that of the viewer, to emphasise his superior status. Decorum does not allow the sitter to be shown in everyday clothes. He wears armour to symbolise valour, or rich clothes as a sign of high status, and he is surrounded by objects associated with power and magnificence – classical columns, velvet curtains, and so on.[16] His posture and expression communicate dignity.

Genre is equally important in the case of poetry, and somewhat more obvious. The rules for the different genres were summarised in formal treatises and in the *Art poétique* (1674), an essay in verse by one of the major poets of the reign, Nicolas Despréaux, better known as Boileau. Louis does not seem to have been the hero of an epic poem, a fact that probably reflects a loss of confidence in the genre rather than the monarch. Jean Chapelain, a poet who advised the government on the literary glorification of the king, argued against the epic on the grounds that epics necessarily included 'fictions' (he was doubtless thinking of the role of the gods in Homer and Virgil) which might harm the king's reputation by making the reader sceptical of his actual achievements.[17] However, a 'heroic poem' in Latin was written on the king's equestrian skills, and Louis was frequently celebrated in sonnets, madrigals and odes.[18]

An ode may be defined as a lyric poem in stanzas combining long and short lines.[19] Its function – like that of the equestrian statue or state portrait – was essentially celebratory. The ancient Greek poet Pindar had written odes in praise of the winners in chariot races. A whole army of poets praised the king's victories in similar fashion. Racine celebrated the king's recovery from illness in 1663 with an ode on his convalescence, describing the 'perfidy' of the 'insolent malady' which had dared threaten the king, comparing Louis to the sun, and his reign to the golden age.[20] Many echoes of this ode can be heard in the minor poets of the reign, especially in 1687, when the king was recovering from a serious operation.[21]

In prose as well as poetry the image of the king was embedded in triumphalist rhetoric. The panegyric or oration in praise of a particular individual on various occasions (from birthdays to funerals) was a favoured genre in seventeenth-century France as in classical antiquity. Regular competitions were held for the best panegyric on Louis in French, while the Jesuits were well known for their skill in composing these orations in Latin. Jacques La Beaune's Latin 'panegyric to the most munificent Louis the Great, father and patron of the liberal arts' (1684) is a good example of the genre, an oration delivered in the Jesuit college in Paris before being sent to the printer[22] (Figure 6).

Sermons were a form of oration much appreciated at the time. Preaching was an art, of which the masters (besides Bossuet) were Valentin-Esprit Fléchier, the Jesuits Louis Bourdaloue (who gave ten cycles of Lent and Advent sermons at court between 1672 and 1693) and Charles de La Rue, and the Oratorian Jean-Baptiste Massillon, who preached with great success at Versailles at the end of the reign.[23] Fléchier's funeral oration for Marshal Turenne and Bourdaloue's for Condé were considered classics of their genre.[24] Court preachers (chosen by the king himself) compared the French monarchy to the sacred monarchy of Saul and David described in the Old Testament and eulogised Louis long before his funeral. Bossuet's sermon on the death of the queen (1683) included many references to the virtues of the king. So did his sermon on the death of the Chancellor, Michel Le Tellier (1686), and many other sermons at the time of the Revocation of the Edict of Nantes (below, pp. 102ff).[25] Yet preachers were allowed to remind the king of his duties, and to criticise his actions (in vague and general terms), especially if they were preaching in Lent.[26]

History too has to be regarded as a literary genre. A work of history was expected to include a number of literary set-pieces such as the 'character' or moral portrait of a ruler, minister or commander, the vivid narrative of a battle, and the presentation of debates through speeches attributed to leading participants (but frequently invented by the historian).[27] Hence there was nothing odd about the appointment of Boileau and Racine as historiographers royal.

Styles

For narrative painting and state portraits, the appropriate style was the so-called 'grand' or 'magnificent' manner [*la grande manière, la manière magnifique*].[28] This style involved idealisation. As Bernini remarked while he was working on a bust of the king, 'The secret in portraits is to exaggerate what is fine, add a touch of grandeur, and diminish what is ugly or petty or even suppress it when this is possible without flattery' [*Le secret dans les portraits est d'augmenter le beau et donner du grand, diminuer ce qui est laid ou petit, ou le supprimer quand cela se peut sans intérêt de la complaisance*].[29]

6. *Louis as Protector of Arts*, from La Beaune, *Panegyricus*, 1684. British Library, London

There were important variations of style within this grand manner: on one side, the style art historians generally call 'baroque' and associate with Bernini, characterised by movement – rearing horses, theatrical gestures, and so on; on the other, the ideal of 'classicism' associated with Poussin, characterised by restrained gestures, a calm dignity, and a greater concern for what was true, natural or at any rate plausible [*le vrai, le naturel, le vraisemblable*], at least in details. Louis took his artists Lebrun and van de Meulen with him on campaign so that they would represent his conquests with accuracy.

Like the epic, the ode was one of the genres for which the so-called 'high style' was required, the equivalent of the grand manner in painting. The aim was the expression of elevated thoughts in an elevated language, employing euphemism or periphrasis to avoid technical terms or references to ordinary life. The incompatibility between the 'barbarous' place-names of Flanders and Holland and the high style was a problem for the poets of the time.[30] Boileau's solution to this and other problems was to discuss them in his poems themselves. He wrote semi-formal epistles as well as formal odes. He also introduced an ironic note, which broke with the tradition of the panegyric and has sometimes been interpreted as subversive, although it may be no more than an attempt to adapt an ancient genre to the requirements of the modern world.[31]

Sermons too, at least those preached before the king, were supposed to be in the high style. The great preacher Massillon was criticised by his rival Bossuet for falling short of the sublime. As for history, it was the prose equivalent of the epic. Historians were meant to celebrate heroic actions and so to write in the high style required by the 'dignity' of their subject. Racine was only using the standard vocabulary of his time when he described the reign of Louis as 'a continuous series of marvels' in which one 'miracle' followed hard on the heels of another [*un enchaînement continuel de faits merveilleux . . . le miracle suit de près un autre miracle*].[32]

Whether in verse (like some of the journals of the 1660s) or in prose, the *Gazette*, on the other hand, employed a 'low' style close to ordinary language and did not avoid technical terms or foreign place-names. The style of the *Gazette* tended to be plain, short on adjectives and other embellishments, but long on information. The tone was cool (except in the case of special issues commemorating victories, etc.), thus suggesting impartiality and so reliability. The rhetoric of the *Gazette* took the form of the apparent rejection of rhetoric.

Like the poets, historians and writers of inscriptions were experts in euphemism, for political and aesthetic reasons alike. The capture of Strasbourg by French troops in 1681 was commemorated by a medal bearing the legend 'Strasbourg Received' [ARGENTORATUM RECEPTUM]. The legend on the medal celebrating the bombardment of Algiers in 1683 was 'Algiers struck by lightning' [ALGERIA FULMINATA], implying an elegant classical reference to Louis as Jupiter, and at the same time presenting the action of the French warships as a force of nature.

It is obvious enough that hyperbole is a rhetorical figure, which constantly appears in this literature of praise. Another is synecdoche, Louis being the part that stands for the whole, with the achievements of ministers, generals and even armies being attributed to the king in person (cf. p. 74). Ezechiel Spanheim, combining the experience of a diplomat at Versailles with that of an ex-professor of rhetoric at Geneva, analysed the techniques of Louis' panegyrists. 'They present him as the sole author and the inspiration of all the successes of his reign, attributing them entirely to his wisdom, his prudence, his courage and his direction' [*On s'attache à le faire seul l'auteur et le mobile de tous les heureux succès de son règne, à les attribuer uniquement à ses conseils, à sa prudence, à sa valeur et à sa conduite*].[33]

Another recurrent figure of rhetoric is metaphor, as in the classic comparison of the king to the sun. This particular metaphor is worked out in such detail, in the decorations of Versailles and elsewhere, that we may view it as a form of architectural allegory.[34]

Allegory

The language of allegory was well known at this time, at least among the elites. Classical gods, goddesses and heroes were associated with moral qualities – Mars with valour, Minerva with wisdom, Hercules with strength, and so on. Victory took the form of a winged woman, Abundance that of a woman with a cornucopia. Kingdoms such as France and Spain (Figure 7), and cities such as Paris and Besançon, were also represented in the form of women (sometimes wearing regional costume), while rivers took the form of old men.[35] The allegories were not always easy to decode, even for contemporaries, but the interest in literary and pictorial enigmas was part of the taste of the time.[36]

Louis was often represented together with allegorical figures of this kind. The Grande Galerie at Versailles, for example, is populated by

7. *Allegory of the Peace of the Pyrenees* by Theodor van Thulden, oil on canvas, *c.* 1659. Louvre, Paris

personifications, some of them classical, like Neptune or Victory, others modern, like the Académie Française, in the form of a woman with a caduceus, or Holland, in the form of a woman sitting on a lion, which holds seven arrows to symbolise the seven provinces. Thanks to the language of allegory, the artist was able to represent events with little visible surface, such as the king's decision to rule in person.

The king himself was sometimes depicted indirectly or allegorically. Jean Nocret's portrait of the royal family (Figure 8), for example, is a 'mythological portrait' or *portrait historié* in the Renaissance tradition of identifying individuals with particular gods or heroes.[37] The cycles of mythological paintings in the Louvre, Versailles, the Tuileries and other royal palaces were also designed to be read allegorically, with Louis in the place of Apollo (Figure 9), Jupiter, Hercules or Neptune. A competition organised in 1663 for the best painting of the heroic actions of the king demanded that they be 'represented under the form of Danaë, adjusting it to the story of the recovery of Dunkirk'.[38] The famous Fountain of Latona at Versailles, which represents the peasants who mocked Apollo's mother being turned into frogs, has been interpreted with some plausibility as a reference to the Fronde (see p. 40).[39]

Representations of the past were another kind of allegory. They should often be understood as indirect references to the present (and seventeenth-century viewers were trained to do this). When Louis asked Charles Lebrun to paint scenes from the life of Alexander the Great, he was not only expressing admiration for Alexander but identifying with him (Figure 10). Louis' subjects too were expected to identify him with Alexander. Racine's tragedy *Alexandre le Grand*, the literary equivalent of Lebrun's cycle of paintings, was dedicated to the king on its publication in 1666.[40]

Louis XIV was also identified with his predecessor and namesake St Louis (otherwise known as Louis IX, king of France from 1226 to 1270). He was represented in painting and in sculpture as St Louis.[41] He was advised to follow in the footsteps of his predecessor. The scholar Charles Du Cange compared the two monarchs in his dedication to the king of an edition of a thirteenth-century biography of St Louis. 25 August, the feast of St Louis, was celebrated in increasingly elaborate style during the reign. The custom grew up of including in the celebrations a panegyric, not only of Louis IX but of Louis XIV as well.[42]

Louis was also identified with Clovis, the first Christian king of France, and with Charlemagne. Although the king himself was not

8. *The Family of Louis XIV* by Jean Nocret, oil on canvas, 1670. Château de Versailles

the hero of an epic, such poems as *Clovis* (1657) by Jean Desmarets (dedicated to the king) and the epics on *Charlemagne* (1664, 1666) by Louis Le Laboureur and Nicholas Courtin respectively, may be viewed as descriptions of his past (or future) deeds at one remove. He was even identified with Christ, for example, as the Good Shepherd (Figure 11).

The historical novels of the period were not infrequently *romans à clef*, in which the hidden meaning was only intelligible to connoisseurs of the world of the court. *Clélie* (1654–61), for example, by Mlle de Scudéry, celebrated Louis as 'Alcandre', while Bussy Rabutin's *Histoire amoureuse des Gaules* (1665) was a transparent allegory of intrigues at court.[43] Even works of scholarship might have an allegorical meaning. It was no accident that the abbé Jean-Baptiste Du Bos, who was attached to the Ministry of Foreign Affairs, published a history of the League of Cambrai against Venice, at just the time that there was a league of European powers against France.[44]

9. 'Louis as Apollo'. *Triumph of Louis XIV* by Joseph Werner, gouache, 1664. Château de Versailles

10. 'Louis as Alexander the Great'. *The Family of Darius at the Feet of Alexander* by Charles Lebrun, oil on canvas, *c.* 1660. Château de Versailles

11. *Louis XIV as the Good Shepherd*, probably by Pierre Paul Sevin, on vellum

12. 'The ill-fated monument by Bernini'. *Model for an Equestrian Monument to Louis XIV* by Gianlorenzo Bernini, *c.* 1670. Galleria Borghese, Rome

The Portrait of the King

At this point it may be possible to create our collage of the visual and literary images of Louis XIV, their assembly into a composite portrait.[45] The king is generally portrayed in armour, Roman or medieval, or in the 'royal mantle' decorated with fleurs de lis and fringed with ermine. He combines these archaic costumes with a late seventeenth-century wig. In his hand is an orb, a sceptre or a baton, all symbols of command. His figure is usually impassive and immobile, and this pose too symbolises power. It is probably what contemporaries are referring to when they comment on the 'air' of grandeur or majesty in royal portraits.[46]

As for the expression on the royal visage, it tends to vary between ardent courage and a dignified affability. A smile was apparently considered inappropriate for a king of France. Indeed, it has been suggested that it was the indecorous smile on the face of the equestrian statue by Bernini (Figure 12), which led to its rejection, or more exactly – since it would have been a pity to waste the marble – to its recycling into an ancient Roman hero.[47]

It may be useful to focus on a single image. An obvious example is the famous state portrait by Rigaud (see Figure 1), all the more interesting because it is known that Louis particularly liked this work and ordered copies of it.[48] The classical column (with an allegorical figure of justice at the base) and the velvet curtain are reminiscent of the Renaissance state portrait. However, the painting is less traditional than it may appear. It is a skilful compromise between opposing trends.

In the first place, it combines idealisation with realistic details. One recent historian has described the portrait as 'true to life even to the tired eyes and the sunken mouth after the 1685 extraction of teeth in the upper jaw'. Augustus was always represented at the age he was when he took over power, and Queen Elizabeth I was portrayed with what art historians call 'the mask of youth', but Louis was allowed to age discreetly in his portraits. Yet Rigaud has placed this old head on a young body. Another historian has remarked on the elegant legs and the 'ballet pose' of the feet, a reminder of the king's dancing days.[49]

The portrait also achieves a certain equilibrium between formality and informality. It represents the king in his coronation robes, surrounded by his regalia, crown, sword and sceptre, the symbols of his power. Yet Louis also wanted to be a modern monarch by the standards of the early eighteenth century, the first gentleman of his kingdom, and there is a studied informality in the way in which he holds his sceptre, the point down, as if it were the cane he usually carried in public (Figure 18). Rigaud may be alluding to Van Dyck's informal portrait of Charles I at the hunt, in which Charles (who also liked to carry a cane) makes a similar gesture (Figure 13).[50] Louis wears the medieval sword of justice at his side, but like an ordinary sword rather than a sacred object. Like Boileau, Rigaud presents the king as carrying his dignity lightly and adapts the classical–Renaissance tradition to the modern world.

Rigaud's portrait suggests that the artists of the period had little to learn from Goffman about the importance of what he calls 'front' in the presentation of an individual.[51] Louis is usually portrayed surrounded by a whole cluster of dignified or dignity-bestowing properties such as orbs, sceptres, swords, thunderbolts, chariots and various kinds of military trophy. Goddesses such as Minerva and female personifications of Victory or Fame often stand or hover near the monarch, when they are not actually crowning him with laurel. Rivers such as the Rhine raise their hands in wonder at the king's exploits. The props also include various figures in attitudes of subordination, including defeated enemies, cowering captives, foreign ambassadors bowing to the king, and so on.

13. 'A model for the Rigaud portrait'. *Portrait of Charles I* by Anthony van Dyck, oil on canvas, *c.* 1635. Louvre, Paris

Monsters are trampled under foot – the python of rebellion, the Hydra of heresy, the three-headed Cerberus and the three-bodied Gerion (the latter two symbols of the triple alliance of Louis' enemies).

The literary representations of Louis have the advantage for the modern reader of making their meaning clear by the use of adjectives. As in ancient Assyria and imperial Rome, a standard set of epithets was applied to the monarch. One poet managed to squeeze fifty-eight adjectives – from *agréable* to *zelé* – into a single sonnet.[52] Louis was generally described as august, brilliant (like the sun), constant, enlightened, generous, glorious, handsome, heroic, illustrious, immortal, invincible, just, laborious, magnanimous, munificent, pious, triumphant, vigilant and wise. In a word, he was 'great', an adjective officially adopted in 1671.[53] LOUIS LE GRAND was often written in capital letters in the middle of a text in lower case.

The reader (or listener) was also informed that Louis was accessible to his subjects; that he was the father of his people; the protector of arts and letters, a field in which he showed sound judgement and 'delicate taste';[54] the most Catholic king; the tamer (or extinguisher) of heresy; the restorer of the laws; 'more feared than the thunder' [*plus craint que le tonnerre*];[55] 'the arbiter of peace and glory' [*l'Arbitre de la Paix et de la Gloire*];[56] the extender of the frontiers; the second founder of the state; 'the most perfect model for great kings' [*des grands rois le plus parfait modèle*];[57] 'our visible god' [*notre visible Dieu*]; and the most powerful monarch in the universe.[58]

The image of the king was also associated with the heroes of the past. He was described as a new Alexander (his favourite comparison, at least in the 1660s), a new Augustus (finding Paris brick and leaving it marble), a new Charlemagne, a new Clovis, a new Constantine, a new Justinian (codifying the law), a new St Louis, a new Solomon, a new Theodosius (destroying the heresy of the Protestants as the first Theodosius destroyed that of the Arians). Charles-Claude de Vertron, of the Academy of Arles, produced a collection of parallels between Louis and other princes who had been called 'great', from Cyrus of Persia to Henri IV of France.[59]

The necessity for keeping the possibility of allegory constantly in mind is one of the reasons for the remoteness of much of this literature from modern readers, who are likely to find personifications such as Victory, with her wings and her laurel, or Abundance, with her cornucopia, somewhat odd, if not absurd. Another difficulty is the change in attitudes to the high style, which sounds insufferably pompous to modern ears. Today, we are likely to perceive the doubling of adjectives, formerly a sign of the 'copiousness' of the good orator, as unnecessary redundancy, 'inflated rhetoric'. Indeed, for many of us, 'rhetoric', like 'formality' or 'ritual', has become a pejorative term: 'mere rhetoric'. As for the praise of important people, that sounds to our democratic ears like servility, like cringing. These shifts in mentalities, values and the 'horizon of expectations' form a major obstacle to understanding the art and literature of the age of Louis XIV. They encourage anachronistic judgements.

Given this cultural distance, it may be wise to adopt the strategy of anthropologists, specialists in understanding other cultures, in order to make the art, the ritual and the literature of the period intelligible to modern readers and viewers. The 'theatre state' of nineteenth-century Bali has already been described (p. 7). In some parts of Africa, among the southern Bantu for example, or in Mali, the tradition of the praise-poem or panegyric still flourishes, as it once did in ancient Rome and Renaissance Europe.[60] The concept of the praise-poem as a recurrent genre or of Boileau as a *griot* (the term for 'bard' in Mali), may help diminish our natural – or more exactly, cultural – resistance to the eulogies of Louis so common in seventeenth-century France. At the very least it should encourage us to make distinctions.

In the first place, a particular epithet like 'heroic' applied to Louis in a particular poem should not be taken out of context and treated as a lie invented by the writer to flatter the monarch. If one is writing an ode to the king or another form of panegyric, this is the kind of adjective one has to use. The idea of writing a panegyric was a normal one in the seventeenth century. The rhetoric of praise and blame (epideictic rhetoric, as it was called) was one of the three major divisions of oratory.

The flattering adjectives applied to the king might of course be laid on more or less thickly, and Boileau, for example, commented harshly on some of his colleagues for exceeding the appropriate dose. Louis himself objected on occasion. Racine has recorded the king's remark to him that 'I would praise you more, if you praised me less' [*Je vous louerois davantage, si vous ne me louiez tant*].

The idea of servility is not an anachronism. The problem is that of deciding when and where it applies, a problem made all the more acute by the fact some poets and courtiers were skilled in praising while appearing not to do so. This was the technique of Boileau, for example, in his famous *Discours au roi* (1665). Boileau claimed to be unable to sing the king's praises [*je sais peu louer*], and criticised the pompous and predictable verses of rival poets who compared the king to the sun or bored him with the narrative of his own exploits. It was also the technique of the historian Paul Pellisson, who explained his technique in a confidential memoir to Colbert: 'It is necessary to praise the king the whole time, but, so to say, without explicit praises' [*il faut louer le Roy partout, mais pour ainsi dire sans louange*].[61] We have returned to the rhetoric of rejecting rhetoric, appropriate to the age of classicism.

A final point, which needs to be borne in mind while reading this kind of literature, is that a panegyric was not necessarily pure praise. It was a tactful form of advice, at least on occasion, describing the prince not as he was but as one hoped he might be. Racine, for example, dedicating his *Alexandre le Grand* to the king, told him that 'history is full of young conquerors' and that much more unusual is the accession of a king who at the age of Alexander already behaves like Augustus [*qui à l'âge d'Alexandre ait fait paraître la conduite d'Auguste*]. Again, when La Fontaine sang the praises of Louis, which was not very often, it was for his peaceful exploits, not his military ones.[62]

Such advice was most freely given in the early years of the reign, which will be discussed in the following chapters.

LOUIS XIV TERRASSANT LA FRONDE
GROUPE COMMANDE EN 1654 A GILLES GUERIN

III
SUNRISE

La majesté règne dans ce visage
Où la douceur à la bonté se joint:
Mais, s'il est tel au levant de son âge,
En son midi, quel ne sera-t-il point?

Baudouin, *Le prince parfait*

CONCERN WITH the image of Louis began with his birth, which was celebrated all over France with bonfires and fireworks, bell-ringing and cannon, and the solemn chanting of the *Te Deum*, and commemorated by sermons, speeches and poems, among them Latin verses by the Italian philosopher Tommaso Campanella, exiled in France, in which he wrote of the baby as a kind of Messiah in whose time the golden age would return.[1]

Indeed, the conception of an heir to the throne and the first movement of the infant in the womb had already been a matter for celebration, a celebration all the more enthusiastic because by 1638 it had come to seem extremely unlikely that Anne of Austria and her husband Louis XIII would ever produce a child.[2] It was for this reason that the epithet of 'god-given' was applied to the boy, *Louis le Dieudonné*.

Less than five years later, the death of his father in 1643 brought young Louis back to the centre of the stage. His accession to the throne in 1643 was marked by a major change in his image. Louis had been shown like other children as a swaddled baby or in the robe commonly worn by boys below the age of seven. From 1643, he began to be represented wearing a royal mantle, with gold fleurs-de-lis on a blue ground, and also the collar of the Saint-Esprit, an order of chivalry founded in 1578 by his predecessor Henri III. At the age of five or six Louis was already shown sitting on a throne, holding a sceptre or a baton of command. He was sometimes represented in armour (modern or ancient Roman).

14. 'The symbolic defeat of rebellion'. *Louis XIV Crushing the Fronde* by Gilles Guérin, marble, 1654. Musée Condé, Chantilly

To paint a small child in armour may seem quaint or playful to a modern viewer. It is likely, however, that portraits took this form because armour symbolised the military prowess expected of kings, warlike virtues which could always be exercised at second hand, through generals and their armies. When the French defeated the Spaniards at the battle of Rocroi in 1643, an engraving of the time showed the king on his throne congratulating his general, the duc d'Enghien (Condé). The engraving is entitled 'les premières victoires de Louis XIV'.[3]

Ritual was another means for the presentation of the young king to his people. He made a state entry into Paris in 1643 to celebrate his accession. In the same year he held his first *lit de justice* (literally a 'bed of justice'), in other words, a formal meeting with the supreme court of the kingdom, the Parlement of Paris, in order to alter the provisions of his father's will and allow his mother Anne of Austria – guided by Cardinal Mazarin – to rule France as Regent.[4]

The Parlement was not a parliament in the English sense of a representative assembly. All the same, its magistrates saw themselves as the guardians of what they called the 'fundamental laws' of the kingdom. In 1648, at much the same time that the English Parliament was putting Charles I on trial, the Parlement of Paris played a leading part in a political movement known as the Fronde. This movement was viewed by its participants (nobles and magistrates) as a protest against the destruction of the ancient French constitution by Cardinals Richelieu and Mazarin, while it was seen by the court as a rebellion against the monarch. The Fronde may be described as, among other things, a conflict between two conceptions of kingship, limited versus 'absolute'.[5]

According to the first view, the power of the king of France was limited by the so-called 'fundamental laws' of the kingdom, of which the Parlement of Paris was the guardian. According to the second view, prevalent at the court, the king had 'absolute power' [*pouvoir absolu*]. The phrase was usually defined negatively as power without limits [*sans contrôle, sans restriction, sans condition, sans réserve*].[6] Louis was considered an absolute monarch because he was above the laws of his kingdom, with the power to exempt individuals from their operation. However, he was not considered to be above the law of God, the law of nature or the law of nations. He was not expected to exercise complete control over the lives of his subjects.

The Fronde, which was defeated in 1652, had a considerable effect on the way in which the young king and his government was presented in public. For example, in 1654, a statue of Louis standing on a prostrate warrior (symbolising the Fronde) was placed in the courtyard of the Hôtel de Ville in Paris (Figure 14). In the same year, a ballet danced at court, *Pelée et Thétis*, represented Apollo (in other words, the king) destroying a python (another symbol for disorder).[7] A series of paintings in the king's apartments in the Louvre also celebrated the defeat of the Fronde. For example, an image of the goddess Juno striking the city of Troy with a thunderbolt was clearly intended to make the spectators think of Paris and the Queen Mother.[8]

The rituals of the *lits de justice* of the 1650s were yet another means by which the government tried to demonstrate the defeat of the Fronde, re-establish the idea of absolute monarchy and show the king as the representative of God on earth. As one of the leading parlementaires, Omer Talon, declared to the king – on his knees – on one of these occasions, 'Sire, the seat of Your Majesty represents to us the throne of the living God [*nous représente le trône du Dieu vivant*]. The estates of the realm offer you honour and respect as if to a visible divinity' [*comme à une divinité visible*].[9]

Similar points were made in the course of the king's coronation in 1654 and his state entry into Paris in 1660. The rituals were traditional ones, but precisely for this reason, relatively small variations would be perceived – by one section of the public, at least – as carrying a political message.

The coronation

Louis' coronation and anointing [*le sacre*] took place in 1654, having been delayed by the troubles of the Fronde. The ritual took place, as was customary, in the cathedral of Rheims, whose archbishop had the right to crown the new king (a right exercised in this case by his proxy, the Bishop of Soissons).[10] The ceremony included an oath sworn by the king, promising to maintain the privileges of his subjects, and the question to the congregation whether they accepted Louis as king or no. There followed the blessing of the royal insignia, including the so-called 'sword of Charlemagne', spurs and what the historian Denys Godefroy called 'the ring with which the said Lord marries the Kingdom' [*l'anneau duquel ledit Seigneur épouse le Royaume*].[11]

Then came the moment of consecration. The king's body was anointed with chrism, holy oil from the Holy Ampulla, the bottle said to have been brought from heaven by a dove when Clovis, the first Christian king of France, was baptised by St Rémy. The bishop placed the sceptre in the king's right hand, the 'hand of justice' in his left and the 'crown of Charlemagne' on his head. There followed the homage of the major noblemen of the kingdom, and the release of a number of birds into the air.

The ritual was watched by foreign ambassadors and (with more difficulty, from outside the cathedral) by a crowd of ordinary people. It was followed by other celebrations, including the performance of a play by the Jesuits of Rheims. Those who missed the proceedings could read the descriptions in a number of pamphlets and also look at the engravings of the coronation officially commissioned from the artist Henri d'Avice. The scene was also commemorated in a tapestry designed by one of the leading painters of Louis' reign, Charles Le Brun.

The meaning of the proceedings for the participants and onlookers, especially the image of the king projected by the ceremony, is not altogether clear. What the historian needs to discover is not so much 'what actually happened' as how contemporaries interpreted what had happened. It cannot be assumed that everyone saw the proceedings in the same light. On the contrary, the *sacre* seems to have been interpreted in two very different ways by different people.

This ritual of inauguration and consecration was essentially a medieval one. It had been codified by Louis VII, at a time when the king was not 'absolute' but shared power with his nobles, and the royal oath and the formal approval of the new ruler by the assembly expressed this idea of kingship. The duc de Saint-Simon, a strong supporter of this traditional idea of limited monarchy, still interpreted the ritual in this way in the early eighteenth century.

It is unlikely that the circle round the king viewed the *sacre* as an expression of the idea of limited monarchy. Such a view would make it difficult to understand why the government staged the performance at this time, so soon after the Fronde. A minor but possibly revealing detail suggesting an attempt to reinterpret the traditional ritual is the fact that Louis took the oath sitting down, although his predecessors had taken it standing up.[12]

The meaning of the *sacre* for the relatively new dynasty of the Bourbons was surely to show their legitimacy by establishing contact with earlier rulers, from Clovis to St Louis. The ceremony also projected the image of sacred kingship. We might say – indeed, contemporaries did say – that the chrism made Louis Christ-like and that the *sacre* made him sacred.

Louis later claimed in his memoirs (like the theorists of absolute monarchy) that his consecration did not make him king but simply declared that he was king. He added, however, that the ritual made his kingship 'more august, more inviolable, and more holy'.[13] This holiness may be illustrated by the fact that two days later, the young king performed for the first time the ritual of the royal touch.[14] It was traditionally believed that the kings of France, like the kings of England, had the miraculous power of curing scrofula, a disease of the skin, by touching the sufferers, and saying 'the king touches you, God cures you' [*Le roi te touche, Dieu te guérit*]. The healing power of the royal touch made a powerful symbol of the sacred character of kingship. On this occasion Louis touched 3,000 people. In the course of his reign he was to touch many more.

The royal entry

The royal journey to Rheims and the king's reception there was one of a number of state visits to cities, which often took the ritualised, triumphal form of a royal entry, a genre of ritual that goes back to the late Middle Ages. As we have seen, Louis made a formal entry into Paris in 1643 to celebrate his accession. He re-entered Paris in 1649 and 1652, to demonstrate the defeat of the Fronde. He made a state visit to Lyons in 1658. The most important of the royal entries, however, was that of the king and queen into Paris in 1660, following the royal wedding[15] (see Figure 4).

The entry into Paris was not an event sponsored by the government. It was an official welcome to the king on the part of the city, organised by the *prévôt des marchands*, the equivalent of the mayor, and his aldermen or *échevins*. However, the government does seem to have supervised both the ceremonies and the décor, which were described in detail in a number of contemporary publications.[16]

The royal entry took place on 26 August 1660. In the morning, the king and queen were enthroned on a high dais to receive 'the respect and submission' of the City and its corporations (including the University and the Parlement) who marched past the dais in procession while their representatives did homage to the king, as the nobility had done at the time of the *sacre*. The *prévôt des marchands* solemnly presented the king with keys symbolising his possession of the City.[17] On the other hand, the president of the Parlement of Paris played a relatively small part in the ceremonial proceedings, making 'a profound reverence' to the king and passing on. It seems to be no accident that the Parlement was given such an attenuated role, in 'expiation', as one contemporary has put it, of the part it had played in a rather different scene, that of the Fronde.[18]

In the afternoon came the entry proper, a cavalcade in which the king and his new queen rode through the city, passing through a number of gates and arches with decorations expressing the significance of the occasion, variations on the theme of the triumph of peace, commemorating the Peace of the Pyrenees between France and Spain, signed in 1659 and sealed by Louis' marriage to the infanta Maria Theresa, daughter of King Philip IV. One gateway bore the inscription LODOVICO PACIFICO, 'To Louis the Peaceful'. Another took the form of Parnassus, with Apollo and the nine Muses representing the arts and sciences, released from captivity by the peace. At the Marché Neuf, a triumphal arch bore the inscription LUDOVICO PACATORI TERRARUM, 'to Louis who has given peace to the world', and showed Hercules (in other words, the king, according to the printed commentary) receiving an olive branch.[19]

A striking feature of these decorations, compared to later fêtes, is the moderation of their praises of the king. Louis shared his glory not only with his queen but with his mother, Anne of Austria, and with his chief minister, Cardinal Mazarin. Anne, who watched the entry from her balcony, also made an appearance on one arch of triumph as the goddess Minerva, offering wise advice, on another as Juno, and elsewhere as a pelican, symbol of the mother who sacrifices herself for her children. Mazarin, who actually negotiated the peace treaty, was unable to take part in the entry on account of his gout, but his empty carriage had an important place in the cavalcade. He appeared on a triumphal arch as the god Mercury, and elsewhere as the hero Atlas, sustaining the world by his efforts. One of the Latin inscriptions referred to his hard work, ASSIDUIS JULII CARDINALIS MAZARINI CURIS. Such homage to a minister was literally unimaginable later in the reign. After the death of Mazarin Louis would be represented ruling alone.

The way in which Louis performed his role as protagonist in these performances struck the imagination of contemporaries, including ambassadors, who had an unusual opportunity to see the king in close-up. They stress the maturity of the child-king, his gravity, his poise. The Venetian envoys noted that in 1643, when he was only five, Louis laughed rarely and scarcely moved in public.[20] It may be that contemporary observers saw what they expected to see, and exaggerated what they thought they saw. All the same, the fact that they were impressed is itself significant.

The Spaniards were famous in the seventeenth century for the gravity of their formal behaviour, and Louis was of course the son of a Spanish princess, Anne of Austria. The letters of Cardinal Mazarin to the king give the impression that he too gave Louis lessons on the manner of presenting himself in public, including the art of simulation and dissimulation. In 1652, when he received the leading *frondeur*, the Cardinal de Retz, without showing him any sign of his imminent arrest, the adolescent king showed that he had learned his lesson. That Louis was well aware of his role is suggested by a remark he made on that occasion, 'that there should be no one on stage' [*qu'il n'y ait personne sur le théâtre*].[21]

Louis also appeared on stage in a literal sense, as a dancer. Between 1651 and 1659 he appeared in nine *ballets de cour* devised by the poet Isaac Benserade, playing a variety of roles which included Apollo destroying the Python and also the rising sun – for which the king wore a magnificent golden wig (Figure 15). It was not unusual for a king to dance in a court ballet – Louis XIII had done so regularly – but the king's skill in dancing was noted by a number of his contemporaries, including the courtier Bussy-Rabutin. In this way he made an important contribution to his own image.

There are relatively few visual images of Louis between the early 1650s and the year 1660, when he suddenly appeared as a young adult with an incipient moustache and a short wig. The wig has been explained as a response to an illness in 1658 in which Louis lost a good deal of hair. The custom of wearing wigs was spreading among the European nobility at this time, making it difficult to say whether Louis was following or creating a fashion. In any case, a wig gave the king the extra height he needed to impress. From this time onwards, he would not be seen in public without one.

The royal image should be seen as a collective production. Painters, sculptors and engravers made their contribution to it. So did the king's tailors, his wigmaker and his dancing-master. So did the poets and choreographers of the court ballets, and the masters of ceremonies who supervised the coronation, the royal entries and other public rituals.

Who wrote the script for the royal drama? In a sense the answer to this question is 'tradition' rather than any single individual; portraits followed models, and rituals followed precedents. However, it is reasonable to suppose that the production had a director: Cardinal Mazarin.

Mazarin was the leading figure in the government between 1643 and 1661. He gave Louis his political education. He was also a leading

15. 'Louis on stage'. *Louis as Apollo*, anonymous costume design, 1654. Cabinet des Estampes, Bibliothèque Nationale, Paris

patron of the arts, who appreciated the work of painters such as Philippe de Champaigne and Pierre Mignard, and writers such as Corneille and Benserade. He was a great lover of opera, and it was thanks to Mazarin that three Italian operas were commissioned for performance in Paris: *Orfeo* (1647) by Luigi Rossi, *Peleo e Theti* (1654) by Carlo Caproli (combined with Benserade's ballet on the same theme) and *Ercole Amante* (1660) by Francesco Cavalli (a subject chosen in allusion to the royal wedding). The scenery was also designed by Italians, Giacomo Torelli and Gasparo Vigarani.

Mazarin loved the arts for their own sake, but he was also aware of their political uses. This awareness is best documented in an episode of 1660, when the cardinal planned to commemorate the Peace of the Pyrenees by a grand staircase leading up to the French church of La Trinité des Monts in Rome.[22] Mazarin had Bernini in mind as architect, and it seems he produced a design. However, awkward political problems were raised by the erection of a statue of Louis XIV in a public square in Rome, and indeed by a monument commemorating a peace which had been made without the pope's mediation. Before these problems were resolved, Mazarin died. But the concern with the politics of the arts in general, and the commemoration of the peace of 1659 in particular, revealed in the cardinal's correspondence, suggests that he may also have inspired the themes of the Paris entry of 1660, celebrating not only the royal wedding but the peace, Anne of Austria and the efforts of the cardinal himself.

In 1660, the king still played the part he was given by tradition and Cardinal Mazarin. From 1661 onwards, Louis would be actively involved in writing (or at least revising) his own script.

16. *Portrait of Louis XIV Surrounded by Attributes of the Arts* by Jean Garnier, oil on canvas, 1672. Château de Versailles

IV

THE CONSTRUCTION OF THE SYSTEM

> Il y a bien, Monsieur, d'autres moyens louables de répandre et de maintenir la gloire de Sa Majesté . . . comme sont les pyramides, les colonnes, les statues équestres, les colosses, les arcs triomphaux, les bustes de marbre et de bronze, les basses-tailles, tous monuments historiques auxquels on pourrait ajouter nos riches fabriques de tapisseries, nos peintures à fresque et nos estampes au burin.
>
> Chapelain to Colbert, 1662

WHETHER OR not there was a master-plan for the presentation of the king in the age of Mazarin, such a project can certainly be documented in the period which followed. On the death of the cardinal in March 1661, Louis declared his intention of ruling without a first minister. He wanted to exercise 'absolute power' [*pouvoir absolu*], in other words power that was not shared with others. This did not, of course, mean that the king ruled without advice or assistance. Among his assistants, the most important figure was Colbert.[1]

Jean-Baptiste Colbert had been in the service of Mazarin, who recommended him to the king. He served Louis from 1661 onwards as a member of the *conseil royal des finances* or Council of State, and from 1664 as *surintendant des bâtiments* or superintendent of the king's works. In these capacities Colbert supervised royal patronage of the arts, playing Maecenas to Louis' Augustus. Colbert's reputation was and is that of an austere, hard-working man who grudged spending the state's money on anything that was not useful. It should be added, however, that Colbert considered the arts as useful in the sense that they contributed to the king's glory.

In the age of Mazarin, royal patronage had been put in the shade by that of the cardinal himself and that of his assistant Nicholas Fouquet, who was complimented by Corneille in the preface to his *Oedipe* (1659) as 'no less the superintendent of belles-lettres than of finance'. In fact, between about 1655 and 1660 Fouquet virtually replaced the king as the kingdom's leading patron, building a splendid house at Vaux-le-Vicomte and employing a galaxy of talented artists and writers, including the playwrights Corneille, Molière and Quinault, the poet La Fontaine, the painter Lebrun, the sculptors Anguier and Girardon, the architect Le Vau and the garden designer Le Nôtre.[2]

Colbert intended to re-establish the king's dominance as a patron (Figure 16). His wide-ranging concern for the king's glory is revealed in his official correspondence, especially his correspondence with Jean Chapelain. Chapelain, a poet and a critic, had won the favour of Cardinal Richelieu by writing an ode in his praise. He became a member of the Académie Française when it was founded in 1634–5. In response to a request from Colbert, Chapelain wrote him a long report in 1662 on the uses of the arts 'for preserving the splendour of the king's enterprises' [*pour conserver la splendeur des entreprises du roy*].[3]

The plan, whether Colbert's or Chapelain's, was an ambitious one. The report concentrates on literature, especially poetry, history and panegyric, listing the strengths and weaknesses of ninety men of letters of the day and their aptitude for the service of the king. However, Chapelain also refers to a variety of other media and genres: medals, tapestries, frescoes, engravings, and finally various kinds of monument 'such as pyramids, columns, equestrian statues, colossi, triumphal arches, marble and bronze busts'.

A good many of these media had already been used to glorify the king, notably in the Paris entry of 1660. All the same, it is extremely interesting to have this documentary evidence of a grand design so early in the history of Louis' personal rule and in the career of Colbert as a royal counsellor. The plan was put into practice in the next decade, when we can observe the 'organisation of culture' in the sense of the construction of a system of official organisations which mobilised artists, writers and scholars in the service of the king.

As in the age of Richelieu, the Académie Française played an important role, together with its committee, the so-called 'little academy' [petite académie], established in 1663 and transformed into the Académie des Inscriptions in 1696.[4] Other new foundations included the Académie de Danse (1661); the Académie Royale de Peinture et de Sculpture, which had been founded in 1648, but was reorganised in 1663; the Académie Française de Rome (1666), a training-school for artists; the Académie des Sciences (1666); the Académie d'Architecture (1671); the short-lived Académie d'Opéra (1671), replaced by the Académie Royale de Musique (1672); and the abortive Académie des

Spectacles (its foundation in 1674 was never registered).[5] All these institutions were located in Paris, but later in the reign provincial academies were founded on the model of the Académie Française (below, p. 155).

The academies were bodies of artists and writers most of whom worked for the king. They also acted as patrons, commissioning works which would glorify Louis. For example, the Academy of Painting and Sculpture admitted new members on the basis of a 'reception piece', which was supposed to deal with *l'histoire du roi*.[6] In 1663 they began holding competitions with a prize for the best painting or statue representing the 'heroic actions' of the king. From 1671 onwards, the Académie Française held competitions for the best panegyric of the king, on a different subject each year. At the end of the reign, several academies were employing a composer to write music in the king's honour.[7]

Other kinds of institution formed part of the system. There was the state factory of the Gobelins (opened in 1663), for instance, employing some 200 workers (including a number of painters) to produce furnishings for royal palaces as well as the famous tapestries of *l'histoire du roi*[8] (Figure 17). There was also the *Journal des Savants*, founded in 1665, and published by the royal press, which printed obituaries of scholars, descriptions of experiments and especially reviews of books (a new idea at the time). The journal, which was edited by men of letters in the entourage of Colbert, spread news about the world of learning, and in the process advertised the king's patronage.[9] The censorship of literature was made more strict in 1667 under the direction of the new lieutenant de police, La Reynie.[10]

What was the significance of these foundations? Were they the expression of a coherent government policy for the arts? Were they limited to the glorification of the king, or did they have wider aims? To answer these questions it is necessary to take a closer look at royal patronage of the different arts and sciences.

In the case of literature, Chapelain's advice was taken seriously. From 1663 onwards, pensions amounting to about 100,000 livres a year were awarded to a number of writers and scholars. Some of them were French, including a poet described by Chapelain as 'a young man named Racine'.[11] Others were foreigners – Dutchmen, Germans and Italians. As in the case of other gifts, these 'gratifications', as they were called, were naturally made in the expectation of returns.

The rules of the game were explained by Chapelain – at times with remarkable candour – in his letters to Colbert and to the foreign scholars concerned. The contradictions between these rules can probably be found

17. 'Louis as patron of the Arts'. *The Visit to the Gobelins* from the 'History of the King' series by Charles Lebrun, tapestry, *c.* 1670. Collection Mobilier National, Paris

wherever gifts are given. However, they were particularly acute in a period of transition from the traditional ideal of royal magnificence to the sense of publicity characteristic of print cultures.

On the one hand, as Chapelain informed the Italian poet Girolamo Graziani, 'His Majesty makes gifts to people of merit for no other motive than that of acting in a royal manner in every way and absolutely not in order to be praised' [*Sa Majesté gratifie les gens de mérite par le seul motif d'agir en toutes choses royalement et point du tout dans la vue d'en attirer des louanges*].[12] The point was, as he told Colbert, that the gratifications 'will seem the more noble the more they seem distinterested' [*paroistront d'autant plus nobles qu'elles paroistront plus désinteressés*].[13] A medal was struck to commemorate the king's liberality to writers and artists, with the legend BONAE ARTES REMUNERATAE, and the date 1666.

On the other hand, the recipients of the gratifications were left in no doubt of what was expected from them in return. 'The king is generous', wrote Chapelain to the Dutch scholar Nikolaes Heinsius, 'but he knows what he is doing and he has no wish to appear a fool' [*Le Roy est généreux, mais il sait ce qu'il fait et ne veut point passer pour dupe*].[14]

'It is necessary for the honour of His Majesty', Chapelain explained to Graziani, 'that his praises should seem spontaneous, and to seem spontaneous they have to be printed outside his realms' [*Il importait en effet pour l'honneur de Sa Majesté que son éloge parût fait volontairement et, pour paraître volontaire, il fallait qu'il fût imprimé hors de ses États*].[15] Most of the beneficiaries (so Chapelain told the German lawyer, Herman Conring) 'have agreed to put the great name of the king at the head' of their works.[16] One of them was instructed to couch the dedication to the king 'in the most respectful and magnificent terms that you possibly can' [*dans les termes les plus respectueux et les plus magnifiques que vous pourriez*].[17] Another was advised to insert into his panegyric of Louis the king's resolution to give public audiences every week.[18]

Poets, lawyers and natural philosophers were all cultivated for different reasons, but particular attention was given to historians. The appointment of historiographers royal was by now a tradition in France.[19] All the same, Colbert and Chapelain made unusual efforts to find historians who would record and celebrate the king's achievements. Of the ninety writers on whom Chapelain wrote reports, eighteen were historians. In 1662, there were six official historians already *en poste*; including Mézéray.[20] In spite of this *embarras de richesses*, Chapelain lobbied – unsuccessfully – for the appointment of Nicholas Perrot d'Ablancourt, who was best known as a translator, while Colbert secured the appointment of André Félibien to a new post, that of 'historian of the king's works' [*historiographe des bâtiments du roi*]. In this capacity, Félibien published official descriptions of the paintings, tapestries, buildings and fêtes commissioned by the king.[21]

Government patronage was extended to the natural sciences, witness the foundation of an Académie des Sciences, the construction of an astronomical observatory, and the launching of a scientific journal. Although the idea of an academy of sciences seems to have originated with a private group of scholars, Colbert's hand is easily visible in these enterprises.[22] The Académie was directed by his former librarian Pierre de Carcavy; the Italian astronomer Gian-Domenico Cassini came to France at his invitation; and the *Journal des Savants* was originally edited by three more of his protégés, Denis de Sallo (a friend of Chapelain's), Amable de Bourzeis (once a writer in the service of Richelieu) and Jean Gallois (formerly tutor to Colbert's children).

The fact that state patronage of science was rare at this time deserves emphasis. The English Royal Society had been founded a few years before the French Académie des Sciences, and began publishing its

Philosophical Transactions two months later than its French rival, but despite its title 'Royal', the English society was not funded by the government. But the king of France was publicly associated with scientific research, an association given visual form in an engraving from the end of the decade showing Louis visiting his academy and surrounded by scientific instruments (Figure 18). The visit, it should be added, was an imaginary one.[23]

To show the world that Louis was a cultivated man, Colbert set about adding to the royal collection of paintings, statues, medals, manuscripts, books, and so on, which the king had inherited from his predecessors. Colbert's protégé Charles Perrault was placed in charge of the publication of volumes of engravings of the collections in the *cabinet du roi*, thus advertising the king's taste and his magnificence. Another protégé of Colbert's, the scholar Pierre Carcavy, was placed in charge of the Royal Library. It was Carcavy who inspired Colbert's attempt (via Chapelain and Conring) to buy the famous library at Wolfenbüttel to add to the royal collection.[24]

In the case of the arts, ambassadors and other government agents abroad (notably two Italian clerics, Elpidio Benedetti in Rome and Luigi Strozzi in Florence) were instructed to look out for classical sculptures, paintings by Renaissance masters, and so on. Colbert's correspondence reveals his methods in detail, down to the haggling over prices, the preference for casts and copies because they were cheaper than the originals, and the political pressure exerted on individuals and institutions reluctant to sell their treasures to the king of France, including a Last Supper by Veronese, owned by the convent of the Servi in Venice. Politics served art collecting on occasion, just as art collecting served politics.[25]

It was not sufficient, of course, to buy antiques. Louis had to commission – and to be seen to commission – new paintings and statues. Just as he depended on Chapelain's advice on matters of literature, so where art was concerned Colbert generally listened to Charles Lebrun, *premier peintre du roi*.[26] According to Bernini, who saw the two men together in 1665, 'Colbert behaves to Lebrun as to a mistress and defers to him entirely'.[27] Another contemporary described Lebrun as having established 'a kind of tyranny in painting [*une espèce de tyrannie dans la peinture*] thanks to Colbert's trust in him'.[28] The phrase has appealed to modern historians impressed with the parallel between royal absolutism and the rule of Lebrun over the kingdom of art.[29] The claim is a little exaggerated, since some artists worked for the king independently of Lebrun.[30]

18. *Louis XIV Visiting the Académie des Sciences* by Sébastien Le Clerc, frontispiece from Claude Perrault, *Mémoires pour l'histoire naturelle des animaux*, 1671. British Library, London

All the same, Lebrun was an important patron in virtue of his position as the dominant figure in the Académie Royale de Peinture (an institution he had helped to found in 1648); as the director of the Gobelins, where *l'histoire du roi* was being produced in the form of tapestries; and as the artist in charge of interior decoration in the royal palaces of the Louvre and Versailles.

Artists who were not on good terms with him or Colbert did not receive the commissions they might otherwise have expected, as in the case of Pierre Mignard after the death of his supporter Anne of Austria, in 1666, while Lebrun's protégés tended to have successful careers in the royal service. The engraver Gérard Edelinck, for example, at whose marriage Lebrun was present, became *graveur du cabinet du roi*, or the sculptor Pierre Mazeline, at whose marriage Lebrun was a witness, worked at Versailles and received a pension from the king.

In the case of architecture, Colbert's adviser was Charles Perrault, a man of letters best known today for his rewriting of folk-tales such as Red Riding Hood, who served as commissioner for buildings [*commis des bâtiments*] when Colbert became *surintendant* in 1664. In his memoirs, Perrault described Colbert's plan 'to have many monuments erected to the glory of the king, such as triumphal arches, obelisks, pyramids and tombs', thus confirming the picture that emerges from the correspondence of Chapelain.[31] A tomb, or more exactly a funerary chapel for the royal family in the church of St-Denis, was designed by the architect François Mansart in 1665 and also by Gianlorenzo Bernini. As for obelisks, or pyramids, the decorations for the royal entry into Paris in 1660 included one in wood, while a stone obelisk glorifying the king was designed by Claude Perrault, Charles's brother, in 1666 (Figure 19). Arches of triumph would be constructed in the 1670s (below, p. 78).

Colbert showed little evidence of personal enjoyment of art, music or literature. In a perhaps deliberate contrast to his predecessors Richelieu, Mazarin and Fouquet, his activities as a private patron were extremely limited. His own interests lay in learning rather than the arts, and his protégés included scholars such as Charles Du Cange and Jean Mabillon.[32]

Yet this apparent philistine did more for the arts in his twenty years of power than ministers like Mazarin, who cared more about them for their own sake. Colbert brought a substantial group of artists and writers into the service of the king. A few of them, like the writers Amable de Bourzeis, Chapelain and Jean Desmarets, had previously served Cardinal Richelieu. Others had served Mazarin: the poet Isaac Benserade, for example, the composer Jean Cambefort, the writer

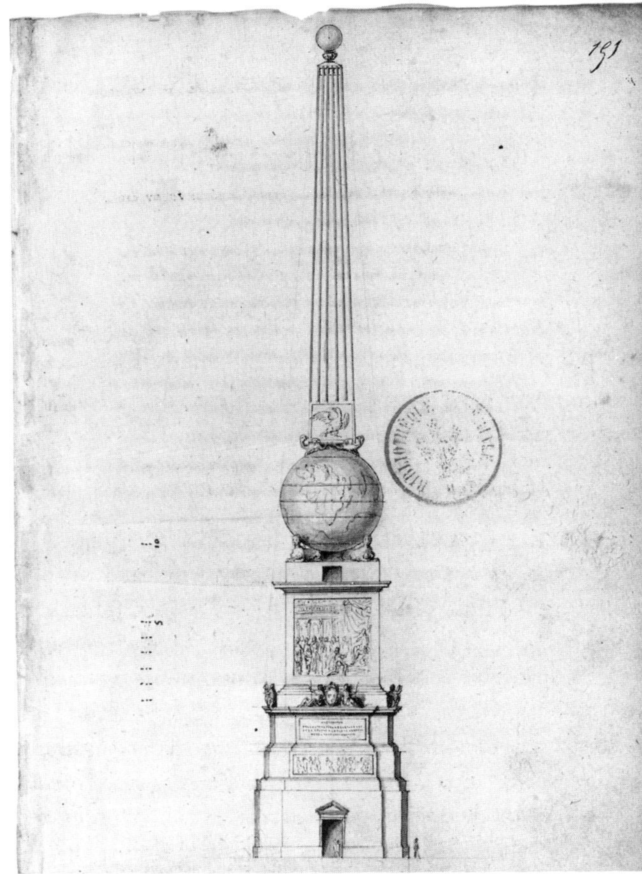

19. *Design for an Obelisk* by Charles Perrault, 1666. Bibliothèque Nationale, Paris

François Charpentier. Some of the most talented were taken over from Fouquet, including Lebrun, Le Nôtre, Le Vau and Molière. Racine came to Colbert's notice via Chapelain, and was pensioned in 1663, when he was still in his early twenties.

There seems to have been a deliberate policy of encouraging foreigners to put their talents at the service of the king. Foreign scholars were pensioned, as we have seen. The Italian astronomer Gian-Domenico Cassini was persuaded by Colbert to move from Bologna to Paris (his pension was 9,000 livres a year). Foreign artists were invited to France to work at the Louvre or Versailles. For example, the Swiss painter Joseph Werner was invited to Paris in 1662, following a favourable report from the French ambassador. The Flemish engraver Gérard Edelinck arrived in 1666. The French translation 'Desjardins' hides the Flemish origins of the sculptor Martin van den Bogaert, who arrived in France around 1670.

Colbert's importance lay in his general vision of the contribution of all the arts to the glory of the king. He depended on specialists for concrete suggestions, notably on Chapelain, Perrault and Le Brun. However, it was the minister who was responsible for the organisation of state patronage, indeed for its bureaucratisation.

In using the term 'bureaucratisation', I do not mean to suggest that the traditional system of patrons, clients and brokers, operative in the world of art as in the world of politics in the early modern period, had come to an end.[33] Artists and writers such as Lebrun and Molière were clients of the financier Fouquet before they were taken over by the king. Chapelain occupied the position of broker in the system of royal patronage of literature. Other brokers also had roles to play. For example, Racine sent his first poem to Chapelain via an intermediary. The composer André Destouches was brought to the notice of the king by the later prince of Monaco. Examples of this kind could be multiplied.

In the course of the reign, however, the arts came to be administered by an increasing number of officials, such as directors, superintendents or inspectors. Lebrun was *directeur de la manufacture royale des Gobelins*. The royal ballets, buildings, devices and music all had their *surintendants*. There was an *inspecteur-général des bâtiments*, an *inspecteur des beaux-arts*, and even an *inspecteur général de la sculpture* (conjuring up an image of statues drawn up on parade).

Another part of the bureaucratisation of the arts was the construction of the system of academies, the equivalent for the arts of the system of colleges, which were developing within the governments of seventeenth-century Europe. Colbert did not only found academies, he regulated the behaviour of their members, as in the case of the Académie Française, who were given fixed working hours together with a pendulum clock to make sure that their sense of time would be as precise as the minister wished.

Equally bureaucratic was the increasing use of committees, like the small group which drew up alternative plans for the Louvre, or, still more important, the petite académie, originally not an academy at all but 'a kind of small committee dealing with everything connected with belles-lettres' [*une espèce de petit conseil pour toutes les choses dépendantes des belles-lettres*].[34]

The members of this committee (Chapelain, Charles Perrault, Bourzeis, Cassagnes and François Charpentier) met in Colbert's house every Tuesday and Friday. Their task was essentially to supervise the creation of the king's public image. They corrected texts before publication, including descriptions of festivals by Félibien and Perrault himself.[35] They examined the designs and composed the descriptions for tapestries and medals. For a few years at least, they worked on a history of the reign.[36] The foundation of this group shows how seriously Colbert took the task of image-making, and how sharp was his sense of publicity.

Like the administration of the state, the creation of the public image of the king was organised from the centre.[37] Teams of artists were directed by committees of patrons. The system might be represented – appropriately enough for an age of increasing bureaucracy – in the form of an organogram. At the top there was the king himself, who intervened from time to time, to commission particular works or at least to choose between alternative projects (below, pp. 67–8, 86). Immediately below Louis came Colbert, who liked to keep all the strings in his hand, despite his other concerns. Then came Colbert's men, three of them in particular. Chapelain advised him on literature, Lebrun on painting and sculpture, and Charles Perrault on architecture. Music (including ballet and opera) was outside Colbert's domain. It was controlled by Lully.

In short, what has been called a 'department of glory' had been founded to organise the presentation of the king's image, or more exactly, a moving picture of the main events of the reign, *l'histoire du roi*. It is time to turn from the organisation to what it produced.

22 (*detail*). *Louis XIV as a Roman Emperor* from Charles Perrault, *Festiva ad capita*, 1670. British Library, London

V
SELF-ASSERTION

Sous un tel souverain nous sommes peu de chose;
Son soin jamais sur nous tout à fait ne repose:
Sa main seule départ ses liberalités:
Son choix seul distribue états et dignités.

Corneille, *Othon*, Act 2, Scene 4

THE LAST chapter was concerned with what might be called the structure of the glorification of Louis XIV, more especially with the creation of that structure from the early 1660s onwards. This chapter deals with the royal image itself from the assumption of personal rule in 1661 to the outbreak of the War of Devolution in 1667. One might describe these years as 'the age of self-assertion'. After the death of his mentor and minister Mazarin, the young king was in a position to take important decisions by himself. Ironically this self-assertion needs to be seen as a collective action in which the king's advisers and image-makers participated.

The myth of personal rule

The image of the young king projected in the 1660s was that of a ruler unusually devoted to affairs of state and the welfare of his subjects. The assumption of personal rule itself became an event to be celebrated, indeed to be mythologised in the sense of being presented in a dramatic manner as a 'marvel'.

The original announcement of the king's intent to rule in person was a semi-private one, made in a speech to the chancellor, delivered in the presence of ministers and secretaries.[1] The official *Gazette* made no mention of it at the time. On the death of Mazarin on 9 March 1661, the journal reported a visit of condolence to the king by representatives of the French clergy, whose spokesman declared that the king was tireless not only in military operations but equally in the conduct of affairs of state [*Sa Majesté, qui a esté infatigable dans les travaux de la guerre, ne l'est pas moins dans la conduite des affaires de son Estat*].[2] The theme was taken up in April by the *Gazette* itself, which noted the king's remarkable application to official business, such as council meetings [*Le Roy, continuant de prendre le soin de ses affaires avec une application toute particulière, se trouva au Conseil des Parties*]. Even a reference to the king's hunting describes this activity as a relaxation from the 'marvellous assiduity' with which the king devoted himself to affairs of state [*des soins que Sa Majesté prend toujours des affaires de son Estat, avec une assiduité merveilleuse*].[3]

A fuller account of the same incident was offered later in the decade in the king's memoirs for the year 1661, a confidential memorandum drafted by the king's secretaries in 1666 or thereabouts, and intended for the Dauphin as part of his education for what the memoirs themselves call the job of being a king [*le métier du roi*]. In this text, Louis explained that he had taken the decision 'above all not to take a first minister' [*sur toutes choses de ne point prendre de premier ministre*]. He is portrayed, in a famous passage, as 'Informed of everything; listening to the least of my subjects; aware at every moment of the number and quality of my troops, and the state of my fortresses; giving orders unceasingly for all their needs; receiving and reading dispatches; replying to some of them myself, and telling my secretaries how to answer the others; setting the level of the receipts and expenditures of my state'.[4]

The event was presented to a wider public in a variety of texts and images. The account in the *Gazette* quoted above was perhaps sufficient to allow the audience to discern a contemporary reference in Corneille's play *Othon*, which had its première at court at Fontainebleau in 1664. The play is set in the reign of the Emperor Galba, one of whose ministers remarks on the unimportance of subordinates to a ruler, who does not rely on them but distributes gifts and appointments himself (see the epigraph to this chapter).

The event was also commemorated later in the reign by means of visual images. The most famous of these is the painting by Lebrun on the ceiling of the Grande Galerie at Versailles, inscribed 'the King takes over the conduct of his dominions, and gives himself up entirely to business' (Figure 20).[5] Louis holds a rudder, to show that he is now the captain of the ship of state. He is crowned by the Graces, while a figure representing France smothers Discord, and a figure of Hymen,

20. *The King Governs for Himself* by Charles Lebrun, ceiling painting, 1661. Château de Versailles

goddess of marriage, holds a cornucopia to signify abundance. Minerva, goddess of wisdom, shows the king Glory, ready to crown him, and accompanied by Victory and Fame. In the heavens, the gods offer Louis their assistance.[6]

A more precise interpretation of the king's personal rule is offered by three medals bearing the date 1661.[7] The first is inscribed 'the king taking over the government' [REGE CURAS IMPERII CAPESSENTE], and represents the 'Order and Happiness' which followed this event, a phrase expanded by the official commentary of 1702 to refer to the reform of abuses, the revival of the arts and sciences, and the restoration of abundance. The other two medals add details to this picture. One of them is entitled 'the assiduity of the king at his councils', despite other calls on his time and even illness, as the commentary explains. The other is 'the accessibility of the king' [FACILIS AD PRINCIPEM ADITUS].[8]

The similarities in phrasing between the inscriptions and commentaries and the *Mémoires* and *Gazette* deserve emphasis. The first medal, like the *Mémoires*, presents the personal rule as the restoration of order after a time when 'chaos ruled everywhere' [*le désordre régnait partout*].[9] The second medal, like the *Gazette*, uses the term 'assiduity'.

The third medal corresponds to the *Mémoires* in noting the king's accessibility to his subjects. Cross-references of this kind between different texts and different media are common in the contemporary representations of Louis XIV, giving the impression of a co-ordinated effort to show the king in particular ways. This impression is confirmed by Chapelain's instructions to the Italian writer Dati to insert a reference to the king's accessibility into his panegyric.[10]

Rivalries

The events of the early 1660s suggest that the young king and his advisers were determined to make an immediate impression on the public, domestic and foreign. The means employed were diplomacy and festivals, both carefully reported in other media.

On the diplomatic front, two events signalled a change of policy, one in London and one in Rome. In 1661, a conflict over precedence between the French and Spanish ambassadors led to what Samuel Pepys called a 'fray' between their followers in the streets of London. The incident was more than an unseemly brawl, marring an official occasion (the arrival of the Swedish ambassador to Charles II). The king supported the action of his representative, and it was the Spanish ambassador to the French court who apologised for what had happened.

In other words, it is likely that the incident was planned, that it was a symbolic assertion of the superiority of the French monarch over his Spanish colleague, Louis' uncle and father-in-law, Philip IV.[11] This interpretation is strengthened by the French reaction in 1662 to an alleged insult to their ambassador to Rome on the part of the pope's Corsican guards. It was the pope's turn to apologise, through his representative Cardinal Chigi, in 1664.

Both diplomatic triumphs found expression in images. Two of the great tapestries designed by Lebrun illustrate the formal apologies of the pope and the king of Spain (Figure 21). The same themes recur in Lebrun's decoration of the Grande Galerie, inscribed *La prééminence de France reconnue par l'Espagne* and *Réparation de l'attentat des Corses*. The Spanish apology was also represented in relief on the great *Escalier des Ambassadeurs*, clearly *pour encourager les autres*. Spain was represented as a woman 'tearing her clothes, to symbolise the resentment of that nation' [*déchirant ses vêtements, pour marquer le dépit de cette nation*].[12] The Dutch scholar Heinsius earned his gratification with a Latin epigram on the affair of the Corsican guard. For good measure, medals were struck

21. 'Tapestry as propaganda'. *Meeting of Philip IV and Louis XIV* from the 'History of the King' series by Charles Lebrun, tapestry, *c.* 1670. Collection Mobilier National, Paris

to commemorate the events, including the commemoration of a commemoration, the erection (and later destruction) of a pyramid in Rome to mark the Corsican incident.[13]

The recovery of Dunkirk, which was purchased from Charles II in 1662, was also celebrated as a major triumph. Colbert asked Chapelain to ask Charles Perrault to write about it.[14] Lebrun painted an equestrian portrait of the king with the newly-recovered city in the background.[15] Dunkirk was also the theme of the first prize competition organised by the Académie Royale de Peinture.[16]

Magnificence

Another method employed to make an impression on Europe was less violent. Ritual, art and architecture may all be seen as the instruments of self-assertion, as the continuation of war and diplomacy by other means. The image of the king as a magnificent and munificent patron was given great stress during the reign. Like his political and military roles, this one too was mythologised. Louis was described by one of his official artists in a lecture to the Académie Royale de Peinture as having 'caused to be born, or shaped, the greater part of the illustrious men who have been ornaments of his reign' [*fait naître, ou formé, la plus grande partie des hommes illustres qui ont fait l'ornement de son règne*].[17]

Other events of this period, which were later celebrated by medals, included the foundation of academies and the award of gratifications to men of letters.[18]

In 1662, one of the major public spectacles of the reign was organised, the *carrousel* in a square opposite the Tuileries. A *carrousel* was a competition for horsemen, which involved running at the ring and other feats of skill popular in the Middle Ages. It had been transformed in the late Renaissance into a kind of equestrian ballet. Louis' appearance on horseback as 'emperor of the Romans' paralleled his appearances on stage, except that the audience was much larger on this occasion. The five teams of nobles were dressed in fantastic costumes, supposedly Roman, Persian, Turkish, Indian and American. Each competitor had his own device on his shield, and the king's was a sun with the inscription 'as I saw I conquered' [UT VIDI VICI]. The king did in fact do well in the competition, and the event was commemorated in a magnificent folio volume of engravings, with an explanatory text by Charles Perrault (see Figure 22). The political importance of the event, the reign's first entertainment of real splendour [*le premier divertissement de quelque éclat*], was underlined in the royal memoirs.[19]

The greatest artistic projects of the decade were of course the reconstruction of the Louvre and Versailles. The Louvre was a medieval palace, rebuilt in Renaissance style in the reign of François I. It was too cramped for the needs of a seventeenth-century court, and the fire which destroyed part of the palace in 1661 put rebuilding high on the agenda. The decision was taken to build a new palace and to commission designs from a number of leading architects, Italian as well as French: Louis Le Vau, François Mansart, Claude Perrault, Carlo Rainaldi and Gianlorenzo Bernini, an artist who had attracted the attention of Cardinal Mazarin.[20]

Bernini was invited to France in 1665. It would be interesting to know whether the invitation was extended because Mazarin had been interested in his work, or to humiliate Pope Alexander VII still further, by depriving him of his greatest artist. When he arrived, Bernini was treated with great honour and pleased the king, but he clashed with Colbert and with Charles Perrault, who criticised his designs, and he failed

22. *Louis XIV as a Roman Emperor* from Charles Perrault, *Festiva ad capita*, 1670. British Library, London

to get the commission, though he did produce a famous bust of Louis.[21]

Colbert (or his man Perrault) produced memoranda arguing that Bernini's project was impractical, ill-adapted to the French climate, insufficiently concerned with security, in short little more than a façade, 'so ill conceived so far as the king's comfort was concerned [*si mal conçu pour la commodité du Roi*]', that with an expense of ten million livres he would be left as cramped as he was before.[22] For his part, Bernini complained bitterly that the French government were concerned only with 'privies and pipes'.

The plan for the Louvre, which eventually gained official approval, was produced by a small committee, consisting of Lebrun, Le Vau and Claude Perrault. The project was executed, and commemorated by a number of medals.[23] However, the king spent relatively little time in this palace. Instead it became the headquarters of the image-makers. Some leading artists were given lodgings and workshops in the Louvre. Girardon, for example, moved there in 1667. The Académie Française was also given rooms in the Louvre, and this event too was commemorated by a medal.[24] It is intriguing to read the correspondence between the king and Colbert on this subject. Colbert suggested that the Louvre would be 'more worthy' of the Académie, but that the royal library would be more comfortable [*plus commode*]. As in the case of the Bernini project, he was still harping on practical considerations. Louis, however, chose the Louvre despite the possible inconvenience to the academicians.[25]

Meanwhile the king had turned his attention to Versailles, at this point a small château, which had been built for Louis XIII in 1624. Soon after the beginning of his personal rule, Louis commissioned Le Vau to enlarge the château and Le Nôtre to design the gardens, provoking a protest from Colbert against the waste of money on 'this house' [*cette maison*, in contrast to the *palais* of the Louvre] because it 'is much more concerned with Your Majesty's pleasure and diversion than with your glory' [*regarde bien plus le plaisir et le divertissement de Votre Majesté que sa gloire*].[26]

To posterity, for whom the glory of the sun-king is so closely linked to Versailles, these words sound strangely. Ought we to credit the young monarch with more political sense, or a more acute sense of publicity, than his minister? It is more likely that at this point in the reign Louis was indeed thinking of his diversions, of a place to hold fêtes or to meet Mlle de La Vallière in relative privacy, and that he had no more idea than Colbert of what Versailles was to become in the course of forty-two years of building and rebuilding.[27]

This famous clash between the young king and the middle-aged minister raises a central problem. Who was taking the decisions? In the case of the Louvre it was Colbert who got his way. The king personally authorised the final plan, selecting it from alternatives proposed by the committee.[28] However, we know that he had been much impressed by Bernini's second project.[29] Colbert seems to have talked Louis out of his preference. Bernini was aware of the problem. He once remarked that if he had stayed in France 'he would have asked the king to deal only with His Majesty directly so far as buildings were concerned' [*il aurait demandé au Roi de n'avoir à traiter de ses bâtiments qu'avec Sa Majesté même*].[30] Louis rated magnificence higher than comfort.

If it was Colbert who won the contest of wills over the Louvre, it was Louis who triumphed in the case of Versailles. So far as music, dance and spectacle were concerned, it was again the king's tastes that counted. Louis continued to participate in court ballets throughout the 1660s, in such roles as Alexander the Great, Cyrus King of Persia, and the chivalric hero Roger. The foundation of an Academy of Dancing in 1661 fits in very well with his personal interests, and so does the appointment of Jean-Baptiste Lully the same year to be superintendent of his chamber music [*surintendant de la musique de chambre du roi*]. The organisation of court festivals was in the hands of a nobleman high in royal favour, the duc de Saint-Aignan, and the king's personal involvement with these spectacles is well known.

It was Louis, for example, who chose the theme, from Tasso, for the *Plaisirs de l'Ile Enchantée* of 1664, as he did later for Quinault's *Amadis*.[31] Molière gives Louis the credit for adding a character to his play *Les fâcheux* (1661) and for suggesting the plot for *Les amants magnifiques* (1670).

The king appears to have shown little interest at this time either in his library or in his collection of statues. These forms of magnificence were simply part of his official personality.[32] On the other hand, he was interested in painting, at least in certain kinds of painting, such as battle-pieces. In 1669 he honoured the Flemish battle-painter Adam-Frans van de Meulen by holding his new-born son at the font.

The king's personal interest in Lebrun's paintings of Alexander the Great is well known. Whether Racine inspired Lebrun or Lebrun Racine, the choice of Alexander by painter and playwright alike – not to mention Benserade's ballet of 1665 on the same theme – paid homage to one young conqueror's identification with another.[33]

23. *Ludovicus Magnus*, medal by Jean Warin, 1671. Cabinet des Médailles, Bibliothèque Nationale, Paris

VI

THE YEARS OF VICTORY

> Voilà comme la Victoire et la Gloire prennent plaisir d'ammasser leur Couronnes sur la Tête d'un Monarque si magnanime.
>
> *Gazette*, 1672

AFTER THE diplomatic offensive of the years 1662–4, it was only to be expected that Louis would choose the royal road to glory, that of a successful foreign war. His first wars were indeed successful; the War of Devolution in 1667–8, and – at least in its early phases – the Dutch war of 1672–8. It is with the image of the conquering hero of these years that this chapter will be concerned. It will focus in particular on one famous incident, the invasion of the Dutch Republic in 1672, and especially the crossing of the Rhine by the king's forces.

The War of Devolution

The War of Devolution was fought to enforce Louis' claim to the Spanish Netherlands, through his wife Maria Theresa, following the death of her father Philip IV in 1665. The ground was prepared by pamphlets presenting a favourable image of Louis as a ruler who wanted nothing more than his just rights. Herman Conring, professor of law at the University of Helmstedt, one of the foreign scholars receiving regular gratifications, volunteered to write in the king's support.[1] The royal press published an anonymous French treatise on 'the rights of the most Christian queen over various states of the Spanish Monarchy'. The treatise was produced by a team working under the direction of Bourzeis (a member of the petite académie), revised by Chapelain and Charles Perrault, and quickly translated into Latin, Spanish and German.[2]

Charles Sorel and Antoine Aubéry also wrote in support of the king's claims. Sorel, a historiographer royal (and former lawyer's clerk), published treatises on the rights of the kings of France, while Aubéry, an advocate at the Parlement of Paris, published *Some Just Claims of the King* [of France] *over the Empire* [*Des justes prétentions du roi sur l'Empire*]. Although the pamphlet was disavowed when the German princes protested, and the author sent to the Bastille, it is probable that the *Just Claims* was officially inspired.[3]

The arguments of the pamphlets were followed in a matter of weeks by the invasion of the Spanish Netherlands by a French army. In this campaign, the king played a prominent role. Following tradition, Louis led his troops in person. Breaking with tradition, Louis took the court with him on campaign, including the queen and two royal mistresses, the duchesse de La Vallière and the marquise de Montespan.

Two artists were also invited to accompany the king, presumably to give greater verisimilitude to *l'histoire du roi*. One of them was Charles Lebrun and the other Adam-Frans van de Meulen, who had recently been appointed court painter. As his name suggests, van de Meulen was a Fleming, who thus found himself participating in the invasion of his own country.

The major events of the war, as it was presented in paintings by these two artists and also in engravings, in tapestries, in medals, in poems and in the contemporary histories of the reign, were the sieges of Douai (Figure 24), Lille, Oudenarde and Tournai, together with a victorious battle near Bruges, and the taking of Franche-Comté (Figure 25). When peace was made at Aix-la-Chapelle in 1668, Franche-Comté was returned to Spain, but Lille was incorporated into France. The end of the war was celebrated by a fête at Versailles to which Le Vau, Vigarani, Lully and Molière all contributed, together with a performance organised by the French ambassador to Mainz entitled 'The Recent Peace' [*Pax nuperrime factum*].[4]

The celebrations of the war also took more permanent forms. The Royal Academy of Painting announced a competition for the best work on the theme 'Louis giving Peace to Europe'. Van de Meulen earned his passage to Flanders with paintings of the king at Oudenarde, Arras, Lille and Dôle. All four paintings were engraved so that they might be circulated more widely, and Chapelain edited a text to accompany them.[5] The series of tapestries designed by Lebrun and dealing with the events of the reign selected no fewer than five incidents from the war – the sieges of Douai (where a cannon ball just missed the king standing

24. 'Louis in the trenches'. *Siege of Douai in 1667* by Adam-Frans van der Meulen, engraving, *c.* 1672. Anne S. K. Brown Military Collection, Brown University Library, Providence, R.I.

25. 'Louis the conqueror'. *Franche Comté Conquered*, engraving by Charles Simonneau, *c.* 1680 after Charles Lebrun. British Library, London

in a trench) and Tournai (where Louis put his head above the parapet); the taking of Lille and Dôle; and the battle near Bruges.[6]

In the later medallic history of the reign, individual medals commemorated the war, the peace, the conquest of Franche-Comté, its return to Spain, and the capture of seven cities: Tournai, Douai, Courtrai, Oudenarde, Lille, Besançon and Dôle. The medal of the siege of Douai, like the tapestry, showed Louis in the trench, and carried an inscription alluding to his role in the campaign, REX DUX ET MILES, the king as leader and as soldier.[7]

The way in which the king is presented as doing everything by himself deserves to be noted. We may suspect that Turenne, a brilliant and experienced general, was the real commander, but he was officially described as carrying out the king's orders. In a private letter, Chapelain described Condé as 'the principal instrument' of the conquest. In public, however, in a poem, Chapelain gave the king the credit for the conquest of Franche-Comté.[8] This pattern would be followed in accounts of later victories. One might explain it equally well by the conventions of panegyric or by the king's notorious reluctance to share his glory.

Following these victories, the king came to be described as 'Louis the Great' [*Louis le Grand, Lodovicus Magnus*]. The epithet seems to have been used for the first time in the inscription on a medal struck in the king's honour by the city of Paris in 1671 (see Figure 23).[9] The example was soon followed on medals and on the triumphal arches erected in Paris at this time. Charles Perrault recorded in his memoirs that 'After the conquests of Flanders and Franche-Comté, M. Colbert proposed the raising of a triumphal arch to the glory of the king.'[10] Charles Perrault's brother Claude produced a design, and the king approved the maquette in 1670.

The arch, on the Place du Trône, was begun but never finished. A memorandum of Colbert's links it with the new Observatory (opened in 1671), as if this too were a monument to the king's glory: 'Triumphal Arch for the conquests of the earth. Observatory for the heavens'.[11] It was at about this time, in 1668, that the king decided to build a completely new château at Versailles, and gave the commission to Le Vau. Like the triumphal arch, the great staircase at Versailles, designed by Le Vau, was intended as a construction 'worthy of receiving this great Monarch when he returns from his glorious conquests'.[12]

Poets and historians also made their contribution to the king's glory. Chapelain, for example, produced sonnets on the invasion of Flanders, the conquest of Franche-Comté and the siege of Maastricht.[13] A certain

P.D. produced a day-by-day narrative of 'the Royal Campaign', complete with poems, a justification of the French claim to the Netherlands and references to the 'marvellous wisdom' of the king, 'which surpasses that of the greatest statesmen of past centuries'.[14] The 73-year-old Jean Desmarets, who had spent his best years praising Louis XIII and Richelieu, devoted a poem to the Franche-Comté campaign. Molière wrote a sonnet on the subject, while Corneille addressed the king 'on his return from Flanders' as a 'great Conqueror', 'covered with laurels', praised his 'great actions' and his 'majestic pride' [*auguste fierté*], and commented on the rapidity of the king's conquests, which gave the poet no leisure to write about them.[15] It was also Corneille who translated into French a Latin poem by the Jesuit Charles de La Rue in praise of the victories of 1667, comparing the king's role in the campaign with that of St Louis in the Crusades and referring once again to his visit to the trenches.[16]

The Dutch war

In the War of Devolution, Louis took artists with him on campaign; in the Dutch war, he took historians. Pellisson was in Flanders in 1677 in his capacity as official historian, while Boileau and Racine took his place in 1678. One might have thought that artists and writers alike had pulled out all possible stops to celebrate the War of Devolution, leaving them with nothing new to say about the Dutch War of 1672–8. The representations of this second war (including the second conquest of Franche-Comté) do indeed have a good deal in common with the first, even allowing for the stereotyping inherent in genres such as the ode and the battle-painting. However, one episode at least, the crossing of the Rhine in 1672, gave poets and painters alike an opportunity to innovate, which they grasped with both hands. I too will take advantage of this opportunity and discuss the images of this incident in particular detail.

One of Chapelain's last contributions to the king's glory was to help spread the official interpretation of the war. In a letter to Herman Conring, he insisted that the king only made war on Holland to make an example of her ingratitude. In a sonnet, which he sent to Colbert, he made the personified republic lament her 'pride', 'insolence' and 'disloyalty'. He also discovered a certain Frischmann, who had composed a Latin poem on the war, and recommended him to Colbert on the grounds that 'it would be advantageous to His Majesty' to have his victories and the justice of his cause celebrated by a German writer.[17]

For a brief sketch of the official version of the occasion of the war we may turn to Racine, who was appointed historiographer royal (together with Boileau) in 1677. The post was no sinecure, especially in wartime, and for some years Racine switched his attention from the theatre to the production of a 'historical panegyric' of the king and an account of his conquests between 1672 and 1678.[18] According to Racine, Louis had already proved himself 'no less an excellent captain than a great statesman' and so had no need of another war. 'Revered by his subjects, feared by his enemies, admired by the whole world, he seemed to have nothing more to do but peacefully enjoy a reputation so solidly established, when Holland offered him still new opportunities to distinguish himself, and opened the way for actions the memory of which will never perish.'[19]

It was the 'insolence' of the Dutch that provoked the king (Corneille too referred to the Dutch people in a poem of 1672 as 'cet insolent Batave'). The republic, according to Racine, 'allied herself with the enemies of France', oppressed the Catholics, competed with French trade 'and boasted that by herself she had set limits to the king's conquests'. Louis decided to 'punish' the Dutch and he led the campaign himself, leaving the pleasures of the court to expose himself to the dangers and fatigues of war. In one day, four fortresses were captured (Rheinberg, Wesel, Burick and Orsoy), an event commemorated by a medal in which Victory holds four laurel wreaths instead of the usual one. The French advance turned into 'a permanent triumph', in which the most famous episode was the crossing of the Rhine.

This triumph was of course reported in the newspapers. The *Gazette* devoted a special issue to the 'glorious action' of 'this marvellous monarch', in a style closer to that of the panegyric than to its usual laconic manner of presentation, noting that the king 'did not spare himself', like 'the lowest officer or soldier in his forces' and also that 'nothing escaped his understanding'. As if describing a painting or statue of the king, the *Gazette* commented, 'See how Victory and Glory take pleasure in heaping their crowns on the heads of such a great-souled monarch' [*un Monarque si magnanime*].[20]

As for what was already known as 'the famous crossing of the Rhine', it was described in the journal as an achievement which even Caesar did not equal, since he made use of a bridge, while Louis, 'more able than the Caesars to resolve every difficulty', surmounted the obstacles to his passage without such mechanical aids. The French army simply swam across. A second special number of the *Gazette* was devoted to the celebrations that followed the king's return, the *Te Deum* in Notre

Dame, and the firework display in the Tuileries, with 'luminous pictures' of Apollo, Victory, Holland 'under the yoke' and the hand of justice, in order to show that justice was 'the sole object' of all the king's exploits.[21]

The poets – Corneille, Boileau, Fléchier, Furetière, Genest, and so on – were not slow to put these exploits into verse. Corneille noted that Spanish commanders such as Alba and Farnese had been unable to follow the Dutch across the Rhine, and put a speech into the mouth of the king declaring the need to surpass the achievements of the Romans. He mentioned a number of the swimmers by name, but told Louis that their valour was simply 'the effect of your presence'.[22] Among the vivid details of the poem is the description of the river itself as 'alarmed' by the king's exploit. Boileau's *Fourth Epistle* and Charles-Claude Genest's ode on the same subject also described the trembling of the river-god.[23]

After the poets, it was the turn of the artists. The Royal Academy of Painting and Sculpture made the passage of the Rhine the theme for the prize competition of 1672.[24] At Versailles, which was being transformed into 'the palace of the sun', the decorative schemes of the 1670s and 1680s would make many allusions to the actions of the king.[25] The decorations of the famous *Escalier des Ambassadeurs* at Versailles, completed in 1680, but destroyed in the eighteenth century, included a bas-relief 'in which the king appears giving his orders for the attack on his enemies. In the air flies Warlike Valour [*la Valeur Guerrière*]. The river Rhine, in the form of an old man, makes a gesture expressing his terror'.[26]

In the Grande Galerie at Versailles, in the 1680s, Lebrun painted nine pictures of the Dutch war, including one of Louis sitting in a chariot holding a thunderbolt in his hand, and accompanied across the Rhine by Minerva, Hercules and personifications of Glory and Victory. (Figure 26). Here too Lebrun showed the river-god as 'seized with fear', as in the verses of Corneille and Boileau.[27] A well-known contemporary description of the decorations of Versailles draws the reader's attention not so much to the images as to the crossing itself, 'an action so bold, so surprising and so memorable that past centuries never saw the like', and to the 'intrepidity' of Louis and 'the grandeur of his courage'.[28]

Lebrun's are only the most famous of the many contemporary images of the crossing. The sculptor Michel Anguier represented it in allegorical form, with Holland in the form of a woman sitting on a lion 'which appeared afraid'.[29] The painter Joseph Parrocel produced a version of the scene for the gallery at Marly, which 'the king found so worthy of his attention, that he had it placed in the council-chamber at Versailles'.[30] Van de Meulen was another artist who produced a memorable image of this incident (Figure 27). The events of 1672 were also commemorated in a series of medals showing the defeat of the Dutch, the capture of their cities and, not least, the passage of the Rhine. The court artists must have been weary of representing winged Victories.[31]

The triumphalist tone was maintained in official representations of the later years of the war, notably the taking of the fortress of Maastricht in thirteen days in 1673, and the second conquest of Franche-Comté in 1674. Pierre Mignard painted a famous portrait of Louis on horseback with the captured fortress in the background (Figure 28), while Desmarets wrote an ode, which declared that Louis had surpassed not only Farnese and the prince of Orange but Pompey and Alexander as well. The old Desmarets and Antoine Furetière (better known for his novel and his dictionary) also wrote stanzas to praise this second conquest of Franche-Comté.[32]

In honour of this conquest, a grand fête took place at Versailles in July and August 1674, after the king's return. On the fifth day of this festival, the victories of the king were represented by trophies, a golden bas-relief of the crossing of the Rhine and a 'mysterious' decoration, in other words a visual enigma which included Hercules (symbolising 'the invincible power and the grandeur of the actions of his MAJESTY'), Minerva (standing for the king's wisdom), a dragon (symbol of envy) and of course a sun, together with an obelisk as a sign of Louis' glory.[33]

The celebrations took a more permanent form on the triumphal arch of Porte St Martin in Paris (Figure 29), bearing the inscription – still visible, in the midst of the traffic – 'to Louis the Great' [LUDOVICO MAGNO] and decorated with reliefs showing the king crowned with laurel and receiving homage (Figure 30). It is significant that this was the fifth arch in a series. The arch on the Place du Trône was apparently the first permanent triumphal arch erected anywhere since the days of the Romans, but it was quickly followed by arches replacing the old gateways of St Antoine, St Denis, St Bernard and St Martin.[34]

In this chorus of praise, one can detect a few pieces of advice, gently suggesting to the king that he had gone far enough and that it was time to give the earth a rest [*Laisse-là tes vertus de guerre/ Mets en repos toute la Terre*].[35] All the same, the war continued. The campaigns of 1676 and 1677 were commemorated by medals of the relief of Maastricht, the taking of Valenciennes, Cambrai and St Omer, and the victory of Cassel, and they were celebrated in poems by Paul Tallemant, by Boileau and,

26. *The Crossing of the Rhine in 1672* by Charles Lebrun, ceiling painting, *c.* 1678–86. Château de Versailles

27. *The Crossing of the Rhine* by Adam-Frans van der Meulen, oil on canvas, *c.* 1672. Musée des Beaux-Arts, Caen

28. 'Louis victorious'. *Louis at Maastricht* by Pierre Mignard, oil on canvas, 1673. Pinacoteca, Turin

29. *Arc de triomphe, Porte St Martin* engraving by Adam Perelle, *c.* 1674. British Library, London

30. *Louis Receiving Homage*, spandrel relief on the triumphal arch at the Porte St Martin, 1674

31. 'The conqueror in repose'. *Louis Resting After Peace of Nijmegen* by Noël Coypel, oil on canvas, 1681. Musée Fabre, Montpellier

once more, by Corneille ('Louis has only to appear and your walls collapse').[36] Celebrations reached their high point in 1678, when the *Te Deum* was sung five times, for the taking of Ypres, Puigcerda and, above all, Ghent (in only six days), and for the peace treaties signed at Nijmegen.

Whatever may have been the case in the brief War of Devolution, in the case of the Dutch war certain discrepancies between the official accounts and the reality of the campaigns were difficult to disguise. In 1672, ten days after the crossing of the Rhine, the Dutch opened their dikes and flooded their country, thus making it impossible for the French army to operate in their waterlogged territory. Louis had to return to France without having won a decisive victory. In 1673, the taking of Maestricht was followed by the retreat of the French army from the Dutch Republic.[37] The shifting of the theatre of operations to

Franche-Comté in 1674 was an admission of the strength of Dutch resistance. So was the compromise agreed at the peace talks in Nijmegen in 1678 (encouraged by the fact that Britain and Spain had joined the Dutch in a Triple Alliance).

In the official accounts, however, difficulties existed only to be overcome by Louis. In one of the rare (and perhaps tactless) references to the flooding of the Dutch Republic, Desmarets describes the king rather than the enemy as breaking 'dikes and barriers' [*comme un fleuve enflé par les eaux des hyvers/ LOUIS domte ses bords, rompt digues et barrières*].[38]

Corneille presented the king as giving the Dutch peace on his terms, rather than accepting a compromise. 'You have scarcely spoken when peace follows, convincing the whole universe of your omnipotence' [*A peine parles-tu, que son obéissance/ Convainc tout l'Univers de ta toute-puissance*].[39] This is how the peace was celebrated in 1679, in verses printed in the *Mercure Galant*, in a ballet presented at the Gobelins, in ceremonies at Toulouse, and so on. It did not reveal the king's weakness but his strength, his 'moderation', his 'goodness' in giving 'repose' to Europe[40] (Figure 31)

Only Corneille's contemptuous references to the Triple Alliance as a 'plot' or a 'mutiny' (as if the three powers were subjects of the French king) betrays his awareness of the situation.[41] It is paralleled by the obsessively recurrent visual image of the king trampling the three-headed Cerberus. The problem of the discrepancies between the official rhetoric of triumph and the reality of French reverses would become more acute later in the reign.

32. 'The image of the image-maker'. *Portrait of Charles Lebrun* by Nicolas de Largillière, 1686. Louvre, Paris. Lebrun is pointing to the painting reproduced in Figure 25.

VII

THE RECONSTRUCTION OF THE SYSTEM

> Venez voir desarmé ce modèle des Rois,
> Peuples qu'il a vaincus sur la Terre et sur l'Onde,
> Vous tous que son seul nom fit trembler tant de fois,
> Quand son bras lui promet la conquête du Monde.
>
> Le Clerc, madrigal on the statue on the Place des Victoires

THE TREATY of Nijmegen was solemnly proclaimed on 29 September 1678 at eleven points in Paris, to the sound of drums and trumpets, and was followed by cannon, fireworks and the singing of the *Te Deum* in the city and the provinces.[1] It was also followed by ten years of relative peace, in which Louis could rest on his laurels and receive the homage of his subjects. It cannot have been easy to think of forms of praise that had not already been employed by this time, but the invention of place-names in the king's honour may be worth mentioning. The fortress in the Saarland constructed in the 1680s was named 'Saarlouis' to make his memory eternal (the town still bears his name, although it is now part of Germany).[2] It was also at this time, in 1682, that the Chevalier de la Salle named part of the North American continent 'Louisiana'.

The decade of peace also allowed money to be spent more freely on the arts. It was in this decade, for instance, that Versailles was reconstructed by Jules Hardouin-Mansart, and redecorated by Lebrun and his collaborators. The palace was redesigned because its function was changing. It was in 1682 that the court moved officially to Versailles, together with the central administration. Louis continued to spend some of his time in other residences, such as Fontainebleau and Chambord, but he became somewhat more sedentary after the death of his wife in 1683 and his secret marriage to Madame de Maintenon a few months later. After the death of the queen the division of the palace into two state apartments was discontinued, and the king's apartment was located at the centre.[3]

It is the image of the Versailles system, as it was reconstructed in this later period of the reign, which is most vividly impressed on posterity, thanks to the famous description of the king, the court and the 'machine' as he calls it, in the memoirs of Saint-Simon.

1683 was not only the year of the death of the queen but of Colbert, the individual who had done most to create another system, the machine for the glorification of Louis XIV, discussed in Chapter IV. Under Colbert's successor Louvois, this system too was under reconstruction.

The palace

From 1675, when he was appointed court architect, Jules Hardouin-Mansart was high in royal favour and attended the king everywhere.[4] It was he who was mainly responsible for the redesigning of Versailles, including the famous Grande Galerie, the *Salons de Guerre et Paix*, and the *Escalier des Ambassadeurs*. The decorations, which were the work of Lebrun and his collaborators, constitute what is probably the most memorable version of *l'histoire du roi* (Figure 32). Printed descriptions of these decorations in the *Mercure Galant* ensured that this account of the reign reached a wider audience than the courtiers. So did the books on the subject published by François Charpentier (of the petite académie), by Pierre Rainssant (keeper of the king's medals) and later by Jean-François Félibien (son of the historian of the king's buildings).[5]

The original programme for the Grande Galerie was a mythological one, the life and labours of Hercules. It is surely significant that the decision, in 1678, to replace this programme by the history of the king's actions was taken at a high political level, that of the *Conseil Secret*.[6] There were nine large paintings and eighteen small ones, dealing with 'the story of the king from the Peace of the Pyrenees to that of Nijmegen'.[7] Of the large paintings, eight were devoted to the war against the Dutch, while one represented the beginning of personal rule (see Figure 20), 'in which the king, in the flower of his youth, with his eye on glory [*envisageant la Gloire*] takes over the helm of the state after his marriage, and . . . considers how to render his subjects happy and humiliate his enemies'.[8] The domestic events of the reign (the reform of justice and finance, the protection of the arts, the policing of Paris, and so on) remained in the background.[9] To ensure that viewers interpreted the images in the right way, the paintings carried inscriptions. The importance attributed to these inscriptions may be judged by the fact that the original ones, by Charpentier, were later effaced by order of

Louvois, on the grounds that they were too 'pompous', to be replaced by simpler texts by Boileau and Racine.[10]

Almost equally spectacular, according to contemporaries, was the *Escalier des Ambassadeurs*, the grand staircase built to celebrate the king's triumphant return from his wars and utilised thereafter for ceremonial occasions such as the arrival of ambassadors for audiences with the king. The staircase, decorated in the 1680s but destroyed in the eighteenth century, can be reconstructed from contemporary descriptions.[11] The main theme was, once again, triumph, emphasised by the numerous trophies and chariots. The defeated enemies of France appeared in the allegorical forms of a hydra and a python, but coats of arms left the viewer in no doubt that references to Spain and the Empire were intended. Bas-reliefs on the staircase represented famous events of the reign, including the reform of justice, the passage of the Rhine, the submission of Franche-Comté and Spanish acknowledgement of French precedence. What the feelings of the Spanish, Dutch and imperial ambassadors may have been as they ascended this staircase must be left to the reader's imagination.[12] The *Salon de Guerre* reinforced the impression of triumph. Its famous bas-relief, in plaster after a marble relief by Antoine Coysevox, showed the king on horseback riding over two captives (Figures 33 and 34).

The court

Today the name 'Versailles' evokes not only a building but a social world, that of the court, and in particular the ritualisation of the king's everyday life. The actions of getting up in the morning and going to bed at night were transformed into the ceremonies of the *lever* and the *coucher* – with the former divided into two stages, the less formal *petit lever* and the more formal *grand lever*. The royal meals were also ritualised. Louis might eat more formally (the *grand couvert*) or less formally (*the petit couvert*), but even the least formal occasions, *très petit couvert*, included three courses and many dishes.[13] These meals were performances before an audience. It was an honour to be allowed to watch the king eat, a greater honour to be spoken to by the king during the meal, a supreme honour to be invited to serve him his food or to eat with him. Everyone present wore a hat except the king, but took it off to speak to the king or if he spoke to them, unless they were at the table.[14]

As the sociologist Norbert Elias has pointed out, in an argument parallel to Marc Bloch's on the royal touch, these rituals should not be

33. *Louis XIV Trampling His Enemies* by Antoine Coysevox, stucco relief, 1681. Château de Versailles

34. *Bust of Louis* by Antoine Coysevox, marble, *c.* 1686. The Wallace Collection, London

dismissed as mere curiosities. They should be analysed for what they can tell us about the surrounding culture – about absolute monarchy, the social hierarchy, and so on.[15] One might reasonably extend this approach to the rest of the king's daily life – his daily mass, his meetings with his councillors, and even his campaigns, his hunting expeditions and his walks round his gardens. It may be thought that to extend the analysis in this way is to dilute the term 'ritual' until it loses most of its meaning. However, observers noted that all the king's actions were planned, 'down to the slightest gesture'. The same events took place every day at the same time, so much so that one could set one's watch by the king.[16]

There were formal rules for participation in this spectacle – who was allowed to see the king, at which times and in which parts of the court, whether such a person could sit on a chair or a stool [*tabouret*] or had to remain standing.[17] The king's daily life was composed of actions which were not merely recurrent but charged with symbolic meaning because they were performed in public by an actor whose person was sacred. Louis was on stage for almost the whole of his waking life. The material objects most closely associated with the king became sacred in their turn because they represented him. Hence (p. 9) it was an offence to turn one's back on the king's portrait, to enter his empty bed-chamber without a genuflexion or to wear one's hat in the room where the table was set for the king's dinner.[18]

The sociological analysis of order in court should ideally be accompanied by a history of the creation and development of the rituals. We should not assume that they were there all the time, difficult as it now is to imagine Louis XIV without them. The question of their origin is at once obvious and neglected, easy to ask and difficult to answer. What might be called the 'invention' of the Versailles tradition remains obscure.[19] Did the domestic rituals begin when Louis took up permanent residence in the palace in 1682? What happened during earlier visits to Versailles, or later visits to other palaces? Did the king create the rituals himself, or were they the work of his advisers or his masters of ceremonies, or did they really follow tradition? Were they created for political reasons?

Given the importance of these daily rituals in the construction of the image of Louis XIV, it is worth summarising what is known about them. Almost all the evidence comes from relatively late in the reign. The fullest, most vivid and most frequently quoted description of what the author calls 'the outer shell of the life of this monarch' [*l'écorce extérieure de la vie de ce monarque*] is to be found in the memoirs of Saint-Simon. This particular section of the memoirs was probably written as late as the 1740s, but it draws on the author's memories of the 1690s, when he was one of Louis' courtiers.[20] Another valuable but less detailed account of these rituals was given by Ezechiel Spanheim, the Elector of Brandenburg's ambassador, in an account of the court of France [*Relation de la cour de France*], written for his master in 1690. Spanheim was ambassador throughout the 1680s, so his lack of comment on possible changes in 1682 is surely significant.

Both Saint-Simon and Spanheim describe the system as a whole. Before 1690, however, the evidence is more fragmentary. Unfortunately, the voluminous Dangeau began his journal only in 1684. In his memoirs for the year 1674, the Italian nobleman Primi Visconti gave a brief description of the king's *petit coucher*, expressing his surprise at the king's being surrounded by his gentlemen of the chamber, even when he was *installé sur sa chaise percée*.[21] In 1671, a former diplomat, Antoine Courtin, published a book on etiquette, which included instructions on behaviour at Versailles.[22] The ambassador of the Duke of Savoy noted the crowd attending the royal *lever* at the Louvre in 1661.[23] Although the court of Henri IV and Louis XIII seems to have been a good deal more relaxed than the court of Spain (below, p. 180), a certain degree of formality is perceptible.

Given the state of the evidence about the invention of tradition at Versailles, a firm conclusion is out of the question. A hypothetical conclusion, which assembles the fragments into a coherent account, might be the following. The king's daily life was already ritualised to a considerable extent before his personal rule began, but the rituals were elaborated thereafter by adapting the Spanish model to French circumstances. The king's interest in dance and spectacle and his role as protagonist in these rituals makes it probable that the changes to their choreography were made or at least closely supervised by Louis himself. The increasingly elaborate setting for everyday life constructed at Versailles made these rituals more glamorous and also more rigid, helping to produce the effect of clockwork.

One major change in the routine of the court can be dated with relative precision. Following his move to Versailles in 1682, the king opened his apartments to the public (that is, the upper classes) three times a week for 'diversions' such as cards and billiards, in which 'the King, the Queen and the whole Royal Family descend from their heights to play with members of the assembly'.[24] This official description of the new institution, the *appartements*, suggests that the point was to demonstrate the king's accessibility to his subjects, a theme emphasised in medals and in the royal memoirs (above, p. 63).

The organiser

Other changes in the presentation of the public image of the king took place in the mid-1680s. It is likely that they were linked with the death of Colbert and the rise of Louvois. Colbert and Louvois had long been rivals, the former predominant in domestic affairs and the latter in foreign policy. Colbert's death in 1683 gave Louvois an opportunity to extend his empire over the arts. The office of *surintendant des bâtiments* was inherited by Colbert's fourth son, the marquis de Blainville, who had been trained to succeed his father in this position. However, the young man had not performed his duties satisfactorily.[25] The king therefore allowed Louvois to buy the office and so gain control not only of the royal buildings but also of the Gobelins and of the academies. He was soon distributing the prizes to artists in his new capacity as protector of the Royal Academy of Painting and Sculpture.[26]

The effects of this change of control in 1683 illuminate the working of the patronage system of the time. It may not be entirely fanciful to compare it to the American 'spoils system' of the nineteenth and twentieth centuries, which may itself be viewed as a survival of an early modern style of political patronage. The main difference is that the absence of formal political parties meant that the seventeenth-century system was more arbitrary (or more flexible). The 'big man' had the freedom to choose whether or not to replace existing office-holders.

The change in the *surintendance* was a threat to the position of Lebrun, who was, as we have seen, a Colbert man, while Louvois supported his rival Mignard. Lebrun did not lose his official positions, but he did lose influence. Another Colbert man who was pushed aside by Louvois was Charles Perrault, who lost his positions as member of the petite académie and as *commis des bâtiments*.[27] The new *contrôleur des bâtiments* – and secretary of the petite académie – was a protégé of Louvois, the sieur de La Chapelle. Conflicts occurred between La Chapelle and Lebrun.[28] Other former clients of Colbert lost their positions. Pierre de Carcavy lost control of the Académie des Sciences and the Royal Library, while André Le Nôtre was forced into retirement.

Pierre Mignard found that his hour had come at last. He was commissioned to paint the Petite Galerie at Versailles, he was ennobled, and on the death of Lebrun in 1690 he replaced him as *premier peintre du roi*. The sculptor Pierre Puget, who had been out of favour in the Colbert years, following clashes with the minister, was given another chance. Another protégé of Louvois, Jean Donneau de Visé, editor of the *Mercure Galant*, obtained a regular pension from the king at this time. The art critic Roger de Piles was another Louvois man, who was sent to the Dutch Republic to spy as well as to buy paintings for the king. The Dutch penetrated his cover, and while in prison, Piles had the leisure to write one of his books.[29]

More important than the change of personnel was the change of policy, or more exactly the change of strategy, since the fundamental aim of glorifying the king remained the same. In his eight years as *surintendant des bâtiments*, Louvois made his mark by promoting a series of grandiose projects. He doubled the expenditure on Versailles.[30] He

35. 'Louis in the provinces'. *Maquette of the Statute for the Place Royale, Lyons* by François Girardon, wax, *c.* 1687. Yale University Art Gallery, gift of Mr and Mrs James W. Fosburgh, B.A. 1933

planned the construction of buildings on the Place Vendôme to house the Royal Library and all the academies. Although he blocked the completion of the Colbert–Lebrun project for a monument to Louis outside the Louvre, Louvois supported what has been called the 'statue campaign' of 1685–6, in other words the idea of commissioning a series of nearly twenty statues of the king, usually on horseback, to be placed in public squares in Paris and in provincial towns: Aix, Angers, Arles, Besançon, Bordeaux, Caen, Dijon, Grenoble, Le Havre, Limoges, Lyons (Figure 35), Marseilles, Montpellier, Pau, Poitiers, Rennes, Tours and Troyes.[31] Some of these statues were never erected (Besançon, Bordeaux, Grenoble), and others only after the king's death (Montpellier, Rennes). All the same, the scale of the operation remains impressive, recalling Roman emperors such as Augustus rather than modern monarchs.

The unveiling (perhaps one should say the 'consecration') of each of these monuments to the glory of the king was itself an occasion for

36. 'Louis victorious'. *Statue of Louis XIV by Desjardins in the Place des Victoires, Paris,* engraving by Nicolas Arnoult, *c.* 1686. Musée de la Ville de Paris, Musée Carnavalet, Paris

37. 'Louis victorious'. *View of the Place des Victoires,* anonymous engraving, early 18th century. Cabinet des Estampes, Bibliothèque Nationale, Paris

38. 'Louis victorious'. *View of the Place des Victoires*, frontispiece from Northleigh, *Topographical Descriptions*, 1702. British Library, London

celebration. The statue at Caen, for example, was solemnly inaugurated on the king's birthday in 1685, with a parade, speeches, trumpets, drums, bells and an artillery salute. The inauguration was itself described in a pamphlet as well as in the *Gazette* and the *Mercure Galant*.[32]

In 1686, the *Mercure Galant* reported that 'everywhere there is a rush to erect statues to him' [*on s'empresse en tous lieux à luy dresser des statues*].[33] Most were equestrian, but some showed the king standing. The most spectacular was the statue by Martin Desjardins for the Place des Victoires, a standing figure of the king in his coronation robes 13 feet high, trampling on Cerberus and crowned by Victory, 'a vast winged woman close behind his back, holding forth a laurel crown over the king's head' (Figures 36, 37 and 38).[34] The foot of the statue bore the dedication 'to the immortal man' [VIRO IMMORTALI] and the marble pedestal carried an inscription listing ten major achievements of the reign. The complex included four bronze captives, six bas-reliefs celebrating the most glorious events of the reign, and four columns bearing torches which were lit every night.[35]

The unveiling of this statue was appropriately magnificent, with parades, speeches, salvos, music and fireworks.[36] In 1687 it was the unveiling of the standing statue of the king by the local sculptor Jean Girouard on the old market-place at Poitiers which was celebrated, on the feast of St Louis.[37] In the same year, on one of his rare visits to Paris, Louis went to see his statue on the Place des Victoires, as well as the Place Vendôme, for which another statue was planned. The two sculptors, Desjardins and Girardon, were in attendance.[38]

The original idea for this statue campaign seems to have come from the royal architect Mansart, and the most spectacular of these statues, on the Place des Victoires, was commissioned by a private individual, Marshal Feuillade (the duc de Richelieu commissioned another for his château at Rueil). Without the support of Louvois, however, these projects would not have stood a chance of success. As for the statues in the provinces, their inscriptions suggest that they were commissioned locally out of spontaneous devotion to the king, and the *Mercure Galant* reinforces this impression. 'The City of Grenoble', for example, is described as charging its aldermen 'to beg His Majesty most humbly to allow them to erect a statue of him on their main square'.[39] Again, 'The City of Caen did not wish to be the last to show its zeal by raising a statue to His Majesty.' Marseilles too asked for a statue.[40]

However, there is evidence that this display of loyalty was not spontaneous at all. The municipalities and provincial Estates were encouraged, if not ordered, to make this gesture by *intendants*, provincial governors and other officials. At Caen, for example, it was the *intendant* Barrillon who took the initiative, at Grenoble the *intendant* Lebret, at Le Havre the duc de Saint-Aignan, and at Rennes the duc de Chaulnes. For their part these officials would hardly have made this suggestion in different provinces at the same time without orders from Paris.[41] Even the inscriptions and other details on some of the monuments to the glory of Louis were laid down by the central government. At Arles, the inscription devised by the local academy was replaced by one composed by the official historian Pellisson. At Dijon, Mansart insisted on additions, which the local Estates had not planned. In the case of Lyons, it was Pontchartrain (to whom the petite académie was responsible after the death of Louvois), who intervened to determine the inscription.[42]

The increasing preoccupation of the central government with the king's image in the provinces deserves some emphasis (below, p. 156). It has been pointed out that the statue campaign concentrated on the so-called *pays d'États* (Normandy, Britanny, Artois, Burgundy, Languedoc and Provence), which had been the last to be incorporated into France and preserved more of their independence. At much the same time came the foundation of provincial institutions on the Paris model, from the royal academy at Nîmes to the opera-house at Marseilles (below, p. 155). The government's new awareness of the need to cultivate public opinion in the provinces may to some extent have been a response to the rebellion of the Breton peasants in 1675 (for which the local elite was blamed).

Louvois also tried to promote the glory of the king through publications, on a characteristically grand scale. Some of these publications were associated with the Académie des Sciences.[43] More directly associated with the image of Louis XIV was another project begun (or at any rate reactivated) by Louvois, the 'medallic history'. The medallic (or metallic) history was planned as an account of the reign in book form, with engravings of all the medals struck to commemorate particular events, arranged in chronological order and accompanied by an explanatory text. The concern of the minister for this project is suggested by the fact that the petite académie, which devised inscriptions for royal medals, was enlarged in 1683, and that one of the new members (besides Boileau and Racine) was a numismatist, Pierre Rainssant, a protégé of Louvois, whose description of Versailles was mentioned earlier in the chapter.[44] In his last years, when war had broken out again, Louvois kept a close watch on the way in which it was reported in the *Gazette*, criticising some articles and correcting the drafts of others.[45]

As in the age of Colbert, team-work was important. All the same, it may not be fanciful to suggest that the projects of this period reflect the personality of the minister (harsh, brutal, with a tendency to go too far) more than that of the monarch. The hands are the hands of Desjardins, Mignard, Rainssant, and so on, but the voice is the voice of Louvois.

The events

Similar accents can be heard in the events of this period, although it was a decade of relative peace. The events chosen for commemoration included two naval actions, two diplomatic occasions, the king's recovery from illness and, dominating the rest by far, the Revocation of the Edict of Nantes.

The naval actions were the bombardment of Algiers in 1683 and of Genoa in 1684, the first city (part of the Ottoman Empire) because it harboured pirates and the second (still an independent city-state) because its government had allowed the construction of galleys for the Spanish navy. The way in which these events were represented on the medals struck to commemorate them tells us a good deal about official attitudes at this time. The inscription on one was 'Algiers struck by lightning' [ALGERIA FULMINATA] (Figure 39), implying an analogy between Louis and Jupiter (often represented with a thunderbolt) (Figures 40 and 41), which is made explicit elsewhere, for example in Lebrun's paintings at Versailles. Another inscription is 'Africa as suppliant' [AFRICA SUPPLEX].[46]

On two different medals of the bombardment of Genoa one side is inscribed 'thunderbolts are hurled at the proud' [VIBRATA IN SUPERBOS FULMINA], and the other 'Genoa corrected' (or chastised) [GENUA EMENDATA] (Figure 42).[47] This is the language of paternalism with a vengeance. Independent states such as the Genoese republic were represented by French official artists and writers as children, to be 'punished' for their faults.[48]

To rub salt in the wound, the doge of Genoa was obliged to come in person to Paris to present his apologies, or, as the *Gazette* described it, 'to make submissions' to Louis [*faire des soumissions au Roy*], as the Algerian ambassador had done (and as the envoys of Spain and the papacy had also done earlier in the reign in the cases of the affairs of the ambassador's coach and the Corsican guards). The doge arrived in Versailles with four senators and made a speech of apology during which he removed his hat every time he pronounced the king's name. After Louis had graciously accepted the apology, and the doge had bowed low three times on his way out, the Genoese were given a dinner, gifts and a conducted tour of Versailles.[49] Their submission was represented and commemorated not only in newspapers and journals, but also by a painting by Claude Hallé (Figure 43); by a tapestry executed at the Gobelins; and by medals with inscriptions such as 'The Submission of Genoa' [GENUA OBSEQUENS].[50]

One embassy which received almost as much attention in the media was that of 'the mandarins sent by the king of Siam' (1686), doubtless because it supported the claim that Louis was 'the greatest monarch in the world'. Four special issues of the *Mercure Galant* were devoted to this visit, and to the admiration for the king which the visitors expressed. It is surely significant that the Siamese were taken to see the Gobelins, the Royal Academy of Painting and a number of works of art, including Lebrun's *History of Alexander*. The embassy was in its turn represen-

39. *Algeria fulminata:* obverse and reverse of medal, engraving from *Médailles*, 1702. British Library, London

40. *Heidelberga Fulminata*, pen and ink design for a medal from 'Projets de Devises de l'Académie avant 1694'. Manuscript Collections, British Library, London

41. *Air*, one of four needlepoint hangings, probably 1683–4. The Metropolitan Museum of Art, Rogers Fund, 1946

42. 'Genoa corrected'. *Genua emendata* by François Chéron, reverse of medal, 1684. Department of Coins and Medals, British Museum, London

43. *Doge of Genoa at Versailles* by Claude Hallé, oil on canvas, 1685. Musée Cantini, Marseilles

ted in paintings in engravings (Figure 44), in bas-reliefs and on medals.[51]

The Revocation

So far as representations are concerned, all the other events of this period were overshadowed by the Revocation of the Edict of Nantes. The king's decision to outlaw Protestantism, which led to the emigration of some 200,000 Frenchmen and women, has often been criticised by historians. The point that requires emphasis here is the importance of favourable comment in the media of the day. Some of the comments can be described as the work of the government, celebrating itself, but others came from outside bodies such as the Jesuits or the secular clergy. To look at contemporary representations of the Revocation in more detail should remind us that the image of Louis XIV did not emanate, like the light of the sun, from a single centre. It was the joint production of official and unofficial writers, artists and patrons.

For official representations of the event, one might begin with the newspapers, especially the *Mercure Galant*, which devoted a good deal of space to the subject. Readers were already prepared for the news by earlier accounts of the conversions of prominent Protestants, suggesting that their 'party' was growing weaker by itself, without any recourse to violence.[52] Every step towards the Revocation was accompanied by applause for His Majesty's most Christian 'zeal'.[53] When the news of the royal edict finally arrived, it was reported with little comment.[54] In subsequent issues, however, a good deal of space was given to poems congratulating the king on his destruction of the 'insolent' heresy:

> Destruire l'Herésie insolente et rebelle,
> C'est l'unique Triomphe ou prétend ce grand Roy.
> Quel autre peut donner une gloire plus belle?[55]

Official representations of the Revocation also included medals, bearing inscriptions devised by the petite académie such as 'true religion victorious' [RELIGIO VICTRIX], 'heresy extinguished' [EXTINCTA HAERESIS], 'The temples of the Calvinists destroyed' [TEMPLIS CALVINIANORUM EVERSIS] or 'Two million Calvinists brought back to the Church' [VICIES CENTENA MILLIA CALVINIANORUM AD ECCLESIAM REVOCATA] (see Figure 58).[56] The statue of Louis by Desjardins on the Place des Victoires included a bas-relief of the Revocation. The Académie Royale de Peinture chose 'the triumph of the Church' and

44. 'The world pays homage to Louis'. *Audience Given to the Siamese Embassy by the King* on the *Almanac for the Year 1687*. Bibliothèque Nationale, Paris

45. 'Louis as Defender of the Faith'. *Allegory of the Revocation of Edict of Nantes* by Guy-Louis Vernansel, *c.* 1685

'heresy trodden underfoot' as themes for diploma pictures. A painting by Guy Louis Vernansel (who became a member of the Académie in 1687) illustrates the second theme (Figure 45). The Church is as usual represented as a woman, defended by Louis, while heretics flee or fall to the ground. Philippe Quinault ended a twenty-year career as librettist for court ballets and operas with an epic entitled *L'hérésie détruite*, while Charles Perrault wrote an ode to the 'newly-converted', congratulating them together with their 'magnanimous' monarch.[57]

The Revocation was also celebrated by the clergy, not surprisingly, since some of them had been urging it on the king. Indeed, it has been argued that on this occasion the clergy used Louis as a 'tool' for their own ends.[58] The most famous eulogy of the king for this particular action is a sermon by Bossuet delivered at the funeral of the former minister Michel Le Tellier and describing Louis as 'this new Theodosius, this new Marcion, this new Charlemagne'.[59] The Jesuits in particular laboured this theme. Philibert Quartier, professor at the Jesuit college in Paris, recently renamed Louis-le-Grand, delivered a panegyric on the king 'for having extinguished heresy' [*pro extincta haeresi*]. The theme of the college ballet in 1685 was 'Clovis', the king who established Christianity in France. Two years later, another Jesuit, Gabriel Le Jay, chose 'The Triumph of Religion' as the theme of his panegyric, inscriptions and devices.[60] With hindsight, earlier ballets and orations may be interpreted as Jesuit encouragement of the anti-Protestant campaign, for instance, *Constantin: le triomphe de la religion* (performed in 1681, the year that Strasbourg was forcibly returned to Catholicism), and *Ludovicus Pius* ('Louis the Pious') (1683).[61]

Other reactions to the Revocation, inside and outside France, were much less favourable. In retrospect, it is clear that this action did the royal image more harm than good. This image would become still more tarnished in the later years of the reign.

46. 'The ageing Louis'. *Portrait of Louis XIV* by Antoine Benoist, wax and mixed media, 1706. Château de Versailles

VIII

SUNSET

'Si l'affaire de Hochstet lui a été plus desavantageuse qu'à ses Ennemis, en ce que ses Troupes ont été obligées de leur céder le champ de Bataille, ils ont perdus beaucoup plus de monde que lui.'

Mercure Galant, October 1704, on the battle of Blenheim

In 1688, Louis XIV was fifty years old. He had been on the throne for forty-five years, and for twenty-seven years he had ruled in person. He was, by the standards of the seventeenth century, an elderly man. No one would have guessed that his reign would last for more than another quarter of a century. The king was not in good physical shape, having had to submit to two operations in the later 1680s. The first led to the loss of most of his teeth. The second, more serious operation was the one to cure a fistula – an illness described in official circles by means of euphemisms such as 'indisposition' – Mlle de Scudéry wrote a madrigal on 'the Indisposition of His Majesty' – or 'discomfort' [*incommodité*].[1] As a result of his illnesses, Louis became more sedentary. Indeed, after taking the court to the siege of Namur in 1692, the king gave up going on campaign altogether.

Louis became increasingly immobile as he suffered more and more from gout. In his last years he was sometimes to be seen in a wheel-chair (his *roulette*) in the palace and gardens of Versailles. He still paid attention to self-presentation, and caught cold one day in 1704 because he spent too long making up his mind which of his various wigs to wear, but he was beginning to withdraw from public view.[2] The public *coucher* was abolished in 1705, and representations of the king's ravaged body became less frequent after the famous portrait by Rigaud of 1701 (see Figure 1) and the wax image by Benoist of 1706 (Figure 46).

47. 'Louis' motto: not unequal to many'. *Nec pluribus impar*, reverse of medal by Jean Warin, 1674. Cabinet des Médailles, Bibliothèque Nationale, Paris

In politics too there was a downward trend. The second half of the long period of personal rule was less successful than the first. It was a period of neither peace nor victory. The proud device 'not unequal to many', NEC PLURIBUS IMPAR (Figure 47), must have seemed increasingly inappropriate at a time when France was unable to defeat the Grand Alliance of her enemies. The war of the League of Augsburg lasted from 1688 to 1697, and the War of the Spanish Succession from 1702 to 1713. These wars were expensive, leaving the state deep in debt, and despite individual successes, especially in the first case, they added little to the king's glory. This was the judgement of contemporaries, French and foreign, as well as the verdict of later historians.

For these reasons the last twenty-five years of the reign may be described as the royal 'sunset'. It will therefore be necessary to look even more closely than before at possible discrepancies between the public image of the king and the reality as contemporaries perceived it, in order to discover how the image-makers dealt with this problem.

In this difficult period, Louis lacked the advice and support of ministers of the calibre of Lionne, Le Tellier and Colbert. The last of the major figures, Louvois, died in 1691. Officials such as Villacerf (a member of the Colbert clan who became *surintendant des bâtiments* in 1691, but resigned after a financial scandal in 1699) or Pontchartrain (who succeeded Louvois in the direction of the academies) were not in the same class. The most able of them was probably the marquis de Torcy, nephew of the famous Colbert, who became Secretary of State for Foreign Affairs in 1696, and included among his responsibilities a concern for the public image of the king abroad, especially during the War of the Spanish Succession.[3] Torcy's concern with pensioning writers and with academies (he founded an academy of politics) suggests a conscious return to the policies of his uncle.

The artists and writers who created this image were also of less distinction than before. There was no new Molière or Racine, only playwrights of lesser calibre, like La Chapelle. The shortage of talent has led historians to speak of a 'crisis of French literature' at this time.[4] There was no effective replacement for Lully (who died in 1687) or Lebrun (who died in 1690). The new decorations at Versailles, Marly and the Grand Trianon were the work of minor talents such as René Antoine Houasse (a former protégé of Lebrun's), Noël Coypel, Charles de Lafosse, Jean Jouvenet and François Desportes.[5] The sculptor Girardon remained active, but he had lost the favour of the king by 1700 and he was in any case over seventy by that time. The Revocation of the Edict of Nantes led to the emigration of some artists in royal service, such as Daniel Marot, who changed his allegiance to William of Orange.

Magnificent spectacles were still presented at court, until the deaths of the Dauphin and Louis' grandson, the Duke of Burgundy, made them inappropriate, but they were the work of relatively minor figures such the composers André Destouches and Michel-Richard de Lalande, or the poet Antoine de Lamotte. Racine survived to 1699 and Boileau to 1711, but Racine had given up writing for the public theatre, while Boileau was no longer producing his best work. The most gifted writer of the younger generation, Jean de La Bruyère, praised the king and his policies on occasion.[6] However, he was best known as a critic of the court society of his time.

There remained the architect Jules Hardouin Mansart, who was made *surintendant des bâtiments* in 1699, the sculptor Antoine Coysevox, who became director of the Royal Academy in 1702, and the portrait painter Hyacinthe Rigaud, who was ennobled in 1709. These three men were gifted artists, but no substitute for the galaxy of talent formerly serving the sun-king.

Court patronage and state patronage – categories that overlap but do not coincide – became increasingly fragmented. What might be called the 'satellite' courts of the Dukes of Burgundy and Orléans became increasingly important centres for patronage of both painting and music. On the death of Louvois, responsibility for the royal buildings and the royal academies was divided, with the result that the petite académie lost its former connection with architecture and concentrated even more on medals and inscriptions.

In any case, the financial problems of the state naturally limited its patronage. The period 1689–1715 might well be described as 'the Great Retrenchment'. The melting down of the silver furniture of Versailles in 1689 is only the most notorious example of the impact of war on the arts. Building and decoration at Versailles was halted for a time. On the death of Louvois, work on the reconstruction of the Place Vendôme was halted at the king's command. The payment of pensions was suspended, and so were the activities of the royal press. The medallic history was delayed, while the Academy of Sciences had to abandon some of its most prestigious projects, such as the *Histoire des plantes*.[7]

Focusing more sharply on the image of the ageing king, this chapter will concentrate on two themes: the representation of wars in an age without victories, and the completion of two major projects for the glorification of the king, the colossal statue for the Place Louis le Grand and the official medallic history of the reign.

Military operations

The events of the war of the League of Augsburg, which lasted for ten years, 1688–97, were celebrated in prose and verse, but not on the scale of the 1660s or 1670s. Thomas l'Herault de Lionnière published a history of the military events of 1689 in the form of a panegyric. Boileau wrote an ode on the taking of Namur, which was also commemorated in paintings and engravings.[8] These events were also marked by no fewer than forty-five medals. Sixteen of these medals represent battles on land or at sea, including Fleurus (in Flanders), Staffarde (in Piedmont), Leuze, Steinkirke, Pforzheim, Neerwinden, Marsaglia and Ter.[9] Twenty medals celebrate the conquest of territories or the capture of cities, including Mons, Nice, Namur, Charleroi and Barcelona – not counting the notorious medal struck to celebrate the destruction of Heidelberg and later suppressed (Figure 48).[10] The viewer is made aware of the scale of the theatre of operations in this 'first world war' as a historian recently called it, by medals of the taking of Cartagena, in South America, and of the defeat of an English fleet in Canada.[11]

48. 'The sack of Heidelberg'. *Heidelberga Deleta* by Jérôme Roussel, reverse of medal, *c.* 1690. Department of Coins and Medals, British Museum, London

At the same time, a comparison with earlier campaigns suggests a certain debasement of the medallic currency. Relatively minor events were commemorated: the saving of a grain convoy from the enemy, the march of the Dauphin to the Scheldt, or the failure of an enemy bombardment to destroy Dunkirk (DUNKERCA ILLAESA), mocked by Addison ('What have the French here done to boast of?').[12] There was even a medal struck for the distribution of medals to French sailors.

The medals for the war of the Spanish succession, 1702–13, reveal by certain eloquent silences that the affairs of France were not going well. Twelve years of war generate only twenty-four medals. Alongside the celebration of nine victories in battle and the taking of eleven enemy fortresses, two medals refer to the relief of French fortresses (Toulon and Landrecies), a revealing admission that France was sometimes on the defensive.[13] Two medals refer not to victories or conquests but merely to the 'campaigns' of 1712 and 1713.[14]

In any case, the names of the victories (Luzara, Fridlingen, Ekeren, and so on) have an unfamiliar and even a hollow ring to any viewer aware of the recent events at Blenheim (1704), Ramillies (1706), Oudenarde (1708) and Malplaquet (1709), engagements in which the armies commanded by the Duke of Marlborough and Prince Eugene of Savoy defeated the French troops. Malplaquet in fact cost the enemy more troops than the French, but the lack of a medal for it suggests that Louis did not regard the event as one fit to celebrate. There was a fall in the demand for winged Victories and laurel wreaths.

The way in which these battles were described in the official press of the time is also revealing. The king's private letters are sufficient testimony to his awareness of disaster.[15] Again, we know that the news of the defeat of the French army and the capture of its commander, Marshal Tallard, at the battle of Blenheim (otherwise known as Hochstädt) in Bavaria was a shock to the court. A letter written by Madame de Maintenon soon after the news reached Versailles commented on the blow to the king (*la peine du Roi*) as well as the calm, resigned manner in which he received the news.[16] The *Mercure Galant* tried to suggest that Blenheim was not altogether a defeat, on the grounds that the enemy 'have lost far more men' than the French, but contemporaries, such as the marquis de Surville, noted the hollowness of the claim and the way in which the government tried to divert attention from the defeat by immediately ordering a *Te Deum* for a naval victory.[17]

Again, if one examines the *Gazette* for 1708, the year of the defeat of the Dukes of Vendôme and Burgundy at the battle of Oudenarde, and also the loss of Lille, one might not have thought that a battle had occurred at all.[18] The *Clef du Cabinet*, an unofficial monthly, tried to suggest that Oudenarde was not a defeat, while the *Gazette* made little reference to the war between the report from Brussels in March 'that the people of this country are extremely discontented with the way in which they are treated by the Allies, who are ruining their commerce', and the news from Spain in July that the French had captured Tortosa, an event celebrated by a *Te Deum*, bonfires and other forms of public rejoicing.[19] The *Mercure Galant* described the engagement as a 'combat' rather than a 'battle', adding that the losses of the Allies had been 'infinitely' greater, and that 'we would have won if it had been possible to break through the hedges'.[20] Oudenarde was thus downgraded to a minor event if not a non-event. In this time of trials there was little to celebrate but the king's calm in the face of disaster, or – to use the stoic term adopted by the petite académie in a medal of 1715 – his 'constancy'.[21]

Instead, Torcy tried another approach, writing in the king's name in 1709 to the bishops and the governors of provinces, and replacing the traditional references to glory by statements of concern for the people. Louis is presented not as a distant figure but as the father of his people, wanting only their 'repose'. 'My affection for my people is as great as that which I have for my own children.'[22] This language was not entirely new; the inscriptions in the Grande Galerie refer on occasion to 'the paternal care of His Majesty for the good of his peoples' [*les soins paternels que Sa Majesté a pour le bien de ses peuples*].[23] All the same, the change of emphasis was quite remarkable.

Domestic affairs

Very few civil or domestic events from this period of the reign, despite its length, were commemorated by medals. An exception was the king's recovery from his operation for the fistula in 1687, an event also celebrated by an extraordinary meeting of the Académie Française, by the king's presence at a dinner at the Hôtel de Ville, by sculptures (Figure 49), and by an avalanche of odes and sonnets, all reported in detail in the press.[24]

Medals were also struck to commemorate the establishment of the order of St Louis (1693), the marriage of the Duke of Burgundy (1697), the inauguration of a statue of the king (1699), the creation of a council of commerce, edicts against luxury and begging, and the accession of Philippe of Anjou to the throne of Spain (all in 1700). It will be noticed that in two of these cases, in a form of circularity which has been noted a number of times already (pp. 16, 64), it was the glorification of the king in one medium that was celebrated in another.

The most memorable domestic events of the latter part of the reign were unhappy ones, from the famine of 1693, the revolt of the Protestants of the Cévennes in 1702 and the harsh winter of 1709, to the deaths of the Dauphin in 1711 and of the Duke and Duchess of Burgundy in 1712.[25] In this situation, there was little else to celebrate but the media themselves. There was a real need for psychological compensation or, as contemporaries such as Surville put it (p. 112), for the diversion of attention.

The foundation of the Order of St Louis was the climax of an identification, or at any rate a parallel, between the two kings, which had been made from Louis' childhood onwards (as it had for his father Louis XIII). In 1648, for example, the ten-year-old king listened to a panegyric on the saint in the Jesuit church of St Antoine on the feast-day of the saint, 25 August. In 1668, the scholar Charles Du Cange published an edition of a medieval biography of St Louis with a dedication to the king and a comparison between the two rulers. At least three images of St Louis with the features of Louis XIV are known to have been made, dating from *c.*1655, 1660 and 1675.[26]

49. 'Louis recovers from illness'. *Allegory of the Recovery of the King* by Nicolas Coustou, marble relief, 1693. Louvre, Paris

In the course of the reign, the comparison was institutionalised, and the feast of the saint became an occasion to honour the king. In 1669, for example, it took the form of a festival at St Germain, with a performance of a play by Molière.[27] It became the custom for the Académie Française to celebrate 25 August with the award of a prize in the form of a medal of the king, and also with a panegyric combining the praises of the two Louis.[28] Motets were composed for the occasion, and in 1703 a medal was presented to the king on that day.[29] The statue of the king erected at Poitiers was inaugurated on the feast of St Louis. The foundation in 1686 of the 'ladies of St Louis' (a school for poor noblewomen at Saint-Cyr) by Madame de Maintenon, like the foundation of the Order of St Louis in 1693, was part of a more general trend.[30] So was the chapel at Versailles, which itself contained a chapel dedicated to St Louis and decorated with scenes from his life.

The unveiling of the statue by Girardon for Place Louis-le-Grand on 13 August 1699 was celebrated with as much fervour as a major victory. The statue itself (see p. 16) was colossal. At the order of the king, René Houasse produced two paintings of the transport of the statue to the square (Figures 50 and 51). Destroyed during the French Revolution, the statue is known not only from engravings (Figure 52) (like the Desjardins on the Place des Victoires) but from reproductions in miniature (of which six survive), yet another form of publicity (see Figure 53).

To inaugurate the monument, the municipality of Paris constructed a 'Temple of Glory' on the banks of the Seine, mounted on a rock (like the famous Bernini statue of the king) in order to show the difficulties of the road to glory (Figure 54). There was also a magnificent display of fireworks, with representations not only of Hercules, Alexander, Clovis and Charlemagne – traditional figures of the king – but also Perseus, Jason, Theseus, Cyrus, Theodosius, Fabius, Pompey, Caesar, Philippe Auguste and Henri IV. The Jesuit Menestrier, now aged sixty-eight, came out of retirement to commemorate the celebrations in an illustrated pamphlet.[31]

Menestrier had also been involved – unofficially – in another great enterprise for the glorification of the king, the long-planned medallic history of the reign. The petite académie began work on the enterprise in the mid-1680s, but at first they did not make much progress. In 1689, Menestrier, who had nothing to do with the academy, published his own medallic history, or *Histoire du roy Louis le Grand par les médailles*. The book included engravings of 122 medals of the domestic

50. *Transport of the Statue of Louis XIV in 1699: Leaving the Capuchin Convent* by René Antoine Houasse, oil on canvas, *c.* 1700. Musée de la Ville de Paris, Musée Carnavalet

51. *Transport of the Statue of Louis XIV in 1699: Arriving at the Place Vendôme* by René Antoine Houasse, oil on canvas, *c.* 1700. Musée de la Ville de Paris, Musée Carnavalet

52. 'The colossus'. *Equestrian Statue of the King*, anonymous engraving of the Girardon statue, *c.* 1697. British Library, London

and international events of the reign, together with *jetons* and a selection of inscriptions, emblems and devices to the glory of the king. The publication was viewed by the Academy as an infringement of its monopoly, as is clear from its protests against later editions of the book.[32] One is reminded of the way in which Antoine Furetière stole a march on the Académie Française by publishing his *Dictionary* in 1684 (ten years before theirs). Team-work is not necessarily more efficient than that of an enterprising individual.

Faced with Menestrier's challenge, and released from their concern with royal buildings (in 1691), the Academy speeded up its work. At the end of 1695, the history had reached 1672. By 1699, the king was expressing his 'impatience' to see the official medallic history in print. In 1702, it was finally published in a sumptuous folio volume from the royal press, at a moment between wars when money for such grandiose

53. 'A reproduction in miniature'. *Equestrian Louis XIV*, maquette for the statue in the Place Louis-le-Grand, 1691. The Metropolitan Museum of Art, New York, Hewitt Fund, 1911

projects was somewhat less difficult to find (Figure 55). There was also a cheaper quarto edition. The *Médailles sur les principaux événements de Louis le Grand* (the word 'history' does not occur, doubtless to distinguish the work from Menestrier's) included engravings of 286 medals, arranged in chronological order; the decision to exclude certain medals was taken at the highest level. The accompanying text includes not only descriptions of the iconography of the medals but also 'historical explanations' of the events commemorated. In other words, the volume provided what so many historiographers royal had been commissioned to produce, but had never published, an official history of the reign. The *intendants* were ordered to keep this work of reference on their desks.

The king himself took part in revising the volume for the second edition, including 318 medals this time, but he never saw the results. By the time the volume appeared, in 1723, Louis had already been in

54. *The Temple of Glory*, engraving by Guérard in C.-F. Menestrier, 179 a 5. British Library, London

55. 'The celebration of Louis celebrated'. Frontispiece to the Academy's *Médailles* . . . , 1702, engraving by Louis Simonneau after a drawing by Noel Coypel. British Library, London

his grave for eight years. Indeed, the last two medals in the volume commemorate the death of the king.

The final scenes

The last illness of Louis XIV was stage-managed to the last, with several death-bed scenes in which the king bade farewell to his courtiers and offered advice to his five-year-old great-grandson and successor. His best-remembered remark was that 'I have loved war too much: do not imitate me in this respect, or in my expenditure, which was too great' [*J'ai trop aimé la guerre: ne m'imitez pas en cela, non plus que dans les trop grandes dépenses que j'ai faites*].[33]

The official accounts of the royal funeral give an impression of magnificence. The ceremony should have been all the more impressive because there had been no funeral for a king of France since 1643. However, the mood of the public, according to contemporary witnesses, was one of relief rather than rejoicing.[34]

Over fifty funeral orations on Louis were published.[35] They gave the preachers a unique opportunity to sum up the reign and to speak without being overheard by the king. Some of these preachers preferred to dwell on the king's death, described as a good death in the Christian sense, and also as a 'magnificent spectacle' of courage and constancy.[36] Others had more to say about Louis' life and reign. They were prepared to criticise his morals, particularly at the time when the young king was a 'slave to his desires'. References were also made to 'the disasters and the suffering brought upon France by wars which were too frequent' [*les maux et les misères que de trop fréquentes guerres ont attiré sur la France*].[37]

All the same, the general tone of these sermons was triumphalist, to the point of evoking, even in the pulpit, the victories in Flanders and the humiliation of Algiers and Genoa. Louis' love of the arts was also mentioned. It goes without saying that the late king's zeal for religion and his works of charity (notably the foundation of the Invalides and St-Cyr) were fulsomely praised.

A final image of the king was projected in his last will and testament, drawn up at Marly in 1714, and a letter written a few days before his death, to be delivered to the Dauphin on his seventeenth birthday, in 1727.[38] The letter advised the future Louis XV never to break with Rome, to prefer peace to war and to keep the taxes down. Should we interpret this text as a recognition of the mistakes of the reign, or a last effort to make a good impression on posterity?

56. 'Delouisfication'. Detail of *Enseigne de Gersaint* by Antoine Watteau, shop-sign, 1721. Schloss Charlottenburg, Berlin

If it was the latter, it seems to have been unsuccessful. The king's death was followed by an outpouring of irreverent comments on the reign (below, Chapter 10). The mood of the Regency seems to have been one of reaction against the king, neatly symbolised by Watteau in his famous image (Figure 56) of the art dealer's shop with a portrait of Louis, no longer in demand, on its way down to the cellar.[39]

57. 'An Historical Study', frontispiece to Titmarsh (W. M. Thackeray), *The Paris Sketchbook*, 1840. British Library, London

IX

THE CRISIS OF REPRESENTATIONS

Le changement des temps et des affaires peut obliger à supprimer ou à corriger.

Bignon

THERE WERE awkward discrepancies between the official image of the king and the everyday reality as perceived by even relatively sympathetic contemporaries. These discrepancies were not of course unique to this particular ruler, but they complicated the task of artists, writers and others concerned with what might be called the 'management' of the royal image.

For example, Louis was not a tall man. He was only about 1.6 metres (5′ 3″). This discrepancy between his actual height and what might be called his 'social height' had to be camouflaged in various ways. His son the Grand Dauphin was taller, but he 'was usually so placed in paintings and engravings that this was not obtrusive'.[1] His wig and his high heels (Figures 1 and 57) helped to make Louis more impressive. The wig also disguised the fact that the king lost a good deal of his hair in the course of an illness he suffered in 1659. His portraits too tended to improve his appearance, although Louis did allow himself to be shown growing older, and even toothless (above, p. 33).

There is another kind of discrepancy to consider. In certain cases, noted above (pp. 54, 112), there were obvious contradictions between the official accounts of the deeds of the king and the information available from other sources. The myth of the invincible hero was obviously incompatible with French defeats, and it is revealing to see how official media deal – or fail to deal – with such incidents. Certain events were celebrated at the time, and suppressed later, as in the notorious case of the destruction of Heidelberg by French troops (above, p. 110). As the abbé Bignon (the official censor, and later head of all the French academies) discreetly put it, 'Changes in the political situation may make it necessary to suppress or correct' information.[2]

It is also possible to find instances of the reverse of suppression, in other words the celebration of events that had not happened, of what the American historian Daniel Boorstin has called 'pseudo-events'.[3] Around the year 1670 Sébastien Leclerc made an engraving of Louis visiting the Académie des Sciences (see Figure 18), at a time when no such visit had taken place.[4]

These examples reveal what might be called 'recurrent' or even 'normal' problems in the official representation of rulers. In the second half of the seventeenth century, however, another kind of problem, or cluster of problems, emerged. I shall refer to this cluster, rather dramatically perhaps, as the 'crisis of representations' of the seventeenth century, and divide it into two parts, the decline of antiquity and the decline of correspondences.

The decline of antiquity as a cultural model in seventeenth-century France is generally discussed under the rubric of the conflict [*querelle*] between the ancients and the moderns, or as Jonathan Swift called it, the 'Battle of the Books'. This debate was at its height at the end of the 1680s. Boileau and La Fontaine defended the ancients, while the Perrault brothers and Fontenelle supported the moderns.[5] The main theme of the debate was whether the ancients, in particular the writers Virgil and Horace, were superior to their modern equivalents. The discussion naturally widened to include the question whether modern culture (including science) was superior to that of classical antiquity. Other issues included the propriety of choosing post-classical heroes (such as Clovis or Charlemagne) as the protagonists of poems and plays, of using a modern language for the inscriptions on monuments (below, pp. 158, 162) of representing modern weapons (muskets, bombs, etc.) on these monuments, and of portraying contemporary figures, such as the king, in modern dress.[6] The moderns 'won' the battle in the sense that the leader of the other side, Boileau, eventually declared himself convinced.

This debate was not a purely literary matter. The participants were well aware of its political implications. If the age of Louis the Great surpassed that of Augustus, then Louis too surpassed Augustus. Charles Perrault went so far as to criticise Alexander for his 'vast pride' and Augustus for his 'cruelty'.[7] An apparently aesthetic decision like the choice of the new 'French order' of columns for the Louvre instead of the traditional Doric, Ionic or Corinthian ones had political implications. Indeed, it was a political message.

On the face of it, the victory of the moderns was a victory for Louis XIV. After all, the leading supporters of the movement were clients of Colbert.[8] All the same, the presentation of the monarch was so closely linked to the prestige of the classical tradition, that any decline in the importance of that tradition created difficulties for artists and writers, difficulties that Boileau, for example, made one of the main themes of his *Fourth Epistle*, on the campaign of 1672.

The second problem is that of the decline of correspondence and of what has been called the 'organic analogy' in an age in which western intellectuals were coming to view the world as a vast machine. It is well known to historians of science, philosophy, literature and political thought.[9] Indeed, it has been under discussion from the 1930s onwards.[10] It has also attracted some attention from art historians.[11] However, so far as I know, the discussion has not been brought into contact with analyses of the representations of rulers.

The myths of medieval and Renaissance rulers depended to a considerable extent on a traditional world view or mentality. If a ruler of this period was represented as (say) Hercules, this was much more than a metaphor saying that he is strong, or even that he will solve the problems of his kingdom with as much ease as Hercules accomplished his various labours. The connection, or 'correspondence' as it was sometimes called, was stronger than that, as it was in the case of the correspondence between a state and a ship (see Figure 20), or a king and a father, or the polity and the human body, or the microcosm and the macrocosm.[12] The ruler was in some important sense of the term identified with Hercules, as if the aura of the demigod rubbed off on him. This is not very precise language but it is difficult to be precise about a process of this kind, which works more at an unconscious than at a conscious level.

These analogies were treated not as human constructions but as objective parallels. Political arguments assumed their reality, claiming for example that the commandment 'Honour thy Father and thy Mother' forbade resistance to kings.[13] We might therefore speak of the 'mystical mentality', noting similarities with the concept of 'mystical participation' [*participation mystique*] put forward early in the twentieth century by the French philosopher-anthropologist Lucien Lévy-Bruhl, but avoiding his term 'primitive'. The word 'mystical' was used by Lévy-Bruhl to refer to non-observable connections or identifications, like the identification made by one tribe between twins and birds.[14]

A good example of this mentality at work might be found in the idea of the mystical marriage between the king and the kingdom. The idea was inscribed in the French coronation ceremony (as we have seen in Chapter 3), and also in the Venetian Wedding of the Sea. In the course of a conflict with his parliament, James VI and I also appealed to this idea as if it were self-evident: 'I am the husband and the whole isle is my lawful wife.' The analogy between the king and the sun is also 'mystical' in the sense of being inaccessible to observation, while performing the important function of 'naturalising' the political order, in other words of making it seem as inevitable and unquestionable as nature itself.

In the course of the seventeenth century an intellectual revolution took place among certain elites in some parts of Western Europe (France, England, the Dutch Republic and northern Italy, at least), which undermined the assumptions of this mystical mentality. This revolution is associated in particular with Descartes and Galileo, Locke and Newton, but many lesser figures also took part in it.

This is not the place for a detailed account of the origins or consequences of this intellectual revolution, of its relation to economic and social change (such as the transition from feudalism to capitalism), or to earlier intellectual movements such as the nominalism associated with the fourteenth-century philosopher William of Ockham (a narrower movement in both the intellectual and the social sense). Suffice it to say here that a crucial consequence of the revolution was the so-called 'decline of magic', in the sense of increasing scepticism on the part of elites about the efficacity of magic, part of the general movement of secularisation or 'disenchantment of the world' [*Entzauberung der Welt*] discussed by the sociologist Max Weber.[15]

The new mentality was one in which the world was viewed as a machine rather than as an organism or 'animal'. The new cosmos was the so-called 'billiard ball universe' of Descartes, in which nothing moves unless touched by something else, and God sets the whole thing in motion, as Pascal put it, with a flick of his finger.

Equally important in this new mentality was the change in the status of analogy: a shift from objective correspondence to subjective metaphor. Symbolism became more self-conscious. With this shift went a devaluation of what was increasingly called 'mere' metaphor, symbol and ritual. For this reason it is tempting to call this intellectual revolution 'the rise of literal-mindedness', though it might be more exact to speak of an increasing awareness of the difference between literal and symbolic meanings.[16] It is at this point that Hercules is reduced to an expression of strength, the lion of courage, and so on, as if viewers and readers felt more at home with abstract qualities than with myths.

In short, a more concrete form of thought was replaced by a more abstract one. The word 'form' deserves emphasis. I am not trying to deny the importance of empiricism in the seventeenth century, the interest in the concrete details of the natural world. The point is that more abstract categories were replacing the correspondences of medieval and Renaissance thought. Together with these changes came the rise of faith in reason and the rise of what it is convenient to call 'cultural relativism', in other words the idea that particular social and cultural arrangements are not God-given or necessary but contingent. They vary from place to place and they may be changed from time to time.

It is likely that only a minority of intellectuals in Western Europe had changed their world-view in this way by the year 1700, but the consequences of the change were profound, from the decline in witch-hunting to the rejection of religious processions as a way of fighting the plague. The meaning of ritual was redefined, notably in a study by a French Benedictine, Claude de Vert, in the reign of Louis XIV, which offered a so-called 'literal' explanation of ritual, a good example of the 'literal-mindedness' just mentioned.

Why, for example, are candles placed on the altar during mass? According to the traditional theory, formulated by Durandus in the thirteenth century, the candles signify that Christ is the light of the world. Claude de Vert, on the other hand, rejects what he calls 'mystical' explanations for historical ones. According to him, the candles were necessary in the days in which the mass was celebrated in the catacombs, and the custom has survived its usefulness (the process that sociologists now call 'cultural lag').[17]

The intellectual revolution had serious political as well as religious consequences. Rulers lost an important part of what Pierre Bourdieu would call their symbolic capital.[18] These consequences can be seen at their most explicit in Locke's famous critique of the analogy between kings and fathers, an analogy assumed to be valid in *Patriarcha*, the book by Sir Robert Filmer which Locke was concerned to undermine.[19] In short, kings were losing their symbolic clothes. They were becoming demythologised and demystified.

For this reason it might not be unreasonable to apply to this period the famous phrase of Jürgen Habermas, 'legitimation crisis'. I am not suggesting that in the middle of the seventeenth century European rulers lost their legitimacy, although Charles I happened to lose his head at just this time. I *am* suggesting, however, that one important mode of legitimation was losing its efficacity.

How does this relate to the image of Louis XIV? As we have seen, Louis like other rulers (and perhaps more than other rulers in his time) was described in the language of paternalism and patriarchy as the father of his people. He was portrayed in the form of St Louis, of Hercules, of Apollo, of the sun. He was considered a sacred ruler, and his royal touch was of course supposed to have a miraculous healing power.

Such power was obviously incompatible with the mechanical universe of Descartes and Galileo. It was mocked by Montesquieu in his *Lettres Persanes*, published a few years after Louis' death, in which the Persian visitor writes home describing the king of France as 'a great magician'.[20] The king's problem was that he was a sacred ruler in an increasingly secular world. He was identified with the sun at a time in which the logic of identification or correspondence was in question. In the royal memoirs, it is explained that the sun is an appropriate image of the monarch because it is 'the most noble' of the heavenly bodies. By this time, Galileo had already offered powerful arguments against using moral terms like 'noble' or 'perfect' about inanimate nature.

The intellectual revolution was not unknown in the circles round the king. After all, one of the leading cultural relativists, La Mothe Le Vayer, had been the king's tutor. Furetière, who gave a reductionist definition of symbols in his famous *Dictionary*, was also a writer of poems in praise of the king. The Academy of Sciences had been founded in 1666 as part of the scheme to present the king as a magnificent patron of learning. The Perrault brothers were involved with the new science as well as with the fabrication of the official image of Louis XIV. Charles Perrault rejected some classical myths as fables fit only for children.[21] Bernard de Fontenelle was not only the librettist for operas, which used classical mythology to glorify the king, but also the author of an essay that undermined the power of myth by reducing it to allegory. He published this essay, *L'Origine des Fables*, after the death of Louis XIV, but he seems to have written it earlier.

What was to be done? One could of course continue as if nothing had happened. Bossuet continued to describe the monarchy as sacred and paternal, and Louis continued to touch the sick (more than 2,000 on Easter Saturday 1697, and 1,800 four years later).[22] At Versailles, the *lever du roi* or 'kingrise' continued to correspond to sunrise. Alternatively, the teaching of Descartes could be banned, as it was in the French universities (a decision for which the king seems to have been personally responsible).[23]

There were other responses to the crisis of representations. A modification in the formula uttered when the king touched the sick was noticed in Louis' time. His predecessors were supposed to have said, *Le roi te touche, Dieu te guérit* – The king touches you, God cures you. The new, more cautious formula was *Dieu te guérisse* may God cure you.[24]

From about 1680, if not before, one can see Louis and his advisers adopting a new strategy.[25] Although the device of the sun was never abandoned, it lost the importance it had had at the time of the ballets of the 1650s or the 1670s. References to Alexander and Augustus declined, as we have seen. In 1679, the original mythological programme for the Grande Galerie, focused on Hercules, was replaced by representations of the king's own actions. The medals, which were produced in increasing numbers at this time (p. 207), also represented the king directly rather than allegorically. The rejection of classical mythology around 1680 would appear to be highly significant.

The new myth of Louis relied on a new rhetoric, modern rather than ancient and literal rather than allegorical.[26] Earlier medals commemorating the king's deeds had modelled their inscriptions on those of Roman emperors. Now, however, we can find examples of statistics. Twenty-two of the medals struck between 1672 and 1700 include figures in their inscriptions. 'Twenty towns on the Rhine taken by the Dauphin in a single month', VIGINTI URBES AD RHENUM A DELPHINO UNO MENSE SUBACTAE (1688); 80 cities captured (1675); 300 churches built (1686); 7,000 prisoners taken (1695); 60,000 sailors enlisted (1680); and 'two million Calvinists brought back to the Church', VICIES CENTENA MILLIA CALVINIANORUM AD ECCLESIAM REVOCATA (1685) (Figure 58), make headlines reminiscent of twentieth-century newspapers.[27] This was after all the age of Colbert and Vauban, who were, among other things, great collectors of statistical data.[28]

The trend was not only visible in France. The British too had their experts in statistics or 'political arithmetic' as it was called in the seventeenth century: William Petty, Gregory King, John Graunt. Early

58. *Vicies Centena Millia Calvinianorum ad Ecclesiam Revocata*, obverse of medal, 1685. Cabinet des Médailles, Bibliothèque

in the eighteenth century, Sir Robert Walpole observed that the British House of Commons took 'figures of arithmetic' more seriously than 'figures of rhetoric' when listening to the arguments made in speeches.

It might also be argued that the great effort which the French government put into the representation of Louis XIV, the sheer number of medals, equestrian statues, tapestries and so on (especially in the second half of the reign), was a response to a crisis, or more exactly to a series of crises.

In the first place, and most obviously, the political crisis of the years of the Fronde, which coincided with the so-called general crisis, or at least with a series of European revolts which made 1648, like 1848, a year of revolutions. In the second place, the political difficulties of the later part of the reign, when French armies were less successful than before and financial problems were more serious. In the third place, I would suggest that the increasing investment in the heroic image of the king (like certain changes in that image) bears some relation to the crisis of representations. As a famous modern analyst of political communication, Harold Lasswell, once remarked, 'A well-established ideology . . .

perpetuates itself with little planned propaganda. . . . When thought is taken about ways and means of sowing conviction, conviction has already languished.'[29]

59. 'Louis the usurper'. *L'habit ursurpé*, anonymous Dutch engraving, beginning of the 17th century. Private Collection

X

THE REVERSE OF THE MEDAL

Le grand-père est un fanfaron,
Le fils un imbécile,
Le petit-fils un grand poltron,
Oh! La belle famille!

Anonymous, *c.* 1708

THE HEROIC image of Louis XIV was not the only image in circulation. There was a 'reverse of the medal', as one manuscript poem from the end of the reign pointed out.[1] A substantial number of alternative images of the sun-king have survived, considerably less flattering than the official ones.[2] Louis was sometimes represented – notably by the Dutch artist Romeyn de Hooghe – not as Apollo but as Phaeton, who allowed the chariot of the sun to get out of control. For some critics, he was not Augustus but Nero. For the biblically-minded Protestants, he was not Solomon or David, but Herod or Pharaoh. Like the official eulogies, the alternative images were generally composed of common-places. In this case too, however, individuals managed to produce ingenious variations on common themes.[3]

The concept of a 'reverse of the medal', however appropriate for a corpus of texts and images in which parody and inversion dominate, is of course too vague for serious analysis. It is necessary to distinguish at least two kinds of dissent from official presentations.

The first was expressed by individuals who regarded themselves – or at least presented themselves – as loyal subjects, making gentle fun of the court, like Bussy Rabutin, or giving the king good, if unwelcome, advice, like Archbishop Fénelon. The second kind of dissent was the work of declared enemies of the king and his regime, many of them writing at a time when their own country (Britain, the Dutch Republic, the Holy Roman Empire) was at war with France. The criticism of the king by the Huguenots began in the first manner and moved towards the second.

The media through which these images of dissent were communicated include paintings, medals, engravings, poems and various kinds of prose text (not only in French but in Latin, Dutch, German, English and Italian). Louis was not the only target. In the course of the reign the satirists also directed their fire at Anne of Austria, at Mazarin, at Colbert, at Louvois, at Madame de Maintenon, at the Duke of Burgundy, at the king's confessor Père La Chaise, and at a number of his less successful generals, such as Villeroi.

The form, style and tone of these texts is extremely varied. Some of them are simple denunciations of 'the French Tyrant', 'The French Machiavelli' [*Machiavellus Gallicus*], 'The French Attila' [*Der Französische Attila*], 'The French Nero' [*Nero Gallicanus*], and so on. However, most of the possibilities of the rich satiric repertoire of the period are also explored, and particular use is made of various types of parody.

For example, there is the parody of the *Pater Noster* (not uncommon in the popular culture of early modern Europe). 'Our father, who art at Marly, thy name is not hallowed, thy kingdom has almost gone, thy will is no longer done . . .' [*Notre père, qui êtes à Marly, votre nom n'est plus glorieux, votre règne est sur sa fin, votre volonté n'est plus faite . . .*].[4] In the age of the romances of Mlle de Scudéry and Mme de Lafayette it is no surprise to find the mock-romance. One of them described the combat between the 'great knight Nasonius' (in other words, William of Nassau) and 'the mighty giant Galieno', 'by some called also Grandissimo'.[5]

Another favourite genre of parody was the mock-will, 'The Testament of Louis the Great' [*Ludwig des Grossen Testament*], for example, as well as the political testaments ascribed to Mazarin, Colbert and Louvois. Another is the mock-diplomatic report, as in the *Relation de la Cour de France*. We also find the mock-catechism, the mock-confession (*Confessio regis gallicae Ludovici XIV*), the mock-wedding (*The French King's Wedding*), the mock-medical account of the pills prescribed for Louis so that he will vomit his conquests, and the mock-epitaph, particularly popular in 1715. The dream framework is used more than once, describing the sleeping Louis visited by the ghost of Mazarin, and Madame de Maintenon by the ghost of her first husband, Scarron (Figure 63).

The tone of these pieces varies from the moralising to the cynical, and the style from the urbane elegance of *Les conquêtes amoureuses du Grand Alcandre* to the charivaresque crudities of *The French King's Wedding*, which claims to describe 'the Comical Courtship, Catterwauling and Surprising Marriage Ceremonies of Lewis the XIVth with Madam Maintenon his late Hackney of State'. The literary tactics vary between direct attacks and the insinuations of 'secret histories' revealed to private eyes.

The main themes of this alternative orchestra, which did not always play in tune, concern the king's ambition, his lack of moral scruple and of religion, his tyranny, his vanity, and his military, sexual and intellectual weaknesses. Let us briefly consider these six themes one by one, constructing a composite dissenting image of the king (as earlier chapters constructed a favourable one), before going on to distinguish different points of view among the senders of the messages.

1. Critics of Louis XIV frequently referred to what one of them called 'The insatiate Appetite of his Ambition'.[6] The general moral criticism was linked to a specific political claim, made in 1667 in a famous pamphlet called 'The Buckler of State' [*Le Bouclier d'Etat*] and frequently reiterated. The claim was that Louis had 'a vast and profound plan' to become 'Master of Europe' and so to achieve a 'universal monarchy'. The critics objected with equal vehemence to the end and to the means adopted to achieve it. According to one of them, the events of the reign were 'speaking Books, where you may read throughout in great characters, LEWIS THE GREAT SACRIFICETH ALL THINGS TO HIS AMBITION AND INTEREST'.[7] The typographical parody of the capital letters used for the king's name in official publications (above, p. 35), should be noted. The most vivid illustration of the King's ambitions comes in a print representing him in stolen clothes (*L'habit usurpé*) (Figure 59).
2. Louis was frequently attacked for his lack of moral scruples, which the pamphleteers linked to the doctrine of 'reason of state' and the ideas of Machiavelli, which he was supposed to have learned from Cardinal Mazarin: 'All Machivilian Policys I have tried/ And all Religious Obstacles defy'd.'[8] Machiavelli had recommended breach of faith to princes: Louis was accused of 'Perjuries', 'Tricks' and 'Frauds' and his Revocation of the Edict of Nantes represented as a breach of faith with the Huguenots.[9] The king was also accused of breaches of international law by 'Invading, Burning, Spoiling, Plundring, Sacking and Depopulating the Territories and Dominions of his Peaceable Christian Neighbours', and especially for the 'Cruelty and Barbarism' of the French invasion of the Palatinate (above, p. 110).[10] This event was described as an example of 'more than Turkish, Tartar, Barbarian Cruelty!' [*O mehr als türckische, tartarische, barbarische Grausamkeit!*], or, to quote the title of a German pamphlet, 'French Reason of State'.[11]

60. 'Louis against Christ'. *Contra Christi Animum*, engraving of the reverse of a medal, from the counterfeit Menestrier, *Histoire du roi*, 1691. British Library, London

3. Another common charge was tyranny, made in 1689 in one of the most famous pamphlets against the king, 'The Sighs of France the Slave' [*Les soupirs de la France esclave*], but often echoed elsewhere, notably in an English pamphlet called *The French Tyrant* (1702). The growth of the absolute, arbitrary, despotic power of the king was contrasted with the destruction of the liberties of the Huguenots, the nobility, the *parlements*, the cities and finally the freedom of the people. Louis was presented as 'the grand Actor of Impiety, Cruelty, Oppression and Tyranny, upon the Stage of the World'.[12] More specifically, he was sometimes described as 'the king of taxes', 'king of tax-farmers', and so on [*le roi des impôts, le roi des maltôtiers*].
4. A fourth charge against Louis was his lack of religion. As he is made to say in one pamphlet (echoing the words of the stage-Machiavelli): 'We think Religion but a Sham.'[13] The king's irreligion was of course exemplified by his treatment of the Huguenots, 'the Sport/ Of my dragoons'.[14] It was also revealed by what the dissenters claimed to be an alliance with a non-Christian state, the Ottoman Empire. A satirical medal represented Louis together with the Ottoman Sultan Suleiman III, 'Mezomorto' Dey of Algiers and James II, with the words 'AGAINST THE SPIRIT OF CHRIST [CONTRA CHRISTI ANIMUM]' underneath them (Figure 60). On the reverse was the image of the devil, with the legend 'THE FIFTH IN THE ALLIANCE' [IN FOEDERE QUINTUS]. Another mocking reference to the alliance was the title of the pamphlet *The Most Christian*

61. *Venit, Vidit sed non Vicit*, reverse of medal, 1693. Dept of Coins and Medals, British Museum

Turk (1690), and yet another was *The Koran of Louis XIV* (1695). The king's irreligion was also exemplified by the blasphemy and paganism of the official cult of the sun-king.

5. This cult also allowed the hostile image-makers to draw attention to what they called the king's 'enormous vanity' [*un amour propre d'une grandeur immense*].[15] One German pamphlet concentrated on this theme and bore the title 'Self-praise Stinks' [*Eigenlob stinckt gern*]. The accusation is illustrated by references to the 'extravagant praises' of the king's 'flatterers' in poems, operas, and so on, praises, which have 'blown up his Ambition, by comparing him to the Sun'.[16] The pamphlets also refer to the erection of Versailles at a vast cost, also out of vanity, and to the statues of Louis, especially the one erected on the Place des Victoires.

6. In contrast, the dissenters emphasise the many weaknesses of this mere mortal. The charge of intellectual mediocrity, made by Spanheim and Saint-Simon, was not for publication. Swift's reference in print to the king's 'vile disease', in other words his fistula, was relatively unusual at the time.[17] The weaknesses of the king on which the pamphleteers concentrated were military and sexual. The themes were in fact closely linked, as in the gibe 'you flee wars but run after girls' [*Bella fugis, bellas sequeris*].[18] They were neatly illustrated in an engraving of Louis in retreat with his 'harem' (Figure 62) and a medal representing Louis in a chariot, which four women are pulling away from the front line

62. 'Louis as womaniser'. *Louis' Retreat With His Seraglio*, anonymous engraving, 1693. Department of Prints and Drawings, British Museum, London

63. 'Maintenon attacked'. Engraved frontispiece to *Scarron apparu à Madame de Maintenon*, 1694. British Library, London

64. 'Louis humbled'. Engraved frontispiece from *Nouvelles Amours de Louis le Grand*, 1696. British Library, London

(somewhere in the Netherlands) towards Versailles. In flagrant contrast to the official image of the royal hero, Louis was presented as battle-shy. He was mocked for his defeats. As the inscription on the medal of the four ladies goes, VENIT, VIDIT SED NON VICIT (Figure 61), a reference not only to Caesar but to the *impresa* devised for Louis at the *carrousel* of 1662, UT VIDI VICI.

The idea that Louis was better at making love than at making war is also the central theme of the *Amorous Conquests*. The setting is once again the Netherlands and the hero's name, 'Le Grand Alcandre', is a malicious reference to the Alexandrian compliment paid to the king in a novel by Mlle de Scudéry (above, p. 29). War is a metaphor for sex. The story concentrates on four of the king's mistresses, La Vallière (described as '*d'une médiocre beauté*'), Montespan (who has other lovers), Fontanges and finally Maintenon (Figure 63), 'who now acts the prude' [*qui fait maintenant la prude*].[19] The conclusion is that 'the Great Alcandre, although raised above the others, was no different from common men in humour and temperament'.[20] Today, this conclusion may seem rather flat, but it becomes subversive when viewed in the context of the official campaign to present the king as a hero.

The military metaphor recurs in *The New Loves of Louis the Great* in which Louis is represented on his knees before his latest discovery, Mme de St Tron (Figure 64). Hearing of his latest defeats on the battlefield, the king admits that he prefers Venus to Mars, while Maintenon tells him rather tartly that 'Your Majesty is not going to win any battles at Meudon, at Marly, at Versailles.'[21] War is again a metaphor for sex. In *The French King's Wedding*, on the other hand, sex has become a metaphor for war. Louis is presented here – in the year of Oudenarde – not as a womaniser but as an impotent dotard, an 'old fumbling Monarch', equally unsuccessful on the sexual and military fronts:

> The Plagues of War and Wife consent
> To send the King a Packing;
> You cannot give your Spouse Content,
> For she'll be always lacking.

The reference to Maintenon as 'wife' shows that the King's second marriage was now an open secret.

As in the case of the official images of the king, it is worth looking at the ways in which particular events were represented – indeed, manipulated – by the dissenters. That medals were struck to commemorate the defeat of French armies at Blenheim, Oudenarde, Ramillies, and so on goes without saying. Indeed, a medallic history of the campaigns of 1708–9 was published in Utrecht in 1711.[22] When the French lost Namur in 1695, the English poet Matthew Prior celebrated the event with a parody of Boileau's verses in praise of its capture three years earlier.

It may be more rewarding to examine the images of more ambiguous events, or non-events, beginning with the notorious medal of the four women pulling Louis away from the battlefield. The inspiration for this image was obviously the occasion when Louis took not only the queen but also La Vallière and Montespan on campaign in the Netherlands during the War of Devolution.[23]

Another revealing example of the manipulation of events is the image of Louis in alliance with the Grand Turk. In 1681, the Emperor Leopold was hard-pressed. Louis XIV annexed Strasbourg, the Hungarians rebelled against imperial rule and the Turks took advantage of the situation to assemble an army in Belgrade in order to invade the Holy Roman Empire. Louis did not actually make an alliance with the Turks. On the other hand, despite an appeal from the pope, he did nothing to help the emperor when the Turks were besieging Vienna. It is this non-event that underlies the image of Louis' diabolical alliance (above, p. 140).[24]

In the case of the Revocation of the Edict of Nantes, there was no need for invention. The event itself was a gift to the Dutch, English and German propagandists. All they had to do was to describe and condemn 'the most cruel and the most violent persecution that there ever was in France', and they did this with gusto, in medals, prints and pamphlets.[25]

Of course, these events had been celebrated by the official French media (above, p. 102). The intimate relation between the two opposite images of Louis, the hero and the villain, deserves further comment.

Subjects that were taboo in official discourse, notably the king's mistresses and his secret second marriage, were of course emphasised by the dissenters. Despite this obvious difference, the two opposed groups of artists and writers chose the same themes again and again, producing inverted images of each other's work. As we have seen, the hostile images rely heavily on parody. They imitate the forms of some of the official media, such as medals and inscriptions, while inverting their content.[26] They refer to 'sunset' or 'solstice' (in the sense of the shortest, darkest day of the year).[27] For them, Louis was not the sun but 'this gilded meteor'.[28] Instead of Apollo, it is Phaeton to whom they compare the king.[29] Instead of Constantine, it is Julian the Apostate.[30] Louis used the proud motto, 'not unequal to many' [NEC PLURIBUS IMPAR]. It was inevitable that in the age of the Grand Alliance someone would describe him as 'the Frenchman who is already unequal to many' [*Gallus iam pluribus impar*].

The pamphlets regularly describe the king as cowardly rather than brave, vainglorious rather than glorious, 'unjust' rather than 'just', and so on. His official title of 'Louis the Great' provoked a number of ripostes. He was 'Petit' rather than 'Grand', or 'grown so impudently great', or 'great only in his ambition'.[31]

Another official title, that of 'the most Christian king', was also a standing invitation to parody, as in the titles of such pamphlets as 'The Most Christian Mars', 'The Most Christian Turk', 'The Most Christian needs to become Christian' [*Christianissimus christiandus*] or 'The Most Christian King's Antichristian Bombardment'.[32]

Royal patronage of learning and the arts was not ignored by the dissenters, but it was condemned rather than celebrated. The paintings in Versailles were presented as examples of the king's arrogance, the academies were viewed as an instrument of despotism, while the royal pensions to writers and even the construction of the Observatory were interpreted as ways of distracting scholars from politics and from the criticism of the government.[33] The Louvre was compared to the Golden House of Nero. The charge of extravagance was a repeated one.[34]

The dissenters frequently drew attention to what we might call the cult of the royal personality, interpreting it in terms of flattery, vanity, blasphemy and paganism. 'Such have been the Humours of this King's Flatterers, that they have more and more blown up his Ambition, by comparing him to the Sun . . . as if they intended to set him up for an Idol for all the World to fall down before . . . those Parasites strive, by glorious Epithets, to make him appear White and Shining, almost, if not altogether, to the height of Blasphemy.'[35]

The cult of Louis was the central theme of several pamphlets, notably 'Self-Praise Stinks' [*Eigenlob Stinckt Gern*], 'Extract of some Flowers' [*Extract etzlichen Flosculorum*] and 'The Praise of Louis Deceived' [*Laus Ludovici Delusa*]. The *Extract* attacks the flattery of the king by the official historian Périgny, while *Eigenlob* is a critique of the *Parallèle* (1685) by Charles-Claude de Vertron (another historiographer royal), who compared Louis favourably with other rulers who had been called great, from Alexander to Charlemagne. In similar fashion, Matthew Prior writes as much against Boileau as against the king:

Pindar, that Eagle mounts the Skies;
While Virtue leads the noble Way:
Too like a Vulture Boileau flies,
Where sordid Interest shows the Prey.

Since hir'd for life, thy Servile Muse must sing
Successive Conquests and a glorious King;
Must of a Man Immortal vainly boast;
And bring him laurels what so'er they cost.[36]

The statue of Louis on the Place des Victoires gave an opportunity to the dissenters, which they were not slow to exploit. Three years after its erection, the *Sighs* (1689) noted that Louis allowed 'Statues on the pedestal of which are engraved blasphemies in his honour', with a footnote to the inscription VIRO IMMORTALI (the discussion of a single example in the plural is a well-known rhetorical technique).[37] An English pamphlet described the statue as 'Crowned with Rays and Stars, as the old Romans used to do their God Jupiter . . . they have in one place made the Figures of Europe, Asia, Africa and America, Kneeling at his feet, as if he gave Laws to the whole Earth.'[38] Another pamphlet declared that 'the French . . . offer incense at this very day to the Divinity of Lewis the Great, and below his Statue, the Head of which is environ'd with a Glory, there are written these Blasphemous words, *Numini Ludovici Magni* . . . they make their Oblations to the immortal man, *Viro immortali*.'[39] A German 'Description of the Praise-Seeking and Arrogant Monument' [*Beschreibung der Ruhm-süch- und Hochmüthigen Ehren-Seule*], published in 1690, discusses nothing else but this monument.[40] In 1715, a poem against the late king referred to the statue of

Cet homme qu'un indigne et basse flatterie
Sur un piédestal criminel
Expose à tous les yeux comme étant immortel.

Even the laurel wreath was used against Louis. A poem jokes about the hesitation of Victory in the act of crowning the king, while a parody-medal of the monument shows Victory removing the laurel, a nicely literal example of what the Russian critic Bakhtin calls 'uncrowning'.[41] The visual parody was perhaps the most effective way to undermine the official image. An engraving, which was circulating in Paris in 1694, replaced the figures at the corners of the pedestal by four women who kept the king in chains – La Vallière, Fontanges, Montespan and Maintenon.[42]

The chronology of these attacks on Louis is worth noting. It is impossible to draw up an exact list even of the pamphlets because of the difficulty of defining the genre – when does a text including unfavourable remarks become an attack? What is possible is to discuss a corpus of seventy-five texts (listed in Appendix 3), which deal with Louis in person in some detail. Four texts (including the famous *Buckler of State*) date from the 1660s, the decade of the War of Devolution. Six texts date from the 1670s, the decade of the attack on the Dutch Republic. The trickle only became a stream in the 1680s, with sixteen texts, including the famous *Sighs of France the Slave*, and other criticisms of the Revocation of the Edict of Nantes. The stream became a flood in the 1690s, with thirty-five texts (seven from the year 1690 alone). Then it begins to dry up; there are only fourteen texts from the period 1700–15.

Who was responsible for this unofficial image of the king? All too little is known about the organisation and distribution of this corpus of texts and images. The place of publication, where stated, cannot always be trusted. Sometimes the place is 'Vrystadt' or 'Villefranche', a common joke of the clandestine printers of the period. Sometimes it is 'Paris', 'Versailles' or even 'Trianon'. The most common place-name on the title-page of French texts is 'Cologne', and the most common printer 'Pierre du Marteau', who may never have existed and certainly did not print all the books ascribed to him over a period of more than a century.[43]

In some cases, bibliographer-detectives have followed typographic clues, and the trail has led to the Elsevir family of printers in Leiden and Amsterdam. It is likely that a good deal of the anti-Louis literature in French was printed in the Dutch Republic and smuggled into France. The Dutch already had a tradition of printing books in foreign languages for export, and the Huguenots who fled to the Netherlands in the 1680s not infrequently made their living as writers or booksellers. It is likely that some of them were deeply involved in these forms of clandestine communication. The great *coup* of the underground presses in 1691 was to counterfeit the medallic history by Menestrier (above, p. 115), slipping into it five extra plates of satirical medals, with a note that 'the five plates of medals which follow, are no less relevant to the HISTORY OF LOUIS THE GREAT than the earlier ones: but Father Menestrier had his reasons for not inserting them in his work.'[44] (see Figure 60)

The creators of these dissenting images are generally as anonymous or pseudonymous as the printers, but it is possible to identify at least a few artists and writers. The leading artist was the Dutchman Romeyn de Hooghe, most famous as an etcher but active as a painter, sculptor, medallist and writer as well. What has been called his 'cartoon-crusade' against Louis began at the time of the war of 1672 and continued till his

65. 'Louis as satyr'. *Louis and Madame de Montespan At a Feast* by Joseph Werner, oil on canvas, *c.* 1670. Zürich, von Muralt collection

death in 1708. It includes a representation of the 'atrocities against the French Protestants' in 1685, and memorable images of Louis as Phaeton or as a crippled Apollo.[45] Another committed opponent of Louis XIV was Nicolas Chevalier. He was a Huguenot pastor who left France after the Revocation of the Edict of Nantes and became a bookseller and a medallist in the Dutch Republic, combining his activities in a medallic history of the campaigns of 1708–9.[46]

Other artists seem to have worked for whichever side paid them. The Swiss artist Joseph Werner we have met before (p. 57) at the court in the 1660s, painting the young Louis as Apollo. Having failed to make a career in France, Werner went to Germany and painted the ageing Louis as a satyr in a bacchanal (Figure 65). Should we interpret this shift from glorification to satire in terms of personal disappointment or merely a change of patron?[47] And what are we to make of Nicolas Larmessin? This engraver-bookseller is best known for his series of frontispieces to the annual *Almanach Royal*, an important contribution to the glorification of the king. However, he was imprisoned in the Bastille in 1704, accused of making or selling a cartoon of the king and Madame de Maintenon.[48]

The authors to whom the pamphlets are attributed are a similar mixture of the committed and the mercenary. They include some names well-known at the time. The *Buckler of State* was the work of Franz Paul von Lisola, a lawyer from Franche-Comté, who became a diplomat in the service of the Emperor Leopold.[49] *Machiavellus Gallicus* is generally attributed to Johan Joachim Becher, who was also in Leopold's service, combining the roles of alchemist and economist.[50] *The Sighs of France the Slave* is generally thought to have been written by the Huguenot pastor Pierre Jurieu.[51]

The most famous name is still to come. It is generally agreed that Gottfried Wilhelm Leibniz wrote the pamphlet 'The Most Christian Mars' [*Mars Christianissimus*]. A critique of Louis XIV may seem a long way from the philosphical and mathematical studies for which Leibniz is famous, but he spent much of his adult life in the service of two German princes, the Elector of Mainz and the Duke of Brunswick, and even devised a plan to divert Louis from Germany by proposing the invasion of Egypt.

Other writers against Louis were professionals, notorious rather than famous in their own day. One of the most picturesque was the Milanese Gregorio Leti, a convert to Calvinism and author of a number of anti-papal pamphlets, who came to France and presented a panegyric to Louis XIV in 1680, and five years later began to write against him. The famous *Conquêtes amoureuses* is generally attributed to a French nobleman, Courtilz de Sandras, who seems also to have written on both sides.[52] *Christianissimus christiandus* was the work of a turncoat journalist, the Englishman Marchmont Needham.

Three major literary figures in Britain all added details to the alternative image of the king: Jonathan Swift, Matthew Prior and Joseph Addison. Swift made uncomplimentary references to the 'restless tyrant' in a poem celebrating William III's expedition to Ireland. Prior, who was employed as a diplomat at this time, circulated his 'ballad' on the taking of Namur among members of the British government. Poetry like diplomacy was a continuation of war by other means. As for Addison, he slipped some sharp remarks about Louis into his apparently innocent *Dialogues on Medals*, as well as accepting an official invitation to write a poem celebrating Blenheim.[53]

The propaganda campaign against Louis was obviously considerably less co-ordinated than the campaign in his favour. Journalists in London, medallists in Nuremberg, Huguenot exiles in the Dutch Republic and French critics of the king could not easily communicate with one another. It was, ironically, the official image of the king that gave the attacks their coherence.

The most important and the most difficult question has been left until last. How effective was this campaign? Who read the pamphlets or looked at the medals? And what did they think of the criticisms? The reception of the unfavourable images of Louis, like the responses to the official representations of the sun-king, will be discussed in the next chapter.

66. 'The silver throne'. Engraving of the Royal Throne, from *Mercure Galant*, December, 1686. Bibliothèque Nationale, Paris

XI
THE RECEPTION OF LOUIS XIV

Etudiez la cour et connoissiez la ville.

Boileau

UNTIL NOW this book, like earlier studies of representations of Louis XIV, has concentrated on production rather than consumption, the image projected rather than the image received. However, no study of communication can be considered complete, as historians of literature and art have come to realise, without some discussion of the reception of the message, the nature of the audience and the ways in which that audience responded.[1]

In other words, we must study not only 'who says what' but also 'to whom' and 'with what effects', refining this formula (above, p. 13) to take account of the processes of interpreting messages and appropriating them for purposes for which they were not originally intended. In the case of Louis XIV, the documentation concerning the intended audiences at least is relatively rich, and the records also allow a few fascinating glimpses of individual responses.

Domestic recipients

For whose benefit, to convince whom, was this image displayed for more than seventy years? It is unlikely that it was intended for the mass of Louis' subjects, the twenty million Frenchmen and women alive in 1643, or 1661, or 1715 (the population of France at the end of the reign was more or less the same as it had been at the beginning). Louis' media were not mass media. Medals were distributed on special occasions such as the inauguration of the Languedoc canal or the statue on the Place des Victoires, but they were not struck in great numbers. All Parisians could see the arches of triumph and the statues erected in their city, but few of them would have been able to understand the Latin inscriptions or even to decode the iconography. Versailles was open to any adult male wearing a sword, and swords could be hired at the entrance, but only a minority were in a position to do this. The royal apartments were opened three days a week for what was described as 'all persons of quality' [*toutes les personnes d'une qualité distinguée*].[2]

Similarly, the festivals may have resembled modern television in their glitter, their glamour and their simultaneous appeal to eye and ear, but they were produced for a small audience at court. The *ballet de cour* was an intimate theatre. The panegyrics in prose and verse were addressed in the first place to an audience of one, the king himself, and they might be read by him (or to him) when they were still in manuscript, although the texts were often published later. The king's *Mémoires* were also originally written for an audience of one – the Dauphin. This confidential document was not published until 1806.

Who then was, or were, the public? The question is a good deal more difficult to answer than it may look. For one thing, the concept of the 'public' was only just coming into existence at this time. The French used phrases such as 'the public good', 'to preach in public', and so on, but not 'the public' *tout court*. The concept of 'public opinion' was not yet known – the first reference to *l'opinion du peuple* dates from the last year of the reign, 1715.[3] The phrase *la voix publique*, in the sense of 'public voice' or perhaps 'public choice', was only a partial substitute. 'One says that a man has the public voice in his favour, in the sense of universal applause' [*On dit qu'un homme a la voix publique pour luy, pour dire, l'applaudissement universel*].[4]

It might be argued that the signifier was lacking because the signified was also lacking. The public might be defined as a social group, which, like a social class, needs self-consciousness in order to exist.[5] This self-consciousness was encouraged by the growth in the media of communication. The official fabricators of the image of Louis XIV thus made an important contribution to the creation of public opinion in France. In that sense they made it easier for unofficial as well as for official images to circulate.

On the other hand, the media of the seventeenth century – like the media of today – were shaped in their turn by the needs and desires of the public, or at least by what the communicators believed to be the needs and desires of the public. The image of the omniscient and omnipotent monarch cannot be dismissed as nothing but the product of a circle of propagandists and flatterers. The similarity between the French hero-king and the heroes of other cultures suggests that the official image was – up to a point – the expression of a collective need. It is pure speculation, but it is tempting to suggest a link between the rise of the centralising state in the seventeenth century and the rise of the cult of the king, who represented – indeed, incarnated – the power of the centre.

It would of course be a mistake to treat seventeenth-century audiences and spectators as monolithic. Indeed, I should like to suggest that the broadcasters of the time were trying to reach three audiences in particular. The three targets at which they were aiming were posterity; the French upper classes, both in Paris and the provinces; and foreigners, especially foreign courts. Let us examine these different groups in order.

Odd as it may seem today, the king's publicists were trying to reach *us*, or more exactly, to reach posterity as they envisaged it. As the royal memoirs puts it, kings owe an account of their actions 'to all the ages'.[6] A draft of a letter written by Charles Perrault for Colbert describes painting and sculpture as arts which according to the king should make a special contribution to 'the transmission of his name to posterity'.[7] One reason for the prominence of obelisks in designs for monuments was that they symbolised eternal fame. The monuments themselves employed materials such as marble and bronze in order to last for centuries. Medals of the events of the reign were buried in the foundations of buildings – the Louvre, for example, in 1665, the Observatory in 1667 and the Pont Royal in 1685.[8]

The best evidence for the government's preoccupation with posterity is surely the effort put into finding suitable authors for an official history of the reign. Of the ninety writers about whom Chapelain reported to Colbert in 1662, no fewer than eighteen were historians. At least twenty individuals held the post, or claimed the title of *historiographe du roi*, or were commissioned by the government to write on history (Appendix 3). The king himself was involved in the writing of official accounts of particular campaigns.[9]

The image of the king was also projected for the benefit of the king's subjects, 'the peoples over whom we reign' [*les peuples sur qui nous régnons*]. In the first place, for the courtiers, especially the higher nobility, for whom attendance at court was virtually compulsory. Saint-Simon tells the story of the king's displeasure with him for leaving the court without permission. The higher nobility was expected to attend the king at court, not only to cut them off from their local power-bases but also to dazzle them with the king's glory. The courtiers, male and female, formed the main part of the everyday audience for the plays, ballets, operas and other performances at court (not forgetting the royal *lever*). On special occasions, the numbers would rise. Six hundred ladies and gentlemen participated in the *Plaisirs de l'Ile Enchantée* of 1664, and 1,500 in the still more elaborate *Divertissement* of 1668. The fact that women participated on equal terms with men and in more or less equal numbers is worth underlining.

In a famous phrase in his *Art poétique*, Boileau characterised the French literary public as *la cour et la ville*, 'the court and the city' (in other words, Paris).[10] The court tended to look down on the city as 'bourgeois', a term that was coming into use in the 1660s to refer to lawyers and other commoners. As for the king, the traditional view that his experiences during the Fronde (above, p. 40) turned him against the city has something to be said for it. After the royal wedding and the state entry into the city, which may well have been witnessed by 100,000 people, Parisians had few opportunities to see their ruler in person.[11] He spent relatively little time in the palace of the Louvre, and took part in relatively few public events in Paris after the *lit de justice* of 1673 (above, p. 40). It was not until 1687 that the king visited the Hôtel de Ville, to demonstrate that he had forgotten the Fronde and was prepared to make peace with the city.[12]

All the same, Louis' praises reached this urban public. The *Gazette*, which was printed in the Louvre, could be read by Parisians while the news was still fresh. Performances for the court were often repeated in Paris. Molière's *La Princesse d'Elide*, for example, was first played at Versailles in May 1664 as part of the *Plaisirs*, but repeated at the theatre of the Palais-Royal in Paris the following November. In 1665, Racine's *Alexandre* was played in the same theatre, and also in the rival Hôtel de Bourgogne. In 1673 the theatre of the Palais Royal was transferred to Lully, and his operas were produced there.

The royal academies of literature, painting, architecture and music were all located in Paris. So was the royal factory of the Gobelins, which exhibited its tapestries on the occasion of major festivals. John Locke, for example, viewed them on the feast of Corpus Christi 1677, noting that 'In every piece Lewis le Grand was the hero'.[13] The major theatres and the opera were in Paris. The rebuilding of the Louvre, the construction of the Invalides, the erection of triumphal arches and the royal statues on the Place des Victoires and Place Louis-le-Grand (Place Vendôme) stamped the image of the king on the city. The transformation was commemorated by a medal with the inscription 'Paris decorated' [ORNATA LUTETIA].

There is also evidence of increasing official preoccupation with a provincial public. Six provincial academies on the model of the Académie Française were founded between 1669 and 1695 at Arles, Soissons, Nîmes, Angers, Villefranche and Toulouse, while scientific academies on the model of the Académie des Sciences were founded at Caen (which already had an academy for the humanities), Montpellier and Bordeaux.[14] An opera house combined with an academy of music on the Paris model was established in Marseilles in 1684. Like their Parisian models, these institutions were often concerned to promote the glory of the king. The academies of Arles and Angers offered prizes for eulogies of Louis, the academy of Soissons organised celebrations for the feast of St Louis, and the humanist academy at Caen was involved in the erection of a statue of the king.

Louis also made a number of state visits to French cities, giving the inhabitants an opportunity to see him in person. He went to Rheims, as was customary, for his coronation in 1654. He made a formal entry into Lyons in 1658. In the period of his personal rule, he visited a number of cities, most of them newly acquired, including Dunkirk (1662, 1671), Lille (1671, 1680), Dijon, Besançon and Strasbourg (all 1683) and Cambrai (1684).

The government expected happy events such as victories or the births of new members of the royal family to be celebrated in Paris and the provinces. Messages were sent to bishops instructing that the *Te Deum* be sung in their cathedrals on appropriate occasions, and even specifying the individuals and groups who were expected to attend the service.[15]

Celebrations often took a more elaborate form. In 1678, for example, there were public rejoicings for the peace of Nijmegen at Abbeville (where a portrait of the king was displayed), Caen, Chartres, Le Havre and Montpellier.[16] In 1682, the birth of the Duke of Burgundy was widely celebrated in the provinces, from Rennes to Marseilles, but above all in the province of Burgundy and its capital, Dijon.[17] The festivals for the birth of another grandson, the Duke of Anjou, in 1684, above all in Angers, followed the same pattern.[18] In 1687, festivals celebrating the king's recovery from illness were organised in Arles and other cities.[19] Celebrations of this kind, which generally included eulogies of the king, might be organised by the local *intendant*, by the municipality or by members of the various provincial academies.

Regular information about the king reached the provinces via journals, above all the official *Gazette* and the *Mercure Galant*. The editor of the *Mercure* (who received a royal pension from 1684 onwards) addressed his readers as if they were all provincials, eager for news of Paris, the king and the court (above, p. 95). The journal was written in the form of letters addressed to a lady in the provinces – the concern with female readers deserves emphasis.[20] A striking indicator of the government's increasing preoccupation with the provinces is provided by the spread of these official journals. By 1685, the Paris *Gazette* was also printed in five provincial towns (Bordeaux, Lyons, Rouen, Toulouse and Tours); by 1699 their number had increased to twenty-one and by the end of the reign to thirty.[21] The *Mercure Galant* was also printed in the provinces, in Bordeaux, Lyons and Toulouse.

The 'statue campaign' of the 1680s was also directed at major cities in the provinces: Arles, Caen, Dijon, Lyons, Montpellier, Pau, Poitiers and Troyes. In addition, triumphal arches were erected at Tours, Besançon and Montpellier (all 1693) and Lille (1695). There were plans for similar arches at La Rochelle, Marseilles and Metz.[22] The geography of these arches resembles that of the equestrian statues (above, p. 97) and the state visits. They were concentrated on the periphery, in the territories that had been acquired most recently, enjoyed most privileges – and rebelled most frequently. The naming of a fortress in the newly-conquered Saarland 'Saarlouis' (above, p. 85) is part of this general trend.

The famous messages to the provinces of 1709, to persuade them of the need to carry on the war (above, p. 112), should be seen as the culmination of this trend. Open letters to the provincial governors and the bishops, signed by Louis but written by Torcy, described the government's efforts to make peace, the bad faith of the enemy and the king's devotion to his people. These letters were printed by local presses all over France.[23]

This description of the representations of Louis before a domestic public has concentrated, like the government, on the elites. A single edition of the *Gazette* is unlikely to have been more than 2,000 copies, while the price varied between 1 and 4 sous. The more exclusive *Mercure Galant* cost 25 sous for a monthly issue in the 1680s. Given their cost of production, medals are likely to have circulated among a small group, like the official medallic history, a magnificent but expensive folio volume.[24] *Jetons* were distributed in greater numbers – more than 26,000 in 1682, for example – but they were still confined to a minority of the population.[25]

DE PAR LE ROY,

ET MONSIEVR LE MARQVIS DE SOVCHES,

Preuoſt de l'Hoſtel de ſa Maieſté, & Grande Preuoſté de France.

ON faict à ſçauoir à tous qu'il appartiendra, que Dimanche prochain iour de Paſques, Sa Maieſté touchera les Malades des Eſcroüelles, dans les Galleries du Louure, à dix heures du matin, à ce que nul n'en pretende cauſe d'ignorance, & que ceux qui ſont attaquez dudit mal ayent à s'y trouuer, ſi bon leur ſemble. Faict à Paris, le Roy y eſtant, le vingt-ſixieſme Mars mil ſix cens cinquante-ſept. Signé, DE SOVCHES.

Leu & publié à ſon de Trompe & cry public par tous les Carrefours de cette Ville & Faux-bourgs de Paris, par moy Charles Canto Crieur Iuré de ſa Maieſté, accompagné de Jean du Bos, Jacques le Frain, & Eſtienne Chappé Jurez Trompettes dudit Seigneur, & affiché, le vingt-ſixieſme Mars, mil ſix cens cinquante-ſept. Signé, CANTO.

67. *Notice advertising the royal touch*, 1657. Bibliothèque Nationale, Paris. An advertisement of 1692 refers to payments to the sufferers.

This is not to say that ordinary people had no image of their king. State visits to cities allowed anyone who wanted to catch at least a glimpse of Louis. An official account of the king's visit to Cambrai in 1684 commented on the 'extraordinary' crowd, which assembled to watch the king take supper.[26] The custom of the royal touch was another opportunity for ordinary Frenchmen and women to see their ruler face to face. To suggest that Louis touched 350,000 people in the course of his reign would be a conservative estimate. These people might be said to have testified with their feet to their belief in sacred kingship. However, it should be borne in mind that those who were touched in this way were given 15 sous apiece, and that this fact was advertised in advance (Figure 67).[27]

Ordinary people also participated in the public prayers for the success of the French armies, ordered in 1672, 1683 and 1709. The king's letter of 1709 to the governors of his provinces was read aloud 'to the whole army' by Marshal Villars, as an English spy testified.[28] Since some 650,000 Frenchmen entered the army in the years 1701–13 alone, the institution deserves study as a means of diffusing official images of the king throughout the nation.[29] The visual images of the king could break through the barrier to communication imposed by illiteracy, and some of them, notably the statues, were highly visible. Even the tapestries of the history of the king were displayed in public on occasion, for example at the Gobelins during the feast of Corpus Christi.[30]

All the same, the image-makers rarely refer to ordinary people. Charpentier was exceptional in recommending the use of the vernacular on public monuments to allow the *menu peuple* 'the pleasure of participating for once in the magnificence of the state and the glory of their prince'.[31] In any case, his recommendation was not followed. In a nation of peasants, official efforts to give the king a good public image concentrated on the cities. It is rare indeed to encounter a statue of the king in a village. The only example known to me is a sculpture in Guimiliau (Finistère) representing Louis XIV as St Louis.[32] It cannot be coincidence that the date, 1675, is also that of the revolt of the Bretons against the king.

Foreign recipients

The foreign public for *l'histoire du roi* was considered no less important than the domestic one. In 1698, for example, the petite académie was asked by Pontchartrain to draw up a list of medals suitable for presentation to foreigners.

Cardinal Mazarin described the young Louis as 'the greatest king in the world' [*le plus grand roy du monde*][33] (Figure 68). The phrase may seem pure hyperbole as well as pure ethnocentrism, but it was repeated and amplified by the panegyrists. A medal struck to commemorate the treaty of Nijmegen represented Louis as 'the universal peacemaker' [PACATOR ORBIS], and showed Victory presenting him with a globe. The image of the four continents or 'the four corners of the world' (Australia being unknown) acknowledging the supremacy of the sun-king was to be seen on the *Escalier des Ambassadeurs* and elsewhere.[34] The inscriptions on the monument to Louis on the Place des Victoires included a reference to the embassies of 'distant nations', and mentioned those from Muscovy, Guinea, Morocco, Siam and Algeria. A festival at Grenoble in 1701 represented Louis on his throne receiving homage from the nations of the world, including 'Siamese, Tonkinese, Algerians,

68. 'The reception of the medallic history'. *Portrait of Graf von Dehn* by Nicolas de Largillière, *c.* 1702. Herzog Anton Ulrich-Museum, Braunschweig

Chinese, Iroquois'.[35] These five examples are precise references to events of the reign.

These images corresponded to a concrete project, with aims well beyond the frontiers of Europe. The attention given to the Siamese embassy of 1686 (commemorated by a medal, p. 98), and the Persian embassy of 1715, in particular, bear eloquent testimony to this project.[36] In order to impress the representatives of 'oriental despotisms', as the French viewed them, Louis received the Ottoman and Persian ambassadors on 'an unusually high throne' [*Un Trône fort élevé*][37] (Figure 66).

There were good practical reasons (p. 143) for the king to cultivate the Ottoman sultan – hostility to the Holy Roman Empire gave them common interests. Algiers and Morocco were dependencies of the Ottoman Empire. Algiers had been bombarded into submission to France in 1684 (p. 97). As for Persia, the diplomatic initiative was taken not by the king but by the shah. In the hope of obtaining the aid of a French squadron in his attempt to take the port of Muscat on the Persian Gulf, Shah Hussein sent an envoy to Louis in 1715.

Louis XIV had at least a foothold in the Americas. The city of Quebec was founded by French settlers in 1608 and became the capital of the province of New France in 1663. A bust of the king was installed on the Place Royale in 1686, at the time of the 'statue campaign' in the French provinces (above, p. 93). The Iroquois, who resisted French domination, were forced by the French governor, Frontenac, to sue for peace in 1696. It was from Quebec that the explorer Robert de la Salle set out for Louisiana, a region – much larger than the present state of the Union – which he annexed in 1682 and named after Louis XIV.

The death of Louis XIV was even commemorated in Spanish America, thanks to the fact that he was the grandfather of the reigning monarch, Philip V. A catafalque was displayed in the cathedral in Mexico City, a sermon was preached by Archbishop Lanciego, and a panegyric of the late king '*Luis XIV El Grande*' was published, describing him as a 'mirror of princes'[38] (Figure 69).

Official contacts with the Far East went back to 1661, when Louis offered his friendship to 'the kings of Cochin-China, Tonkin and China'.[39] The Jesuit Joachim Bouvet went to China and entered the service of the Emperor Kangxi, who ruled from 1662 to 1722. Bouvet described the greatness of Louis to Kangxi. What impression the king made on the emperor unfortunately is unknown. By Chinese standards, the ruler of twenty million people must have appeared nothing but a

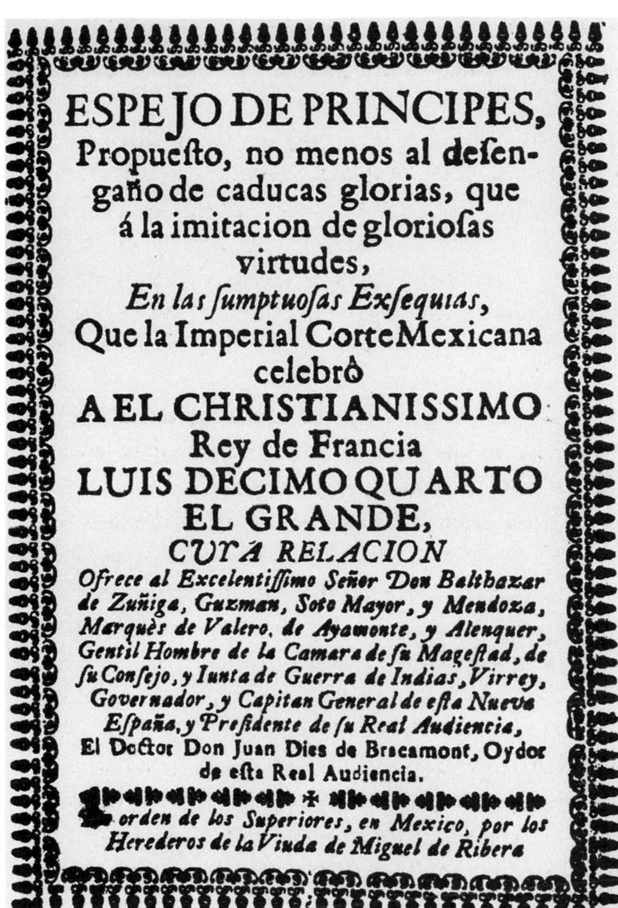
ESPEJO DE PRINCIPES,
Propuesto, no menos al desengaño de caducas glorias, que á la imitacion de gloriosas virtudes,
En las sumptuosas Exsequias,
Que la Imperial Corte Mexicana celebrô
A EL CHRISTIANISSIMO
Rey de Francia
LUIS DECIMO QUARTO
EL GRANDE,
CUYA RELACION
Ofrece al Excelentissimo Señor Don Balthazar de Zuñiga, Guzman, Soto Mayor, y Mendoza, Marquès de Valero, de Ayamonte, y Alenquer, Gentil Hombre de la Camara de su Magestad, de su Consejo, y Iunta de Guerra de Indias, Virrey, Governador, y Capitan General de esta Nueva España, y Presidente de su Real Audiencia,
El Doctor Don Juan Dies de Bracamont, Oydor de esta Real Audiencia.
orden de los Superiores, en Mexico, por los Herederos de la Viuda de Miguel de Ribera

69. 'Louis in the New World'. Title-page of *Espejo de Principes*, Mexico, 1715.

petty princeling. However, Bouvet was sent back to Versailles to give Louis an account of the Chinese court.[40]

These contacts served religious, economic and political ends. The Jesuits were primarily missionaries, following in the footsteps of St Francis Xavier, the apostle of the Far East, and Matteo Ricci, the founder of the China mission. Colbert was concerned with the promotion of trade with Asia. The desire to spread the news of the king's glory and thus to increase it was another reason for the cultivation of relations with these distant kingdoms.

All the same, most effort went into impressing the other courts of Europe with the greatness of Louis XIV. A good deal of the king's time was taken up with the ritual of diplomacy, including relations with very small states. To take a fairly normal month as an example, Louis spent

November 1682 in Fontainebleau and Versailles. At Fontainebleau he gave two audiences to the ambassador of Savoy (with whom a royal marriage was being negotiated) and one each to the envoys of Hanover, while the envoys of Savoy and Bavaria presented their respects before leaving (the *congé*). At Versailles, he gave audience to the envoys of Wolfenbüttel and Parma, while those of Hanover and Zell took their leave.[41] On a special occasion, such as the death of the queen, the entire diplomatic corps would come one by one to present their compliments, or in this case condolences.[42]

The ambassadors formed a substantial part of the audience for court festivals, plays, ballets and operas. They were often presented with gifts, which would enhance the king's image abroad – medals and tapestries of the events of the reign, volumes of prints representing objects in the royal collections and jewelled portraits of Louis himself. Presentations of this kind fulfilled several functions simultaneously. They were examples of royal munificence, they diffused his image and they might serve other purposes as well. It is reasonable to assume that the gift to the pope of a tapestry representing the doge of Genoa apologising to Louis was intended as a warning.[43]

Performances abroad were another means employed to increase the king's reputation in other parts of Europe. In 1668, the ambassador to the court of the Elector of Mainz received instructions from Paris to organise a musical drama on the theme of 'the peace lately made' [*Pax nuperrime factum*] at Aix-la-Chapelle (above, p. 72). In 1682, the birth of the Duke of Burgundy was celebrated by French ambassadors in public in Venice, Rome, Madrid, Berlin and even in republican Switzerland.[44] In 1688, the French ambassador in Rome celebrated the capture of the fortress of Philippsburg with a firework display.[45]

Texts glorifying Louis in foreign languages show the importance accorded to foreign readers. The inscriptions on monuments and medals were in Latin, despite the protests of 'moderns' such as Charpentier and Desmarets, not only in order to follow classical precedent but also to communicate more effectively with educated people all over Europe.[46] Some of the numerous panegryrics on the king were composed in Latin. The choice of language sometimes marked an academic occasion – Jacques de La Beaune, for example, author of a eulogy on Louis as patron of the arts (above, p. 23) was a professor at the Jesuit college of Louis-le-Grand. On the other hand, translations of panegyrics into Latin (like Charles de la Rue's versions of Corneille) must have been intended for an audience outside France. Accounts of the king's coronation and of the famous *carrousel* at the Tuileries were also available in Latin.[47] Some of the prints representing *l'histoire du roi* carry inscriptions in Latin. Pamphlets justifying the War of Devolution and the War of the Spanish Succession were also translated into Latin, and so was the official medallic history.[48]

Latin was used by so many kinds of people for so many purposes in this period that texts in that language do not allow us to make an accurate assessment of the group for whom the messages were intended. A clearer impression of the main target audiences may be obtained from translations into various vernaculars.

Spanish, or Castilian, was the language of the court of Madrid, with whom the king's rivalry was particularly intense in the 1660s (above, p. 64). It is not surprising to find that the official defence of the War of Devolution (supposedly fought in defence of the rights of Louis' Spanish queen) was immediately translated into Castilian. It is intriguing to find that an account in Spanish of the famous *divertissement* of 1668 (above, p. 78) the *Brief Description of the Splendid Banquet* by a certain Pedro de la Rosa, was published at the time – not in Spain but in Paris, suggesting that the translation was inspired by the government. Apart from these, Spanish texts glorifying Louis are rare before the era of his grandson Philip V. Pamphlets justifying the War of the Spanish Succession were translated into Spanish and distributed via the French ambassador to Madrid.[49] The famous Rigaud portrait of the ageing Louis was originally commissioned to hang in Philip V's palace in Madrid.

German was the language of the court of the Holy Roman Emperor, another of Louis' main rivals on the European stage, so it is not surprising to find translations into that language. One of the contemporary descriptions of the royal wedding was translated into German.[50] So was the official justification of the War of Devolution, and the medallic history. A translation into German of Félibien's description of the Gobelins tapestries of the four elements and the four seasons – descriptions which include the praises of the king – was published at Augsburg in 1687.[51]

It was also at Augsburg that a German engraver, Elias Hainzelmann, made a print celebrating the king's conquest of heresy (Figure 70), a reminder that Europeans were not unanimous in criticising the Revocation of the Edict of Nantes. Some pamphlets justifying the War of the Spanish Succession were translated into German,[52] and a large number of attacks on Louis were also published in German in this period (Appendix 3).

70. *Louis as the Conqueror of Heresy*, engraving by Elias Hainzelmann, 1686. Bibliothèque Nationale, Paris

The translation of the praises of the king into Italian suggests the desire to impress the pope and perhaps the courts of Turin, Modena and elsewhere. A description of the king's coronation was published in Italian in 1654, and a description of the royal wedding in 1660. Girolamo Graziani, secretary to the Duke of Modena, was pensioned by Louis in order to glorify him. Graziani not only wrote sonnets on the king's victories but he circulated French justifications of the War of Devolution.[53] Elpidio Benedetti, best known as one of the artistic advisers of Colbert (above, p. 54), was also the author of a panegyric on the king, *The Glory of Virtue in the Person of Louis the Great*, published in Lyons, presumably for the export market.[54] Another panegyric of the king, by Pellisson, was translated into Italian. So were a number of pamphlets justifying the French position during the War of the Spanish Succession.[55]

Relatively little effort seems to have been made to convince the English or the Dutch of the king's greatness. In the Dutch case, the use of French by the ruling elite made the effort appear unnecessary. The same argument could not be used of English. However, it was only at the time of the War of the Spanish Succession that a serious attempt was made to convince the English public of the justice of the French cause. A statement by Louis that his 'sole aim is to maintain peace' was translated into English and put into circulation by the French envoy to London. The envoy also tried to recruit Sir Charles Davenant to write pamphlets supporting the French cause. Some pro-French accounts of military operations (written by Donneau de Visé, editor of the *Mercure*) were published in English translation.[56]

Responses

The crucial question is the most difficult one to answer. How did these various publics react to the presentation of Louis as a glorious, invincible, magnificent monarch? The best that can be done is to offer individual examples, faces in the crowd. Whether these reactions are typical of the groups to which the individuals belonged it is impossible to say, but their variety, at least, may be instructive.

One might begin with contrasts within the higher nobility. The duc de Saint-Aignan, a favourite of the king's, worked hard to promote his master's glory. He offered a prize, advertised in the *Mercure Galant*, for poems in honour of the king. He wrote such poems himself. He played an important role in the foundation of the Academy of Arles, which regularly sang the king's praises, and in the erection of a statue of Louis in the city of Le Havre. In a similar way, on a grander scale, the duc de Feuillade, Marshal of France, initiated the famous statue of the king on the Place des Victoires. Indeed, it was he who paid for the statue, although the project was supported by the government and the king gave him the marble. Yet as every reader of his memoirs knows, the duc de Saint-Simon was extremely critical of the king and also of the way in which he was glorified (see p. 184).

Further down the social scale, corporate reactions are easier to document than individual ones, particularly those of the Jesuits and the municipalities. A considerable number of Jesuits contributed to the creation of the royal image in different media, notably Jouvancy, La Beaune, Le Jay, Menestrier, Quartier and la Rue. Performances praising Louis were organised by Jesuits in Paris, Lille, Lyons, Toulouse and other cities. They celebrated Louis not only as a pious monarch who opposed heresy, but also as a conqueror and as a patron of the arts. The concern of the order to encourage Louis to suppress Protestantism hardly seems a sufficient reason for all the money and effort they invested in the glorification of the king.

The municipalities also offer examples of official enthusiasm for the king. In 1676, for example, the consuls of Arles erected a recently discovered fragment of a Roman obelisk as a monument to the king, topped with a golden sun and bearing a Latin inscription composed by Pellisson. The cost to the city was 6,825 livres.[57] But an eighteenth-century story suggests that at Pau the municipality was less than enthusiastic about the proposal that they should erect a statue of Louis on a public square.[58] Where municipalities welcomed the suggestion that they should erect statues of the king, it is difficult to interpret the motives of the town council. They may have been expressing loyalty, currying favour with the central government, or attempting to improve the appearance of their city, and to glorify themselves in the process.[59]

This kind of local reinterpretation or appropriation of messages from the centre is as elusive as it is fascinating, since it depended for success on ambiguity. At first sight the inscription placed (in 1715) on the statue of Louis on the triumphal arch at Montpellier, with its reference to 'peace on land and sea' [PAX TERRA MARIQUE PARTA] appears to be a classic example of official hyperbole. A second look suggests the possibility that the monument celebrated the Peace of Utrecht rather than the monarch.

Below these aristocratic and corporate levels, the evidence is fragmentary. Paris inventories show that some private individuals owned portraits of the king.[60] His image appeared on Paris shop-signs, such as that of the royal engraver Guillaume Vallet, 'Buste de Louis XIV', or the warehouses on the Petit Pont, 'au Grand Monarque'.[61] It also appeared on cheap pottery plates. The manufacture of these objects suggests a certain measure of popular devotion to the king, but the strength and spread of the devotion is impossible to measure. All we can do is cite a few contrasting examples of the reactions of private individuals to the king and his cult.

The concept of a 'private individual' is rather more elusive than it may look at first sight. A painting of Louis XIV touching the sick, for example (Figure 71), was commissioned by a certain Charles d'Aligre, abbot of Saint-Riquier. However, it turns out that the abbot's late father, Etienne d'Aligre, had been Chancellor of France and a cousin of another Chancellor, Michel Le Tellier, the father of Louvois. The role of the administrators, their relatives and clients in the commissioning of works glorifying the king deserves to be studied in detail.

Bearing this in mind, let us pick out a few faces in the crowd. On the negative side, one might begin with a man from Thouars who found himself in court in 1707 after remarking, with brutal simplicity, that 'le roi est un bougre et un voleur'. In 1709, when food was running short, there was what Saint-Simon called a 'flood' of placards against the king. His statues were defaced and an anonymous letter called for his assassination.[62] The traditional contrast between the good king and his evil councillors did not appeal to everyone. In similar manner, if more polite language, Paul-Ignace Chavatte, a cloth-worker from Lille (a city recently incorporated into France) made unfavourable comments about the king in his private journal, criticising Louis in particular for allowing his army to invade, pillage and burn without declaring war.[63]

In contrast, Pierre Gaulthier, dean of Toul, also on the frontiers of France, dedicated a gallery of thirty-one statues 'to the glory of Louis the Great'. The central figure was that of the king, represented 'as he is on the Place des Victoires in Paris' (see Figure 36), except that the statue held a club like that of Hercules to show that he is 'a true Hero, Tamer of Nations'. A curious but possibly revealing detail in the contemporary description of the statue is the reference to 'un petit Ange' about to crown the king with laurel. One wonders how many people viewing the statue on the Place des Victoires interpreted the figure of Victory in this way.[64] Further down the social scale, the journal of a country priest interpreted the Revocation of the Edict of Nantes as a case of piety overcoming self-interest, and described Louis as 'great'.[65]

71. 'Louis the miracle worker'. *Louis XIV Curing the Scrofula* by Jean Jouvenet, oil on canvas, 1690. Abbey church of Saint-Riquier

Foreign reactions to the royal image are most systematically described in the reports of the Venetian ambassadors, whose political neutrality makes their testimonies all the more reliable. The responses of the English – including Addison, Evelyn, Prior and Swift – are more vivid but also more partial. Addison and Prior have been quoted already (pp. 111, 144). John Evelyn commented with some disdain on 'those Royal flatterers Perault, Carpentier, La Chapel [sic]' and on the 'egregious Vanity' of the medal of the statue on the Place des Victoires.[66] In similar fashion an English physician, John Northleigh, who visited France in the 1680s, expressed his disapproval of the 'preposterous' inscriptions on monuments to Louis and 'the Abusive or Blasphemous Application' to the king of words and images associated with Christ (including 'a Glory above his Head').[67] The similarities between these comments and the propaganda against Louis (p. 145) will be obvious. Northleigh and Evelyn may have been persuaded to see the king in this way. However, a response is no less genuine for having been learned.

Again, an English country gentleman denounced Louis in a private letter of 1686 for his 'unparalleled cruelties to his Protestant subjects', and went so far as to rejoice over his illness (news of the fistula clearly travelled fast): 'I heare he stincks Alive, & his Carkass will stinck worse when he is dead, and so will his memory to all eternity'.[68]

The English were not alone in being scandalised by the way in which Louis was glorified. The court of Vienna was shocked by the 'arrogance' of the French ambassador, whose way of celebrating the birth of the emperor's second son in 1682 was to display a device making imperial claims for Louis XIV.[69] Charles XI instructed his ambassador to leave France if the story were true that the king of Sweden had been represented as a suppliant on a bas-relief on the notorious monument on the Place des Victoires (Figure 72). The Great Elector of Brandenburg-Prussia was equally offended by the humiliating representations of his rivers, the Oder and the Elbe.[70] Some inhabitants of Rome were shocked by the celebrations at the French embassy there after the capture of Philippsburg in 1688.[71] According to Saint-Simon, the paintings of *l'histoire du roi* at Versailles played 'no small part in irritating Europe against the king'.

Yet some foreign courts paid Louis the compliment of imitating his style of self-representation. Versailles in particular was taken as a model.

The clearest case of imitation was the court of Spain under Louis' grandson Philip V. The state portrait of Philip by Rigaud echoes the state portrait of Louis by the same artist (Figures 73 and 1). The

72. *The Swedes Reinstated in Germany* by Jean Arnould, relief, 1686. Louvre, Paris

Spanish court was reformed following the French model, and the king became more visible and accessible. The statues in the gardens of Philip's palace at La Granja imitated those of Versailles – Apollo, Hercules, Latona, and so on. The painter Houasse and the architect Robert de Cotte worked for Philip as well as for Louis, and the old king intervened in person in the reconstruction and redecoration of the Spanish palaces. Philip also founded academies of art, language and history on the French model.[72]

In other cases the imitation was more spontaneous. Nicodemus Tessin, *surintendant des bâtiments* to Karl XI of Sweden, the 'pole star' of the North, had been received by Louis at Versailles, as well as meeting Lebrun, Rigaud, Mignard and other artists, and he took their lessons to heart when he was building the royal palace at Stockholm.[73] Again, when Balthasar Neumann was commissioned to build a palace for the

73. 'Louis as exemplar'. *Portrait of Philippe V* by Hyacinthe Rigaud, oil on canvas, *c.* 1700. Louvre, Paris

prince-bishop of Würzburg, he visited France, in 1723, to look at 'Versailie', as he called it, and to submit his plans to the royal architect, Robert de Cotte. It is no wonder that the grand staircase at Würzburg is reminiscent of the *Escalier des Ambassadeurs* at Versailles.[74]

The list of palaces which have been described as imitations of Versailles is a long one, running from Caserta to Washington. The criteria for the description are not always easy to establish.[75] In any case, the palace of the sun is only part of the image of Louis XIV. Hence it may be more useful to examine three courts which found Louis exemplary in more than one respect: London, Saint Petersburg and Vienna.

Charles II took France as his model when he founded the *London Gazette* in 1665, the Royal Observatory in 1675 and Chelsea Hospital (the English Invalides) in 1681. Ironically, Louis' enemy William III imitated him in an even more thorough-going way than his pensioner Charles. William employed the Huguenot architect Daniel Marot, who had been forced to leave France after the Revocation, to help rebuild the palace at Het Loo, including a replica of the *Escalier des Ambassadeurs* at Versailles. William's military actions, like those of his opponent, were commemorated by a medallic history, *L'histoire métallique de Guillaume III* (1692)[76] (Figure 74). In other words, some of the people who opposed Louis most strongly were sufficiently impressed by his image-making to follow his example.

Among private individuals, Joseph Addison, no friend to Louis, recommended the foundation of an Academy of Inscriptions on the lines of the petite académie. The first Duke of Montagu, a supporter of William III, employed a French architect to design Montagu House in London, and a French painter (Lafosse, a favourite of Louis XIV's) to decorate it. His country house, Boughton, in Northamptonshire, 'perhaps the most French-looking seventeenth-century building in England' according to Nikolaus Pevsner, was described at the time as 'contrived after the Model of Versailles, with extending Wings, excellent Avenues, Vista's and Prospects' (Figure 75). His years as ambassador to France had affected Montagu's taste.[77]

Peter the Great was in France in 1717 and he visited Versailles and the Academy of Inscriptions. On his return home he sent the Academy the inscription for his equestrian monument at Saint Petersburg.[78] The tsar also founded an official newspaper on the model of the *Gazette*, a tapestry factory on the model of the Gobelins, and an Academy of Sciences on the model of the Académie des Sciences. His palace of Peterhof in Saint Petersburg (Figure 76) might be viewed as a new

74. 'Another royal rival'. Engraved frontispiece to Nicolas Chevalier's *Histoire de Guillaume III*, 1692. British Library, London

Versailles, in function if not in appearance, allowing for the fact that even by Russian standards of distance it was rather a long way from Moscow. Peterhof was designed in part by J. B. A. Le Blond (a pupil of Le Nôtre, the creator of the gardens of Versailles), and it included a grotto and an area called 'Marly'.[79] Louis' *appartements* also had their Russian equivalent in the assemblies of St Petersburg, although their purpose was rather different – to teach western manners to the Russian aristocracy.

The court of Vienna followed the French example even more closely.[80] The Emperor Leopold I (Figure 77), who ruled from 1658 to 1705, was not only the rival of Louis XIV, but his brother-in-law (having married the infanta Margarita Theresa, younger sister of Maria Theresa). Leopold too was musical, and the ballet and the opera flourished at his court, the

75. 'An English Versailles'. Boughton House, Northamptonshire, exterior. *c.* 1690–1700

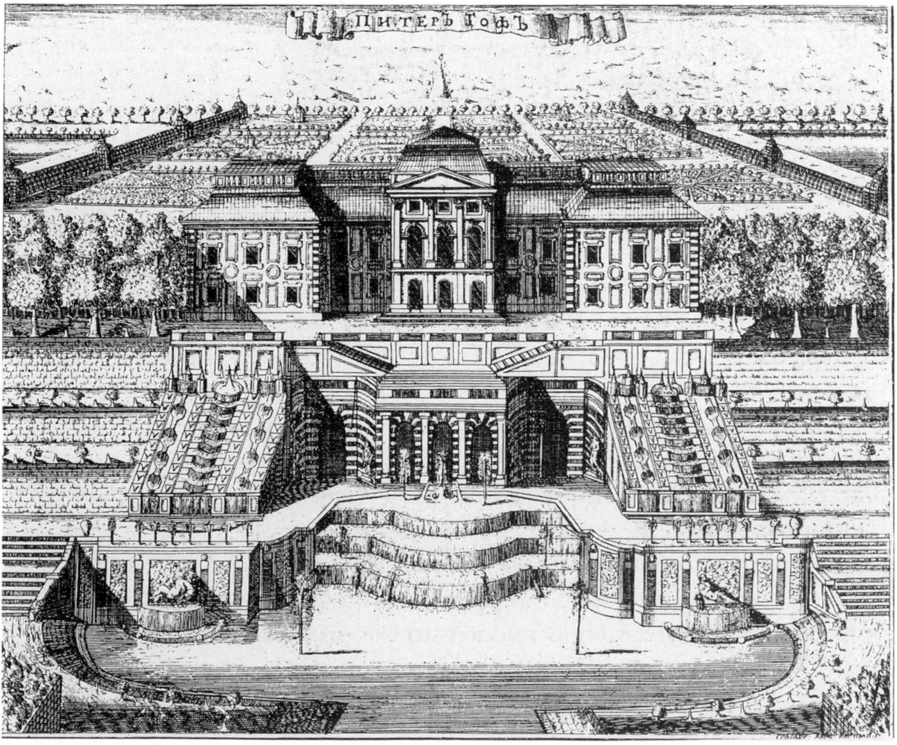

76. 'A Russian Versailles'. *Projected View of Peterhof with Cascades* by Alexis Zubov, engraving, 1717

77. 'Louis' rival'. *King Leopold I as the Conqueror of the Turks* by Matthias Steinl. Kunsthistorisches Museum, Vienna

most notable performance being 'The Golden Apple' [*Il pomo d'oro*] of 1668, a magnificent production in which Jupiter and Juno represent the emperor and his bride.[81]

Leopold's style of rulership was generally sober rather than splendid. 'Modest' was an adjective officially applied to him, and the imperial bedroom was indeed modest compared with that royal bedroom at Versailles. The term 'great' was applied to him not in his lifetime, but after his death in 1705. Leopold's employment of official historians (the Italian noblemen Galeazzo Gualdo Priorato and Giovanni Baptista Comazzi) and his rebuilding of his palace in Vienna, the Hofburg, are normal examples of the kind of patronage expected of princes at the time. Even the comparisons made between Leopold and the Emperor Constantine or the god Apollo (Figure 78) were commonplace enough not to require interpretation as reactions to the image of Louis XIV.

78. *Emperor Leopold as Apollo* by Christian Dittmann and Georg von Gross, engraving, 1674. Bildarchiv, Nationalbibliothek, Vienna

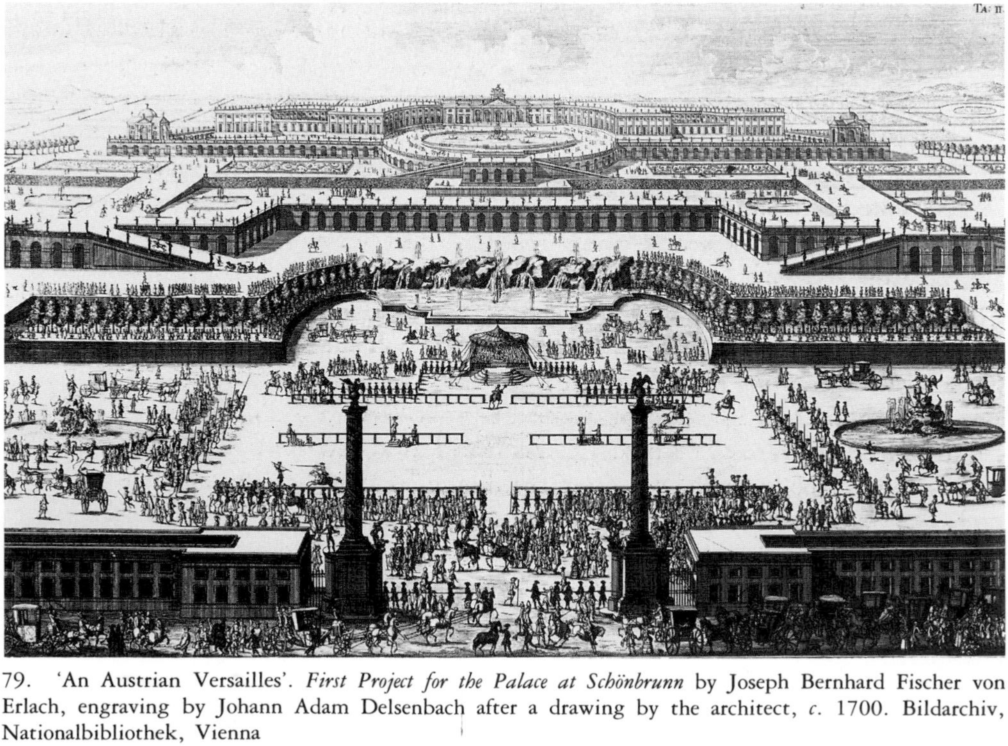

79. 'An Austrian Versailles'. *First Project for the Palace at Schönbrunn* by Joseph Bernhard Fischer von Erlach, engraving by Johann Adam Delsenbach after a drawing by the architect, *c.* 1700. Bildarchiv, Nationalbibliothek, Vienna

80. 'An Austrian Versailles'. *Schönbrunn as the Palace of the Sun* by I. V. Wolfgang, medal, 1700. Kunsthistorisches Museum, Vienna

On the other hand, the *carrousel* staged at the Hofburg in 1667 may be seen as a response to the one at the Tuileries five years earlier, while the foundation of a military hospital in Vienna was inspired by the Invalides. Again, the commission to J. B. Fischer von Erlach to build a new palace outside Vienna, at Schönbrunn (Figure 79), was surely a reaction to Versailles, all the more clearly so because the first project for the palace coincides with the outbreak of the War of the League of Augsburg. Indeed, a medal struck in 1700 by a certain I. V. Wolfgang presented Schönbrunn as the palace of the sun (Figure 80). One might therefore speak of a 'war of images', or of art as the continuation of war by other means.[82] The means chosen was a form of homage to Louis as an exemplar, however unwilling that homage might have been.

The official presentation of Leopold's eldest son and successor Joseph I, who ruled from 1705 to 1711, was still closer to that of Louis XIV. Joseph's election as King of the Romans in 1690 was marked by a triumphal entry into Vienna. He was hailed as a 'new sun', and represented as Apollo on the ceiling of the dining-room at Schönbrunn. His sarcophagus was decorated with reliefs of four victories over the French, including one of the battle of Ramillies. Even in the grave he continued to compete with Louis.[83]

81. 'A model for Louis as conqueror'. *Philip IV on Horseback* by Diego de Velázquez, oil on canvas. Prado, Madrid

XII

LOUIS IN PERSPECTIVE

> Qu'eût dit Louis XIV si on lui avait prouvé qu'en touchant les écruelles il prenait modèle sur un chef polynésien?
>
> Reinach[1]

In this book I have attempted to describe the gradual formation of the image of Louis XIV in the course of his reign, and to consider the audiences for whom it was intended and how it was received. To conclude the study I should like to place this image in comparative perspective. I shall attempt three kinds of comparison. In the first place, between Louis and other rulers of his time. In the second place, comparisons with rulers in earlier periods, concentrating on those who were most familiar to the king and his advisers, artists and writers. Finally, returning to one of the themes of the introductory chapter, I shall juxtapose the image of Louis XIV to those of some modern heads of state.

Louis in his time

Louis XIV was not the only ruler of his age to pay attention to modes of self-presentation. As others competed with him, so he competed with others, learned from them and defined himself by contrast to them. If Louis did not imitate Leopold as much as Leopold imitated him, he envied him the title of emperor (and had indeed tried to obtain it for himself at the time of the imperial election of 1658).

Like other early modern kings, especially after 1648, Louis attempted to present himself as equal to the emperor, and his kingdom as an empire.[2] For example, in the official description of the 1660 entry, the famous phrase from Virgil's *Aeneid*, 'I have given an empire without limit' [*imperium sine fine dedi*] was applied to the kings of France, who were presented as successors to the Roman emperors. The claim was made more explicitly and more fully in 1667 in Aubéry's pamphlet on Louis' rights over the empire (above, p. 72).[3]

Many apparently casual references to Louis reinforce this claim. For example, one of the historiographers royal, Vertron, composed an inscription styling Louis 'the emperor of the Franks' [IMPERATOR FRANCORUM].[4] The frequent references to Louis as 'auguste' or as the greatest monarch in the world should be interpreted as support for particular political claims, as well as a general form of glorification. So should his use of the traditional imperial symbol, the sun, with the implication that there is one supreme ruler in the world as there is one sun in the heavens.

In order to place the fabrication of Louis XIV in historical perspective, it is necessary to go back before 1660, or even 1643. In the generation before his own, two kings were particularly important to Louis as examples to emulate and surpass: one was his father, Louis XIII, and the other was his uncle and father-in-law, Philip IV.

Philip IV paid considerable attention to his public image. The term 'image' is all the more appropriate in the case of a king who impressed foreigners such as the French ambassador by his capacity for remaining virtually immobile, 'like a marble statue', when he appeared in public, with only his lips moving.[5] In fact, Philip did not make many such appearances. The king took part in religious and diplomatic rituals and sometimes went out in a coach, but he preferred to remain withdrawn from view. He ate in public only once a week.

This manner of playing the royal role was not unique to Philip IV, but part of Spanish tradition, in which a calm dignity, or as they called it *sosiego*, was a highly prized quality. Gravity and sobriety should not be confused with a lack of concern with self-presentation – the number of surviving portraits of the king are eloquent evidence of this concern. Philip's interest in court rituals is equally apparent from the care with which he revised the official protocols [*etiquetas*]. The king's immobility and virtual invisibility should therefore be viewed as part of the theatre of the court. The fact that Philip could not be seen for much of the time was a way of making his public appearances all the more dazzling.[6]

'Dazzling' may seem an inappropriate term for a monarch as sober as Philip IV, who generally dressed (like his grandfather Philip II) in dark colours, especially after reaching middle age, wearing a simple collar [the *golilla*] instead of the splendid ruffs that had been the fashion at court (Figure 81). His portraits by Velázquez are equally sober and impress by understatement.[7]

All the same, Philip was compared with the sun and described as 'the planet king' [*el rey planeta*]. He was also known in his own lifetime as 'Philip the Great' [*Felipe el Grande*]. A splendid equestrian statue of the king by the Italian sculptor Pietro Tacca was erected on the Plaza de Oriente in Madrid in 1640. Philip was prepared to spend a good deal of money in order to appear in public in a magnificent setting. It was in his time, in the 1630s, that a new palace, the Buen Retiro, was constructed on the outskirts of Madrid at a cost of some two million ducats, including a magnificent throne room, the Hall of Realms.[8] It was also in Philip's time, in the 1640s, that the palace in the centre of Madrid, the Alcázar, was given its magnificent Hall of Mirrors [*Sala de Espejos*] (Figure 82), to serve as a setting for royal audiences. During the negotiations for Louis XIV's marriage, the French delegates were received there.[9]

Philip made Velázquez his court painter, and put him in charge of the decoration of the royal palaces. In fact 'decoration' is too weak a term, since the paintings in the state rooms transmitted political messages. In the Hall of Mirrors in Madrid, there hung a painting by Rubens representing Philip IV as Atlas, the globe on his shoulders referring to the Habsburg claims to world empire. The imperial theme was reinforced by Titian's famous equestrian Charles V, which hung in the same room, together with portraits of Roman emperors.[10] In the Hall of Realms at the Buen Retiro, there hung five equestrian portraits by Velázquez, and ten scenes of the life and labours of Hercules (the king's mythical ancestor) by Zurbarán. The Hall also included twelve paintings of the major victories of Philip's reign, notably the *Surrender of Breda*, by Velázquez, and the *Recapture of Bahía* by Juan Bautista Maino (Figure 83).[11] The king might dress simply, but his residence had to be magnificent.

Philip's chief minister, the Count-Duke of Olivares, shares responsibility for the fabrication of the royal image with the art-loving monarch and his court painter. Like his contemporary, Richelieu, Olivares was aware of the political importance of paintings, pamphlets, histories, poems and plays. He employed the poet Quevedo (among others) to write both pamphlets and plays on topical themes, while the Italian nobleman Virgilio Malvezzi was appointed court historian in order to

82. 'A model for the Grande Galerie'. *Charles II of Spain in the Sala de Espejos, Escorial* by Juan Carreño de Miranda, oil on canvas. Prado, Madrid

glorify the king.[12] Olivares expected to share in this glory. In the *Recapture of Bahía*, Maino glorifies not only the victorious commander and his monarch but the minister as well. Even Mazarin, whose praises were sung in the 1660 entry (p. 44), did not go as far as this. Olivares also appears in the background to a painting by Velázquez of the heir to the throne, Prince Baltasar Carlos. The political significance of this appearance may be gauged from the fact that the minister was omitted from a copy of the painting made after his disgrace.[13]

Louis XIV, who had a Spanish mother and a Spanish wife, was well aware of Philip IV's style of monarchy. In the course of the negotiations leading to Louis' marriage, the French ambassador was shown the royal apartments in the Alcázar. Louis had a chance to meet his uncle in 1660 (p. 44, see Figure 21).

As the conflict over precedence in 1661 makes abundantly clear, Louis' aim was to surpass Philip. His method was imitation, in the

83. *Recapture of Bahia* by Juan Bautista Maino, *c.* 1633. Prado, Madrid

Renaissance sense of the term – to follow a model in order to go beyond it. Although he never allowed Colbert to become an Olivares, Louis had his own Velázquez in the person of Charles Lebrun, who was the keeper of the royal collection and bought works of art for the king from all parts of Europe.[14] Versailles resembled the Buen Retiro in its conception – a palace on the outskirts of the capital – as well as in its decoration with paintings of royal victories. The Galerie des Glaces, on the other hand, followed – and surpassed – the example of the Sala de Espejos in the Alcázar. The daily rituals of Versailles, so much more formal than the court of Louis XIII, owe something to Spanish precedent. The French courtiers seem to have taken an interest in the Spanish style: at all events, the guide to survival at court by the Spaniard Baltasar Gracián went through at least eight French editions between 1684 and 1702. Louis was probably less accessible and less visible than his immediate predecessors. Saint-Simon, for one, took this view and criticised what he called 'the idea of making oneself more worthy of respect by withdrawing from the gaze of the multitude' [*l'idée de se rendre plus vénérable en se dérobant aux yeux de la multitude*].[15]

The official image of the king emphasised his accessibility. The royal memoirs explicitly contrast the French style of monarchy with those of 'nations' – most obviously Spain – in which 'the majesty of kings largely consists in not allowing themselves to be seen' [*où la majesté des rois consiste, pour une grande partie, à ne se point laisser voir*].[16] The Jesuit La Rue congratulated the inhabitants of provinces conquered from Spain because they would now be able to see their monarch.[17] A similar point was made in one of Louis' funeral sermons, which described the late king as 'very different from those mysterious kings who hide themselves to make themselves respected' [*bien différent de ces rois mystérieux, qui se cachent pour se faire respecter*].[18] Louis certainly appeared in public much more than Philip. His style of self-presentation was majestic but it was also outgoing. When he instituted the custom of the *appartements* at Versailles, he and the queen visited the gaming tables and even took part in the games, thus honouring his subjects (as the *Mercure Galant* was quick to point out) by his familiarity.[19] Louis' style might be described as midway between the stiff Spanish manner and the more demotic style of other seventeenth-century kings, notably Christian IV of Denmark and Gustav Adolf of Sweden, who liked to speak to his subjects in the market-place. It has already been suggested (see p. 33) that the famous portrait of Louis by Rigaud tries to achieve such a balance between formality and informality. Both the display of the regalia and the relaxed pose of the king are features that Spanish royal portraits studiously avoided.

The contrast between Louis and Philip may have been a matter of difference in temperament, but it should also be explained in terms of politics and cultural tradition. The sobriety of Philip, like that of the Emperor Leopold (above, p. 175), was the Habsburg style. It might be argued that a family which had been ruling since the thirteenth century had such legitimation by descent that it did not need very much glorification by other means. In contrast, Louis was a mere third-generation king of France (though an earlier Bourbon had been king of Navarre). Hence the portraits of Louis had to be more flamboyant and more heroic. Louis needed more equestrian statues and more medals than Philip or Leopold. The French government also made much more use of the press than the Habsburgs did. In this respect as in others it followed the model of the government of Louis XIII and Cardinal Richelieu.

Richelieu, together with his assistants the Capuchin friar Père Joseph (for literature) and the *intendant* Sublet des Noyers (for architecture and painting) had been very much concerned to harness artists and writers to the chariot of the state, to present a favourable image of the king and his government. To this end he founded the Académie Française in 1634, a group of forty appointed according to a mixture of literary and political criteria.[20] At Richelieu's request, the nobleman Jean-Louis Guez de Balzac, a member of the academy, wrote a treatise on *The Prince* which portrayed Louis XIII as an ideal ruler. A number of pamphlets were written to justify the policies of the government against internal and external critics. One of them, by the sieur de Fancan, carried the appropriate title *La voix publique*.[21] An official newspaper was founded in 1631, the weekly *Gazette*, printed in the Louvre and edited by a client of Richelieu's, Théophraste Renaudot.[22]

The history of the reign was recounted by a number of official historians such as Charles Sorel (best known as a writer of fiction), Pierre Matthieu, author of *Les merveilles de Louis le Juste* (1627), and Scipion Dupleix, whose *Histoire de Louis le Juste* (1635) also presented the reign as a series of 'marvels' and compared the king to Caesar, Clovis, Charlemagne and St Louis.[23] The use of the title 'Just' in the king's lifetime is worth noting. In similar fashion Henri IV was addressed as 'Henri le Grand' in an ode by the poet Malherbe.

The government also paid attention to spectacle and to the visual arts. Louis XIII was fond of music and the dance, and the *ballet de cour*, like the theatre, flourished in his reign. The political function of some of the performances of the period is obvious, as in the case of the ballet *La prospérité des armes de France* (1640), devised by Jean Desmarets, a founder-member of the Académie Française.

The king showed little interest in visual display, but his mother and Richelieu showed a great deal. It was Queen Marie de'Medici who summoned Rubens to Paris in 1622 to paint a cycle of twenty-four pictures of the reign of Henri IV and of the Regency, scenes from contemporary history combined with allegory which are perhaps the closest precedent to Lebrun's images of Louis XIV in the Grande Galerie at Versailles (Figure 84). The queen also ordered an equestrian statue of her husband Henri IV from the leading sculptor in Florence (indeed in Europe) at that time, Giambologna, while Richelieu commissioned the famous equestrian monument of Louis XIII erected on the Place Royale in Paris.

The cardinal's concern with painting is even more clear. He summoned Simon Vouet and Nicholas Poussin back to France and he tried to

84. 'A model for Louis in triumph'. *Henri IV Enters Paris in Triumph* by Peter Paul Rubens, (detail), *c.* 1625. Florence, Uffizi

attract Italian artists as well. As for engravings, the Fleming Jacques de Bie dedicated to Louis XIII his *La France metallique* (1634), a history of the kings of France in medals, which surely helped inspire the medallic history of Louis XIV.

When he danced in the *ballet de cour*, the young Louis XIV was actually following in the footsteps of his father, who was if anything even more fond of music and the dance. The famous *carrousel* of 1662 followed the precedent of the *carrousel* of 1612. The similarities between Richelieu's programme of the 1630s and Colbert's programme of the 1660s will also be clear. In fact there were close connections and continuities between the two. The sumptuous official publication, *The Triumphs of Louis the Just*, involving historians, artists and poets (among them Corneille), was planned while the king was still alive but published only in 1649.[24]

Mazarin, who was Richelieu's client and Colbert's patron, bridged the gap between the 1630s and the 1660s, and so did a whole group of writers. Jean Chapelain, for example, was a client of Richelieu's before he became an adviser to Colbert. Bourzeis was a literary assistant to Richelieu before he entered the petite académie. Desmarets survived long enough to write panegyrics on Louis XIV's campaigns of the 1660s and 1670s (above, p. 75). When Colbert employed the seigneur de Chantelou to accompany Bernini on his visit to France, he was following the precedent of Sublet des Noyers and Richelieu, who had sent Chantelou to Rome to bring back Poussin.

Precedents

No attempt to place the image of Louis XIV in historical perspective can confine itself to France and Spain or stop in the early seventeenth century. One might start from the fact that the notorious strategy attributed to Louis, that of forcing the upper nobility to come to Versailles in order to weaken them, had already been attributed to Henri IV by an English ambassador, Sir George Carew. It was 'To have them live in court; so they practise not in other places; and there by play, and other unthriftiness, they grow poor.'[25]

In certain respects, the court of Louis XIV resembles the court of the Valois kings rather than that surrounding his father and grandfather. François I was a munificent patron of the arts and literature, presented as such in his own time. He was compared with Constantine and Charlemagne, and was represented in Roman armour. He was honoured by an equestrian statue and a triumphal arch in the Roman manner, although these constructions lasted no longer than the festivals of which they formed a part.[26] Henri III was described as a sun-king, he danced in *ballets de cour*, and he supported an academy. He also appointed a Grand Master of Ceremonies and made court ritual (including that of the *lever* and the *coucher*) more elaborate and more formal.[27] It is unlikely that Louis and his masters of ceremonies were unaware of this precedent.[28] The relation between the other public rituals of sixteenth-century French kings and those of Louis XIV is rather more elusive.[29]

The French debt to Italian Renaissance and Baroque traditions was enormous in almost all media in which the king was represented. The 'Italian connection', as we might call it, is an obvious aspect of Cardinal Mazarin's patronage of the arts (above, p. 46). He had learned to be a patron in Rome, in the circle of Pope Urban VIII, and he tended to favour Italians. He employed an Italian, Francesco Buti, as his artistic adviser in Paris, while Elpidio Benedetti and Luigi Strozzi kept him in touch with Rome and Florence. He brought to France Italian singers, composers, painters and theatrical designers (Giacomo Torelli and Gaspare and Carlo Vigarani).

A specific Italian connection which deserves to be emphasised is the Paris–Modena axis. Francesco d'Este, Duke of Modena, took a great interest in the arts. He consulted Bernini over improvements to his palace, commissioned a portrait bust from him, and employed Gaspare Vigarani as his architect and the superintendent of court festivals. The duke also cultivated relations with the court of France. He visited Paris in 1657, he proposed his daughter as a wife for Louis XIV, and himself married a niece of Mazarin's.[30]

The king of France followed the duke's example in a number of ways. Gaspare Vigarani was called to Paris in 1659 and designed the arches for the royal entry into Paris in the following year, while his son spent two decades designing machines for royal fêtes. The duke's secretary, Girolamo Graziani, was pensioned by Louis XIV in the 1660s and wrote panegyrics of the 'French Hercules' (above, p. 52). It is unlikely to be a coincidence that Francesco I and Louis XIV both asked Bernini to advise on changes to their palaces and to make their portrait-busts.

As these examples show, the Italian connection outlasted Mazarin. It was encouraged by the foundation of the French Academy in Rome (1666), where young artists were able to study. In fact, the habit of study in Italy, and more especially Rome, had been established before it was institutionalised. Lebrun had spent four years in Rome, from 1642 to 1646. Girardon was also in Rome in the 1640s, while Mignard was there for more than twenty years (1635–57).

Italy had a great deal to offer the artists in the service of Louis XIV. In Rome, they could observe the use of obelisks in the transformation of urban spaces into monuments celebrating the popes. In Venice, the use of historical paintings in the doge's Palace as a means of glorifying the regime. In Florence, the suite of rooms – associated with the planets – in Palazzo Pitti (Figure 85), the residence of the Grand Dukes of Tuscany, looks very much like a model for Versailles.[31] These rooms were decorated by Pietro da Cortona between 1637 and 1647, with a combination of stucco, gilding and frescoes glorifying the Medici family. The example was all the more appropriate because Louis XIV's grandmother was a Medici.

An earlier Grand Duke of Tuscany, Cosimo de'Medici, was almost certainly a model for Louis XIV or his advisers. Cosimo, who ruled from 1537 to 1574, turned his Grand Duchy into an absolute monarchy in miniature. He ruled a state with less than a twentieth of the population of France under Louis XIV. Cosimo was the son of a mercenary captain, who was made the ruler of Florence after the childless Alessandro de'Medici had been assassinated. His lack of legitimacy made him all the more aware of the political uses of the arts in creating a good public image.

85. 'A model for Versailles'. Salon of Saturn, Palazzo Pitti, Florence, by Pietro da Cortona, *c.* 1640

For example, Cosimo erected a column in Piazza Santa Trinità in Florence to commemorate his victory over the forces of the exiled republicans. He had twelve medals struck to commemorate events of the reign. He employed Bronzino, Cellini and Vasari to portray him in a heroic manner, stern and lion-like, in paintings, statues and frescoes.[32] He had himself represented with the artists he patronised (Figure 86). He appointed official historians, who were given pensions and access to official documents and were expected to tell a story favouring the Medici. He spent 50,000 scudi on a splendid festival to welcome his son's bride (sister of the emperor) in 1565, with triumphal arches, mock-sieges, fireworks, and so on. He founded two academies, the Florentine Academy, which worked on an Italian grammar and dictionary, and the Academy of Design. These academies were the prototypes of the Académie Française and the Académie Royale de Peinture.

The artists and writers who worked for Louis XIV were great admirers of Renaissance Italy. Jean Chapelain, for example, was well read in

86. 'A model for Louis as patron'. *Cosimo and His Architects* by Giorgio Vasari, ceiling painting. Palazzo Vecchio, Florence

Italian literature, and even wrote verse in Italian.[33] The great debates between ancients and moderns and in painting between the primacy of drawing and that of colour echoed earlier debates in Italy. In his 'poetical history' of the war between the ancients and the moderns, François de Callières placed the army of the moderns under the command of Torquato Tasso. The epics of Ariosto and Tasso were well known and much admired. It is scarcely surprising to find that the Quinault–Lully opera *Armide* (1686) is based on episodes from Tasso's *Gerusalemme Liberata*, or that the *Plaisirs de l'Isle Enchantée* adapted scenes from Ariosto's *Orlando Furioso* to the setting of a tournament. The famous *carrousel* of 1662 owes a good deal to Italian models. The very idea of combining tournament and theatre goes back to the Renaissance courts of Ferrara and Florence.[34]

The devices or *imprese* used in festivals, or on medals, belonged to an Italian Renaissance tradition. So did the medals themselves. So did much of their iconography, especially personifications such as Fame, in the form of a woman, Discord, in the form of a monster, and so on, often taken from that invaluable reference-book for artists, Cesare Ripa's *Iconologia* (1593), which had been translated into French in 1644. The writings of Menestrier on what he called 'the philosophy of images' reveal his awareness of the Italian Renaissance literature on emblems.[35] Indeed, Menestrier might be regarded as a late example of a Renaissance phenomenon, the so-called 'humanist adviser' to artists.

In style, too, Renaissance Italy provided a model, or rather models, since the Florentine and Venetian styles each had their partisans. The 'grand manner' of Lebrun was the style of the High Renaissance and in particular of Raphael. Lebrun rendered simultaneous homage to Raphael, Colbert and the king with *Triumph of Constantine*. This engraving of Constantine in a chariot, crowned by Victory, followed a design by Raphael. It was dedicated to Colbert, and it represented one of the rulers to whom Louis was most frequently compared. Again, the lectures of François Blondel, Director of the Academy of Architecture, show constant awareness of Renaissance precedents. He frequently cites the major Italian architects of that period, such as Alberti, Palladio, Vignola and Scamozzi.

These forms of imitation were not slavish. They are not examples of the 'dead weight' of tradition. French artists and writers chose from the Italian repertoire precisely the models which they could use. Their respect for Italian achievements did not prevent some of them thinking that they could do better.[36]

The relation of the image of Louis to medieval traditions is rather different. In this case what we find are more or less unconscious continuities rather than imitation and competition. The ritual of the *sacre* followed medieval French precedent (p. 41). So did the *lits de justice* of the earlier part of the reign (p. 40). The formal royal entry into a city was a medieval custom, although it had been reconstructed in the Renaissance on the model of an ancient Roman triumph, with chariots, trophies, triumphal arches, and so on. An elaborate ritual was a feature of the court of Burgundy in the later Middle Ages – indeed, it was from Burgundy that some features of Spanish court ritual had been adopted in the middle of the sixteenth century.

Seventeenth-century Frenchmen did not normally admire the Middle Ages. They tended to look down on this age of darkness and to associate it with barbarism and the 'Goths'.[37] All the same, links between Louis and Clovis, Charlemagne and St Louis were taken seriously (Figure 87). In certain respects, medieval rulers offered models for the public presentation of Louis XIV. Louis was anointed with the holy oil supposed to have been brought to Clovis by a dove. He wore the traditional royal mantle, embroidered with fleurs-de-lis. He used the regalia, the traditional symbols of royal authority – crown, sceptre, orb, sword, ring, and so on.[38] The king performed other medieval rites (such as the *lit de justice* and the state entry) which despite their transformation in the sixteenth century were essentially medieval. He touched the sick and he washed the feet of the poor. One might say that Louis was worldly enough to appreciate the advantages of being a sacred monarch, a claim that Bossuet, for example, continued to make on his behalf.[39] He may not have shared the belief of his Merovingian predecessors in the magical potency of long hair, but he wore his famous high wig.

In the course of the reign, the king distanced himself from these medieval models without abandoning them altogether. Unlike medieval rulers, he did not often wear a crown, or hold a sceptre or a *main de justice* (a staff surmounted by a hand, representing the king's role as supreme judge). After he gave up holding the *lits de justice*, Louis did not often sit on a throne. Among the rare occasions when he did so were the audiences given to the Algerian envoys in 1684, the Siamese envoys in 1686 and the Persian envoys in 1715 (see Figure 68). One is therefore left with the impression that a throne had come to be regarded as an archaic survival, so exotic that it was used simply to impress orientals.

Even the representations of the king shifted away from the traditional regalia, and often showed him in ordinary clothes, sitting on a chair or holding a baton rather than a sceptre to demonstrate his authority. The famous state portrait by Rigaud (Figure 1) displays some of the traditional symbols but in a muted form. Louis wears the royal mantle, but it is open so that his modern clothes are visible underneath. He holds the sceptre, but in an unconventional manner. He wears the sword of state, but only the hilt is visible. There is no orb and the *main de justice* is tucked unobtrusively away on a chair.

Another model of rulership known in the king's entourage was that of Byzantium. A magnificent folio edition of Byzantine historians was published in the 1660s with a dedication to Colbert. It was perhaps a pity that the famous guide to court ritual by the tenth-century emperor

87. 'Louis identified with St Louis'. *Louis as St Louis*, Anonymous painting, *c.* 1660. Poitiers, chapel of Jesuit College

Constantine VII Porphyrogennetus was unknown at Versailles, for in more than one respect Louis resembled a Byzantine emperor.[40]

Lights burned before the images of emperors, and there were formal rituals for greeting them in the morning, for standing and sitting in their presence, and even for prostration before them (the so-called *proskynesis*). The emperor was described as 'peace-bringer' (*eirenpoios*), pious (*eusebios*), a benefactor (*euergetes*), as a priest, as an *autokrator* (not so far from an absolute monarch), as God's lieutenant, as the sun. Some of Constantine's coins carried the legend 'the unconquered sun', SOL INVICTUS.

The French king's claim to be *monarque de l'univers* may seem less shocking to modern ears when it is remembered that Byzantine emperors too claimed to rule the whole world (*oikumene*).[41] Like later emperors, Louis was described as 'a new Constantine', a parallel all the more appropriate because (as recent historians emphasise), Constantine himself was well aware of the value of propaganda. Bossuet, who described Louis in this way, probably saw himself as a new Eusebius, the Bishop of Caesarea famous for his panegyrics of Constantine, his persecution of heretics and his history of the Church.[42] The famous arch of Constantine in Rome was an inspiration and a model for the king's triumphal arches, although, as Charles Perrault did not fail to point out, the king's arches were larger.[43]

Byzantine emperors drew on Roman imperial traditions, and here we are on firmer ground. In the age of Louis XIII, Guez de Balzac had suggested the imitation of Roman emperor-worship. Ceremonial specialists such as Godefroy and Saintot studied the rituals of Roman emperors.[44] The critics of the statue on the Place des Victoires (above, p. 145) were more accurate than they may have known in their malicious references to the Roman apotheosis.[45]

The relation between the image of Louis XIV and the classical tradition is a subject well worth a monograph of its own, in the manner of Aby Warburg, discussing seventeenth-century perceptions of antiquity as well as the adaptation of the repertoire of classical forms and images to new functions and new contexts. Architects and artists were well aware of ancient Roman models, even when they chose to diverge from them. Claude Perrault published a translation of the treatise by the Roman architect Vitruvius as well as designing a 'French order' for the Louvre to show that modern France could compete with ancient Rome. François Blondel liked to include modern weapons in his trophies, including muskets, cannon and even bombs (on which he was a particular expert), but he also liked to quote Roman precedents for his designs, including Trajan's column, the Arch of Titus (with its winged victories in the spandrels) and the Arch of Constantine (with its sun).[46]

The survival of ancient monuments in French cities, the Porte de Mars in Rheims for example, made classical precedents familiar to Colbert as well as to his architects.[47] Sculptors went to Rome to study ancient statues and returned to lecture to their pupils on the Laocoön, the Farnese Hercules and the Belvedere torso.[48] Classical statues and plaster casts of statues (including Trajan's Column) were brought to Paris by Colbert for political as well as aesthetic reasons, to impress foreigners and to demonstrate that Paris was a new Rome.[49]

Equestrian statues of Louis often followed the model of the statue of Marcus Aurelius on the Capitol. A plaster cast of this statue was on display in the Académie Royale de Peinture et Sculpture, where the Siamese envoys viewed it in 1686.[50] Girardon was one of the sculptors who followed this model, though he made sure that his statue was bigger.[51] The debate whether or not to gild the statue of Louis on the Place des Victoires invoked the example of Marcus Aurelius.[52] Medallists followed Roman precedent in images and inscriptions alike, although they were prepared to break with these precedents on occasion (p. 131). Artists such as Lebrun and Desjardins, who represented Louis as Hercules, are unlikely to have been unaware that Roman emperors too were represented in this way.

The relation between the literature of ancient Rome (and to a lesser extent, Greece) and that of seventeenth-century France was at once closer and more complex than that of the visual arts, because the writers (unlike the artists, or to a greater extent than the artists) could assume a familiarity with the classics on the part of their readers. Writers exploited this familiarity by playing with quotation and allusion.

If Bossuet was a new Eusebius, Boileau cast himself as a new Horace, with Colbert as his Maecenas and Louis as his Augustus. Like Horace, he wrote odes, epistles, satires and an *Art of Poetry*. The prose portraits of the king by Félibien and others followed the tradition of the classical *ekphrasis* or description of a work of art.[53] The formal panegyrics of the king, and even the habit of delivering them on his birthday, followed classical precedents. The Jesuit La Beaune edited classical panegyrics as well as writing modern ones. Pliny's panegyric on the Emperor Trajan was particularly well known. For those who could not read Latin or Greek, translations were increasingly available.

For example, Benserade translated Ovid's *Metamorphoses* into verse and the king ordered the publication of an illustrated edition, doubtless because it would help viewers to decode many of the allegorical paintings in his honour. Writers regarded ancient Rome as a rival to be surpassed. They also made use of the idea that Rome had been surpassed in order to glorify Louis XIV. It would of course be absurd to reduce the famous 'battle of the books' between the ancients and the moderns to a means of propaganda for Louis XIV. All the same, there was a political element in the literary commonplace that Louis was a new Augustus, or even, according to an inscription on the king's bust at the convent of the Mathurins, 'more august than Augustus' [*Augusto augustior*].[54]

As classicists have shown, Augustus was very much concerned with his public image, so it may be of interest to pursue the comparison a little further.[55] The parallels between the two leaders are indeed striking. Augustus was a small man, and in order to look taller he wore high heels.[56] He presented his own interpretation of his reign in his memoirs, or *Res Gestae*. He was believed to have a special relationship with

88. *The Emperor Claudius*, cameo. Cabinet des Médailles, Bibliothèque Nationale, Paris

Apollo.[57] He was represented as Jupiter. Many statues of Augustus were erected in public places, in the provinces as well as in Rome, portraying him as 'aloof, majestic and heroic'.[58] Private individuals too placed images of Augustus in their houses as a sign of loyalty, while provincial cities honoured him as a god, the saviour of the world, the lord of earth and sea (like Louis XIV, Roman emperors emphasised their power over the world with titles like *Conservator Orbis*, *Pacator Orbis*, *Restitutor Orbis*, and so on).[59] Coins and statues associated Augustus like other emperors (Figure 88) with the figure of Victory. He dedicated two obelisks to the sun. Festivals were organised to encourage the loyalty of the people. With the help of Maecenas, a number of writers were recruited into the service of the regime, including the historian Livy as well as Virgil and Horace.

The differences in the presentation of the two rulers are also worth noting. Augustus replaced a republic and it was necessary to modify the language of political communication (literary and visual) in order to represent his position as leader.[60] He was portrayed as eternally youthful, while Louis, as we have seen, was allowed to grow discreetly old. Augustus made a virtue of simplicity and if he could have seen Versailles he would probably have disapproved of its rich decoration. He was more 'populist' than Louis in the sense of claiming to be concerned with popular approval. He appeared in the theatre to be seen by the Roman people and even to enter into dialogue with them.[61]

The accumulation of precise parallels is remarkable, but it must not be assumed that the similar (or even identical) images had the same meaning in the two contexts. Apollo, for example, was part of the official Roman pantheon. In the age of Louis he was a Christian allegory. The political and cultural differences between the two epochs are fundamental, although they are masked by seventeenth-century reverence for the classical tradition in general and in particular for the age of Augustus [*le beau siècle d'Auguste*].[62]

The Roman cult of Julius Caesar, Augustus and later emperors owed a good deal to Greek and oriental traditions. For example, the mausoleum of Augustus took the form of a pyramid, as if he were another Pharaoh.[63] For Caesar as for Louis XIV, the great hero was Alexander the Great. It was Alexander's achievement not only to conquer most of the known world but also to establish a new style of monarchy on the Persian or Egyptian model, with an elaborate court ceremonial. This was how the oriental *proskynesis* entered the western tradition. The cult of the ruler was also expressed in the foundation of at least thirteen cities with the name of Alexandria, and the project for turning an entire mountain, Mount Athos, into a colossal image of Alexander.[64]

How well the scholars of the age of Louis XIV knew the oriental tradition of ruler-worship it is difficult to say. Blondel and Charles Perrault both discussed Egyptian obelisks as models for their own age, and they were aware of the Egyptian cult of the sun.[65] It would be interesting to know whether they thought of the cosmic hall in the palace of Khusrau (the sixth-century Sasanid king of Persia), discussed in at least one scholarly publication of the time, as a precedent for Versailles.[66] Khusrau, or Cosroès, was also the hero of a contemporary play by Jean Rotrou, set in the palace of Persepolis.[67] It is unlikely, however, that adjectives like 'god-given' applied to Louis were conscious echoes of the epithets of Akkadian and Sumerian rulers.[68] It is even less likely that the image-makers of Louis XIV knew of the traditional association between the ruler and the sun in cultures as remote from them as Japan and Peru.

In Hawaii, too, there was a connection between royalty, divinity and the sun.[69] The recourse to the same image of power in so many different cultures should not surprise us. The implied identification between the political order and the cosmic order is a classic example of the legitimation of a particular set of institutional arrangements by presenting them as natural, indeed as the only possible system.

The twentieth century

So far, the attempt has been made to view Louis in perspective by looking backwards along the corridor of time. Louis has been compared and contrasted with certain other monarchs in order to discover whether or not his mode of self-presentation was unusual. Since the king himself and the artists and writers in his service also looked backwards, it has proved necessary to discuss their attitudes to different periods and rulers in the past.

It is impossible to ignore the fact that our own standpoint is necessarily different from theirs. In the three centuries that separate him from us the representations of rulers have changed in many ways. Whether we are aware of this or not, our view of the seventeenth century is shaped by our own experiences of the twentieth. In order to avoid anachronistic judgements, it may be best to make comparisons explicit. Indeed, we may reach a deeper understanding of both our own age and the age of Louis XIV if we consider both the similarities and the differences between these two periods. I should therefore like to conclude this chapter – and the book – by comparing and contrasting seventeenth-century with twentieth-century media, and the public image of Louis with the images of some more recent heads of state.

Students of the twentieth-century media sometimes operate with rather questionable assumptions about earlier periods, including the so-called 'old regimes', which preceded the French Revolution. Take for example a well-known study of propaganda, written in the 1920s, which suggests that 'times have changed' since Louis XIV, and that the rise of propaganda and 'the new profession of public relations' is a twentieth-century phenomenon, encouraged by the First World War but necessitated by the free competition of ideas in a democratic society.[70]

Another example of a study of the modern world flawed by false assumptions about the old regime is the perceptive and provocative essay on 'the image' published in the early 1960s by the American cultural historian Daniel Boorstin. In this essay Boorstin argues that what he calls the 'graphic revolution' of the late nineteenth and early twentieth centuries (thanks to the steam press, photography, etc.) has led to the rise of what he calls the 'pseudo-event', a term with meanings ranging from an event staged for the sake of the media to one that is reported before it happens.[71] I hope to have shown the utility of this term of Boorstin's for the analysis of seventeenth-century media, including journals, medals and engravings. In the age of Louis XIV, apparently spontaneous actions were sometimes staged with some care, from the public rejoicings on the news of French victories to the erection of statues of the king.

Again, a study written in the 1970s uses phrases such as 'the theatre state' [*l'état-spectacle*] and 'the star system in politics' to describe the world of Kennedy and De Gaulle, Pompidou and Carter. The author contrasts this 'personalisation of politics' and the stress on packaging candidates for power with the system that obtained 'formerly' (whenever that was), when ideas mattered and politicians wrote their own speeches. He explains the difference by the influence of the cinema – including Rossellini's *Louis XIV* – and of advertising.[72]

The exaggeration in this argument should be obvious to readers of this book. Power was already personalised in the seventeenth century. Cardinal Richelieu and Louis XIV employed ghost-writers for their speeches, memoirs and even letters (pp. 8–9). Contemporary politicians may be presented like products, but it might equally well be argued that contemporary products are eulogised in the manner once reserved for princes. 'Hype' derives from hyperbole.

Long before the cinema, the theatre affected perceptions of politics. When the doge of Genoa arrived at Versailles in 1685, a contemporary observer, who happened to be a playwright, Donneau de Visé, remarked that 'the role which he had to play was not easy' [*le Personnage qu'il avoit à soutenir n'estoit pas aisé*].[73] The comparison between politics and the theatre was a common one in our period. For his contemporaries as for posterity, the sun-king was a star.

The means of persuasion employed by twentieth-century rulers such as Hitler, Mussolini and Stalin, and to a lesser extent by the French and American presidents, are analogous in certain important respects to the means employed by Louis XIV.[74] The grandiosity of official architecture and sculpture, for instance, dwarfing the spectators to make them conscious of the power of the ruler. The myth of the hero as omniscient, invincible and destined to triumph over the forces of evil and disorder. The image of the leader working during the night while his people sleep. Long before this image of Mussolini (or indeed, of Napoleon), was current, La Bruyère described how 'we rest, while this king . . . watches alone over us and over the whole state' [*nous reposons . . . tandis que ce roi . . . veille seul sur nous et sur tout l'Etat*].[75] The publication of official newspapers, the organisation of writers into official academies charged with the publication of prestigious dictionaries and encyclopaedias. Even a detail like Mussolini's insistence on printing his title of DUCE in capital letters has its parallel in the typographic presentation of LOUIS. Both rulers were presented in public as a second Augustus.[76] If Lyndon Johnson's private parts were the centre of publicity during his gall bladder operation, so were those of Louis at the time of his fistula.

Looking back along the corridor of history, the suppression of the medal on the destruction of Heidelberg, like the suppression of Olivares from the portrait of Baltasar Carlos, comes to resemble the deletion of Trotsky from the *Soviet Encyclopaedia*. The instructions to French municipalities to volunteer to erect a statue of Louis XIV in the main square of the city (above, p. 96) are good examples of what a historian of revolutionary Russia calls 'the myth of spontaneity'.[77] The naming of Saarlouis and Louisiana, like that of Leningrad, seems an expression of the cult of personality. Chapelain appears to be the perfect *apparatchik*, and the reaction against Louis XIV in the age of the Regency a case of 'delouisfication' on the model of de-stalinisation. Looking the other way, we may view the Soviet Academy of Sciences as, ironically, an act of homage to the France of Louis XIV – or more exactly (p. 172), the successor to an institution founded by Peter the Great in homage to the French academies.

These similarities are surely striking. They remind us not only of the importance of ritual, myth and symbol in politics at all times, but also of the continuity of particular myths and symbols in western societies.[78] However, I do not wish to present a simple argument to the effect that *plus ça change, plus c'est la même chose*. The image of modern rulers, and still more the image of modern regimes, does differ from that of Louis XIV and his contemporaries in certain important ways.

The most obvious of these differences is technological. Louis was presented in public by means of print, statues and medals, while twentieth-century rulers have relied increasingly on photography, the cinema, radio and television. The new electric media have their own requirements. The shift from political speeches to debates and question-and-answer sessions, for example, is one of their effects.[79] All the same, the contrast between what might be called 'the electric rulers' and their predecessors has been exaggerated.

More important is the rise of legitimation by popular election. Louis represented God, but later rulers represented the nation, a point made by an international lawyer in 1758.[80] The French Revolution marks a watershed between old regimes, in which there was no need to persuade the people, and modern states, in which they are the main target of propaganda. Popular newspapers made their appearance. One of them, *Père Duchesne*, is said to have sold as many as a million copies. The illiterate could listen to others reading these texts, or 'read' political images, or participate in political rituals like the Festival of the Federation, which celebrated the Revolution itself. It is no accident that the ideas of political conversion and political propaganda made their appearance at this time.[81]

Since those days, the organisation of persuasion has become still more elaborate and sophisticated, notably in the United States, thanks to the combination of a presidential regime, democratic elections, and an interest in new modes of communication. It has been suggested that image-making became important in American presidential campaigns as early as the 1820s, with the development of the campaign biography.[82] Professional political managers go back to California in the 1930s and 'Campaigns Inc.'.[83] The rise of these agencies is associated with the idea of 'packaging'. As the Republican party chairman remarked in 1952, 'You sell your candidates and your programs the way a business sells its products.'[84] We have reached the age of Saatchi and Saatchi.

It has been argued with some force that the Russian state after 1917 was 'more permeated with propaganda than any other', in the sense of making a conscious effort 'to create a new humanity suitable for living in a new society'. 'No previous state had similar ambitions, and no leaders had paid comparable attention to the issues of persuasion.'[85] Some of the means employed were relatively traditional. The Smolensk Party Committee, for example, stressed the need for 'splendour, grandeur and pomp' as a way of influencing the young, and advocated the foundation of revolutionary holidays. Other means of persuasion were new, notably the use of posters, wall newspapers, short and simple films (the so-called *agitki*), and special propaganda trains and ships with cinemas, libraries and presses on board.[86]

The original aim in 1789 and 1917 alike was to celebrate the revolution itself. There were attempts to sweep away the statues of rulers as well as the rulers themselves. Most of the statues of Louis XIV were destroyed in 1792. After 1917, the statues of the tsars were removed from the squares of Moscow and Leningrad and replaced by those of popular and revolutionary heroes.[87]

In the longer term, rulers returned to the streets as they returned to the presidential palaces. They simply came to be represented in a more demotic style. Examples of this style can be found earlier on occasion, in the age of Gustav Adolf of Sweden, or indeed, that of Augustus (pp. 192–7). The rise of portraits of royal families, the 'domestication of majesty' as it has been called, is a striking indicator of this change of style.[88]

An example from France is that of the French king Louis-Philippe. After he came to power after the revolution of 1830, Louis-Philippe was presented as a ruler accessible to his subjects and indeed not very different from them. His first official portraits therefore showed him – unlike his predecessor Charles X – without conspicuously royal properties such as the crown and the coronation robes, and with his eyes at the viewer's eye level.[89] Such egalitarianism, whether genuine or artificial, would have been unthinkable in the age of Louis XIV. It was a compromise between the ideals of the traditional monarchy and those of the French Revolution.

In similar fashion, one might say that the image of Lenin in the last years of his life was a compromise between the ideals of the Russian Revolution and the tradition of the tsars. Lenin's style of life was modest, and he avoided artists and photographers.[90] However, there was already a cult of Lenin before his death, marked by poems in his praise, biographies, posters, and the naming of schools, factories, mines and collective farms after him.[91]

Today, the dominant language of politics is the language of liberty, equality and fraternity. Power is supposed to derive from 'the people' and public monuments celebrate 'the unknown soldier' or a generalised heroic worker. Elected leaders need to think of the voters, and even undemocratic rulers often claim to derive their power from the people. Social distance is abolished, or appears to have been abolished (thanks as much to the invasion of TV cameras as to conscious choices). The illusion of intimacy with the people is necessary, the fireside chat, handshaking for hours at a time and so on. Dignity is dangerous, because it implies remoteness. The emphasis is now on dynamism, youth and vitality. Mussolini is far from the only middle-aged ruler to have presented himself in public as a sportsman and even an athlete.[92] Photographs are selected to emphasise dynamic qualities. On occasion, the body language of individuals is modified on the advice of publicity agencies and campaign managers so that the candidate will fit the role of popular leader.

Louis claimed to derive his power from God, not from the people. He did not need to cultivate any voters. His media were not mass media. He was presented – indeed, he had to be presented – as someone special, the Lord's anointed, *le Dieudonné*. The contrast between seventeenth-century leaders and twentieth-century ones is not a contrast between rhetoric and truth. It is a contrast between two styles of rhetoric.

GLOSSARY

ABSOLU [absolute]. This is defined by Furetière in his Dictionary as 'sans condition, sans reserve'. Spanheim, for example, referred to the period before 1661 as one when 'le pouvoir absolu du gouvernement étoit entre les mains d'un premier ministre', in other words when Mazarin was in control. One of Louis XIII's official historians, Dupleix, claimed that 'jamais roi ne fut si absolu en France que nostre Louis'.

ACADÉMIE FRANÇAISE. The most prestigious academy, consisting of forty men of letters, founded in 1635.

ACADÉMIE DES INSCRIPTIONS, see PETITE ACADÉMIE.

ACADÉMIE ROYALE DE PEINTURE ET DE SCULPTURE [Royal Academy of Painting and Sculpture]. Founded in 1648.

ACADÉMIE DES SCIENCES [Academy of Sciences]. Founded in 1666.

APPARTEMENTS. A term used at the time not only to refer to the royal apartments in Versailles, but also the custom of opening them to the public three times a week.

BALLET. The *ballet de cour* of this period was a musical drama, which centred on dancing but did not exclude singing.

CONSEIL D'EN HAUT. The 'Council upstairs', so-called from the place of its meetings, was the council of state, in which the most important ministers met weekly with the king and the most important decisions were taken.

CONSEIL SECRET. The French equivalent of what the British call the 'Privy Council'.

ESTATES [Etats]. Regular assemblies representing the three 'estates' or 'orders' (clergy, nobility and 'third estate') in certain French provinces (known as the *pays d'états*): Artois, Brittany, Languedoc, Normandy (to 1650s), Burgundy, Dauphiné and Provence. The Estates-General, representing the whole kingdom, did not meet between 1614 and 1789.

GRANDE GALERIE. The contemporary French name for the room in Versailles best known today as the *Galerie des Glaces* or Hall of Mirrors.

GRATIFICATION. A royal gift, often a pension.

HISTOIRE DU ROI ['the story of the king']. The name given by contemporaries not only to histories of the king's actions but also to the various series of representations of these actions in paintings, tapestries, engravings and medals.

HISTOIRE MÉTALLIQUE ['metallic' or 'medallic' history]. The history of the reign, told by arranging the medals representing the events of the reign in chronological order. There were two medallic histories of the reign of Louis XIV, one unofficial, the work of the Jesuit Menestrier, published in 1689; and the other the work of the petite académie, published in 1702. For further details, see Appendix 1.

INTENDANT. A representative of the central government in the provinces. The *intendants* increased in importance in the course of the seventeenth century, as centralisation became more effective.

JETON. A kind of medal, distributed by the government on 1 January each year.

LIT DE JUSTICE. Literally 'bed of justice', a formal visit by the king to the Parlement, often in order to enforce the registration of royal edicts.

LIVRE. The *livre tournois* was a unit of account. As in the case of traditional pounds, shillings and pence, the *livre* was worth 20 *sous* and the *sou* 12 *deniers*.

PARLEMENT. Not a parliament in the English sense but a court. There were provincial parlements at Aix, Besançon (from 1676), Bordeaux, Dijon, Douai (from 1686), Grenoble, Pau, Rennes, Rouen and Toulouse. The Parlement of Paris was the supreme court of the kingdom.

PETITE ACADÉMIE [small academy]. Originally a committee of the Académie Française, set up by Colbert in 1663 to supervise the glorification of the king. It became independent in 1696 with the name Académie Royale des Médailles et Inscriptions, changed in 1701 to the Académie des Inscriptions et Médailles and in 1717 to the Académie des Inscriptions et Belles Lettres.

SURINTENDANT DES BÂTIMENTS [superintendent of buildings]. The title of the official in charge of royal buildings, or as English contemporaries put it, the 'King's Works'. Colbert held this position from 1664 to 1683.

APPENDIX 1 THE MEDALS OF LOUIS XIV

It is less easy than it might seem to count the medals of Louis XIV, let alone to date them.

In the first place, the phrase 'medals of Louis XIV' is ambiguous. Medals and *jetons* need to be distinguished. *Jetons* were smaller and produced in larger numbers.[1] Another problem is the fact that not all the medals representing the king were struck by the king. The city of Paris struck a famous medal of Louis 'the Great' in 1671, for example (Figure 14).

To calculate the number of medals struck by the king, one might think one would be on safe ground in having recourse to the official medallic history of the reign, published in 1723, which includes 318 medals. However, this total includes two medals representing the death of Louis XIV, medals that should therefore be described as belonging to the reign of his successor. On the other hand, at least two medals were deliberately excluded from the official medallic history, the medal representing the statue on the Place des Victoires, and the medal by Roussel representing the destruction of Heidelberg.[2] We are left with a total of 318 official medals. A comparison between the 1702 and 1723 editions shows other discrepancies. Each collection contains medals omitted from the other. Adding them together one gets 332 medals, and adding the suppressed medals, 334.[3]

Dating these medals is even more difficult. They are often discussed as if the date on the medal was the date when it was struck rather than the date of the event commemorated. In the case of the later medals this assumption is not too far from the truth, but in the case of medals of events before about 1685, it is extremely misleading. It is therefore necessary to distinguish the date of events from the date of the medals representing them, and also from the date of the grouping of the medals into the *histoire métallique*.

1 *The time of events*. If we analyse the corpus of medals according to the date of the event represented, we find the following distribution.

1630s	2
1640s	29
1650s	26
1660s	70
1670s	67
1680s	49
1690s	53
1700s	25
1710s	11
Total	332

2 *The dating of the medals themselves*. Sixteen medals have been attributed to Jean Warin, who died in 1672.[4] In 1675, after Warin's death, his pupil François Chéron was called to Paris and appointed *graveur ordinaire des médailles du roi*. Chéron had been working in Rome for Popes Clement X and Innocent X. It has been suggested that only thirty-seven medals were struck in Colbert's time, in other words 1661–83, but this figure is implausibly low. A contemporary source claims that ninety-nine medals had been struck by the beginning of 1685.[5] The unofficial medallic history published by Menestrier in 1689 includes 122 medals which represent events between 1638 and 1688. Subtracting this figure from 332 leaves 220 medals struck in the period 1689–1715. Of these, ninety-two deal with the period 1689–1715. If these are subtracted from the 220 we are left with 128 medals struck during the period 1689–1715, but representing earlier events of the reign.

3 The dating of the medallic history of the reign also presents problems. The official project for a medallic history is normally dated to *c.*1685 and associated with Louvois.[6] If we are looking for a well-defined project for a publication in book form, this date may well be correct, but vaguer ideas can be found earlier in the reign, notably in letters of Jean Chapelain (1 August 1665 and 28 September 1672). In 1673, the *Mercure Galant* described Jean Warin as engaged on 'l'Histoire du Roy en médailles'.

The task of realising the official project was confided to the petite académie. The work went slowly – the academy had other tasks. Meanwhile, in 1689, Claude-François Menestrier published his famous (but unofficial) *Histoire du roi par les médailles*. This collection of the medals and devices commemorating events between 1638 and 1688 seems to have been a tribute to the king on his fiftieth birthday. It was perhaps in reaction to this unofficial publication that the petite académie was renamed the Académie des Inscriptions, in 1691, and ordered to concentrate on the medallic history. In 1693, the second edition of Menestrier's book was given a new title, *L'Histoire du règne de Louis XIV*, presumably to allow the academy the use of the classic phrase *l'histoire du roi*. When their work was finally published in 1702, however, it was entitled *Médailles sur les principaux événements du règne de Louis le Grand*. For further details, see Jacquiot (1968), Jones (1979a and b), Ferrier (1982) and Oresko (1989).

1 Jacquiot (1968); cf. M. G., January 1682, pp. 53ff.
2 Jacquiot (1968), pp. 433ff, 617ff.
3 Contrast the figure of 312 in N. R. Johnson (1978), p. 52.
4 The inventory listing them is printed in Jacquiot (1968), document 72.
5 Ibid., p. xxvi; M. G., January 1685, p. 99.
6 Jacquiot (1968), pp. x–xi, xxvff.

APPENDIX 2 ICONOGRAPHY OF LOUIS XIV

There seems to be no way of estimating the total number of portraits of Louis XIV in various media executed during his reign. The fullest survey known to me is restricted to surviving works, thus excluding the famous statues of the 1680s.[1] It is also limited to works 'by artists who saw or could have seen the king'. The compilers list only ninety-nine engravings, although they point out (p. 4n) that 671 engravings of Louis can be found in the Cabinet des Estampes of the Bibliothèque Nationale. Their survey also excludes medals and tapestries. Even with these restrictions the total reached is 433 (including sketches and scenes in some of which the king is not prominent). From these I have extracted 287 datable finished portraits for further analysis.

The distribution of the images by decades deserves some comment. Contrary to the medals, there is normally little discrepancy between the date represented and the date of painting, engraving etc. (apart from nos 7, 165 and 271, which are therefore omitted from the following table).

1630s	5
1640s	30
1650s	14
1660s	48
1670s	40
1680s	62
1690s	44
1700s	36
1710s	5
Total	284

The peak in the 1680s is pronounced, and would be even more so if all the statues erected in that decade had survived.

1 Maumené and d'Harcourt (1932).

APPENDIX 3 CHRONOLOGY OF PUBLISHED LITERATURE AGAINST LOUIS XIV

The following list includes only publications that discuss the king (as opposed to France) in some detail. Nearly all of them are anonymous or pseudonymous, while the place of publication is rarely to be trusted.

1665	*Histoire amoureuse des Gaules*
1667	*Bouclier d'état*
c.1667	*Chimaera gallicana*
1673	*Die französische Türckey*
1673	*Das französische Cabinet*
1674	*Machiavellus gallicus*
1674	*Risées de Pasquin*
1678	*Christianissimus christiandus*
1678	*The French King Conquered*
1680	*The French Politician*
1681	*French Intrigues*
1684	*Mars christianissimus*
1684	*Breviarium Mazarini*
1684	*Conduct of France*
1684	*Triomphe de la Vérité*
1685	*Les Conquêtes amoureuses du Grand Alcandre*
1686	*Le Dragon missionaire*
1687	*Mars Orientalis et Occidentalis*
1688	*La France galante*
1688	*L'Esprit de la France*
1688	*Remarques sur le gouvernement du royaume*
1689	*Intrigues*
1689	*Bombardiren*

1689	*Soupirs de la France esclave*
1689	*Laus Ludovici delusa*
1689	*Montespan im Schlaf*
1690	*Eigenlob stinckt gern*
1690	*Der Französische Attila*
1690	*The Most Christian Turk*
1690	*Concursus*
1690	*Nero Gallicanus*
1690	*The Present French King*
1690	*Beschreibung . . . Ehren Saule*
1690	*Solstitium gallicum*
1691	*Ludwig der französische Greuel*
1692	*The French King's Lamentations*
1692	*Monarchie Universelle*
1692	*L'Ombre de Louvois*
1693	*French Conquest*
1693	*Royal Cuckold*
1694	*On the Taking of Huy*
1694	*Giant Galieno*
1694	*La Politique Nouvelle de la Cour de France*
1694	*Scarron apparu*
1695	*Alcoran de Louis XIV*
1695	*Amours de Mme de Maintenon*
1695	*Tombeau des amours de Louis le Grand*
1695	*On the Taking of Namur*
1696	*Grand Alcandre frustré*
1696	*Nouvelles amours*
1697	*Parallèle*
1697	*Chrestien non français*
1699	*Télémaque*
1700	*La Partage du lion*
1702	*The French Tyrant*
1702	*Französische Ratio Status*
1705	*Catechismus van de Konig van Frankrijk*
1706	*Allerchristliche Fragstücke*
1708	*The French King's Wedding*
1708	*Ludwig des Grossen Testament*
1708	*Proben einer königlichen Baukunst*
c. 1709	*Pillers geordeneerd voor L14*
1709	*Curses*
1709	*The French King's Dream*
1711	*Clear View*
1712	*Friendship*
1714	*Arcana gallica*

NOTES

ABBREVIATIONS

D. N. B. *Dictionary of National Biography*

HARI *Histoire de l'Académie Royale des Inscriptions*

M. G. *Mercure Galant*

I INTRODUCING LOUIS XIV

1 Lavisse (1906); Goubert (1966); Wolf (1968); Labatut (1984); Bluche (1986).
2 Sonnino (1964); Thireau (1973).
3 Vries (1947); N. R. Johnson (1978).
4 Burke (1987, 1990).
5 Maumené and d'Harcourt (1932); Jacquiot (1968); Mai (1975); Jones (1979a); M. Martin (1986); Oresko (1989).
6 Recent studies include Beaussant (1981); Verlet (1985); Himelfarb (1986); Néraudau (1986); Pommier (1986); Walton (1986).
7 Ssymank (1898); Ferrier Caveriviere (1981); Marin (1981).
8 Ranum (1980); Fossier (1985); Tyvaert (1974); Klaits (1976).
9 Kantorowicz (1963); Elias (1969); Haueter (1975); Giesey (1985, 1987); Christout (1967); Isherwood (1973); Apostolidès (1981); Moine (1984).
10 L'Orange (1953); Hautecoeur (1953); Kantorowicz (1963).
11 Dilke (1888); Lavisse (1906).
12 Giesey (1985), p. 59.
13 Zwiedineck-Südenhorst (1888); Gillot (1914b); Gaiffe (1924); Malssen (1936); Jones (1982–3).
14 Hartle (1957); Posner (1959); Grell and Michel (1988).
15 Godelier (1982).
16 Quoted in Adhémar (1983), p. 26.
17 Chapelain (1883, 1964); Clément (1868); Jacquiot (1968).
18 For details, see Appendix 1.
19 Grell and Michel (1988).
20 Apostolidès (1981), p. 126; Picard (1956).
21 Walton (1986).
22 Moine (1984), p. 12; M. Martin (1986).
23 Collas (1912), p. 357.
24 McGinniss (1968); Atkinson (1984).
25 Klaits (1976); cf. Speck (1972);

Schwoerer (1977); Vocelka (1981), esp. ch. 1; Kenez (1985), introduction; J. Thompson (1987).
26 Schieder and Dipper (1984).
27 France (1972).
28 Kenez (1985), p. 4.
29 Veyne (1988).
30 Furetière (1690), s.v. 'Gloire'.
31 Rosenfield (1974).
32 Longnon (1927), pp. 33, 37, etc.
33 Scudéry (1671).
34 Clément (1868) 5, p. 246.
35 Longnon (1927), p. 134.
36 Bossuet (1967), book 10.
37 Montesquieu (1973), p. 58.
38 Charpentier (1676), p. 131; M. G., April 1686, p. 223.
39 Naudé (1639), p. 158.
40 La Bruyère (1960), p. 239.
41 Cf. N. R. Johnson (1978).
42 On political myths, Tamse (1975). Cf. Burke (1939–40); Kershaw (1987).
43 Racine (1951–2), p. 209.
44 Geertz (1980); cf. Schwartzenberg (1977).
45 St-Simon (1983–8) 1, pp. 714, 781, 857, etc.
46 Quiqueran (1715), p. 48, Mongin (1716), p. 3.
47 Lünig (1719–20); Longnon (1927).
48 Kertzer (1988).
49 Goffman (1959).
50 La Porte (1755).
51 Pitkin (1967); H. Hofmann (1974); Podlach (1984).
52 Gaxotte (1930), p. 104.
53 Furetière (1690).
54 Saint-Simon (1983–8) 1, pp. 803ff; Gaxotte (1930), introduction.
55 Longnon (1927), p. 53. On the authorship of the memoirs, Dreyss (1859); Sonnino (1964).
56 Courtin (1671), p. 41.
57 Félibien (1688).
58 Courtin (1671), p. 40.
59 M. G., September 1687, p. 178 (Poitiers).
60 At Agde in 1687: M. G., April 1687, p. 141.
61 Visconti (1988), p. 28.
62 Lacour-Gayet (1898), pp. 306, 357.
63 Longnon (1927), p. 280; cf. Hartung (1949).
64 Bossuet (1967), p. 177; *Soupirs* (1689), p. 18.
65 Bossuet (1967), p. 141; Louis XIV (1806) 3, p. 491.
66 Cf. the title of Biondi (1973).
67 Godelier (1982); Bloch (1987), p. 274.
68 Bloch (1924).
69 Boorstin (1962); on communications research in the United States, W. Schramm (1963).
70 Shils (1975); Eisenstadt (1979).
71 Geertz (1980); p. 13; cf. Tambiah (1985).
72 Burke (1987), ch. 12.
73 Trilling (1972), ch. 1.
74 Lasswell (1936); Hymes (1974).

II PERSUASION

1 Lee (1940).
2 Rpr. Félibien (1688), pp. 83–112; cf. Bosquillon (1688); Benserade (1698) 1, pp. 171–2; Guillet (1854) 1, pp. 229–38.
3 Maumené and d'Harcourt (1932).
4 Grivet (1986).
5 Dotoli (1983).
6 Christout (1967); Silin (1940).
7 Quinault (1739), 4.145f, 269, 341, 5, 200, 257, 411; cf. Gros (1926).
8 Félibien (1674); Apostolidès (1981).
9 Möseneder (1983).
10 Pincemaille (1985); Sabatier (1985, 1988).
11 Perrault (1909), p. 60.
12 Combes (1681); Rainssant (1687).
13 Curtius (1947).
14 Tronçon (1662); cf. Roy (1983); Bryant (1986).
15 Maumené and d'Harcourt (1932), nos 79, 178.
16 Jenkins (1947); Mai (1975); Burke (1987).
17 Chapelain (1936), pp. 335–6: Krüger (1986), pp. 227–46.
18 Fléchier (1670).
19 Jump (1974).
20 Racine (1951–2) 2, p. 986.
21 Benserade (1698) 1, pp. 193–4.

22 La Beaune (1684).
23 Bossuet (1961); Bourdaloue (1707); Fléchier (1696); La Rue (1829). On the sermon, Hurel (1872); Truchet (1960), pp. 19ff; Bayley (1980).
24 Perrault (1688–97), pp. 262ff.
25 Bossuet (1961), pp. 310, 340, etc.
26 Truchet (1960) 2, pp. 216–58.
27 Rapin (1677).
28 Poussin (1964), p. 170; Piles (1699) 1, p. 6; Coypel, in Jouin (1883), p. 280.
29 Chantelou (1889), p. 212.
30 Boileau (1969), p. 45.
31 France (1972); Pocock (1980), pp. 74ff.
32 Rapin (1677), pp. 43ff; Racine (1951–2) 2, p. 209.
33 Spanheim (1900), p. 70; on him, Loewe (1924).
34 Sedlmayr (1954).
35 For a convenient summary of conventional views, M. G., December 1684, 3–9. Cf. Ferrier (1978).
36 Montagu (1968); Rosasco (1989).
37 Bardon (1974): Polleross (1988).
38 Montaiglon (1875–8) 1, p. 224.
39 Whitman (1969).
40 Posner (1959); Grell and Michel (1988).
41 Polleross (1988), no. 555.
42 M. G., 1679, 1681, 1682, etc.; cf. Zobermann (1985); Neveu (1988).
43 Scudéry (1654–61); cf. Scudéry (1669).
44 Du Bos (1709); cf. Klaits (1976).
45 On visual portraits of Louis, Mai (1975); on literary portraits, Marin (1981).
46 Guillet (1854), pp. 229ff; Sabatier (1984).
47 Wittkower (1961).
48 Mai (1975).
49 Hatton (1972), p. 101; Blunt (1953), p. 401.
50 On the Van Dyck, Held (1958).
51 Goffman (1959).
52 J. Espitalier (1697), quoted in Römer (1967), p. 119n.
53 Blondel (1698), p. 608.
54 Molière (1971) 2, pp. 1193–4.
55 Racine (1951–2) 1, p. 990.
56 Menestrier (1689).
57 Perrault (1688–97).
58 Robinet (1665), in Rothschild (1881), p. 37.
59 Vertron (1686).
60 Finnegan (1970), pp. 111–46; Curtius (1947); McGowan (1985), pp. 1ff, 11ff.
61 On Boileau, France (1972); on Pellisson, Marin (1981), p. 50. Cf. Pellisson (1735, 1749).
62 La Fontaine (1948), pp. 626ff, 636ff, 730ff.

III SUNRISE

1 Campanella (1915), pp. 195–207.
2 *Gazette* (1638).
3 Maumené and d'Harcourt (1932), no. 151.
4 On the establishment of the Regency, Wolf (1968), ch. 2.
5 Keohane (1980), pp. 220ff.
6 Furetière (1690).
7 The statue was the work of Gilles Guérin, the ballet by Isaac Benserade.
8 Menot (1987).
9 Hanley (1983), especially pp. 307–21.
10 Haueter (1975); Jackson (1984); Le Goff (1986); Coquault (1875), pp. 279–96, 613–32.
11 Godefroy, quoted in Haueter (1975), p. 197.
12 Viguerie (1985).
13 Dreyss (1860) 1, p. 450; cf. the royal letter of 1654, quoted Le Goff (1986), p. 144.
14 Bloch (1924).
15 Möseneder (1983).
16 Especially important is Tronçon (1662).
17 Ibid., p. 9.
18 Möseneder (1983), p. 42. The quotation is from Guy Patin.
19 Tronçon (1662), pp. 21–2.
20 Barozzi and Berchet (1857) 2, p. 401.
21 Quoted Labatut (1984), p. 43.
22 Laurain-Portemer (1968); Lotz (1969); Marder (1980).

IV THE CONSTRUCTION OF THE SYSTEM

1 Meyer (1981).
2 Châtelain (1905).
3 Chapelain (1883) 2, p. 272f; cf. Collas (1912), ch. 8; Couton (1976).
4 Mesnard (1857).
5 Thuillier (1967); Hahn (1971); Isherwood (1973).
6 Dussieux et al. (1854) 2, p. 16.
7 Grove (1980), s.v. 'Bousset'.
8 Gersprach (1893); Florisoone (1962).
9 Morgan (1929).
10 H. J. Martin (1969), pp. 695ff.
11 Chapelain (1883), p. 313.
12 Ibid., p. 422.
13 Ibid., p. 451.
14 Ibid., p. 608.
15 Chapelain (1964), p. 28.
16 Chapelain (1883), p. 384.
17 Ibid., p. 667.
18 Ibid., p. 509n.
19 Ranum (1980).
20 The remaining five were Denys Godefroy, a scholarly archivist; Jean Puget de la Serre, better known as the author of a guide to letter-writing; Charles Sorel, better known as a writer of fiction, who had bought the office as early as 1635; Samuel Sorbière and Henri de Valois, both appointed in 1660.
21 Thuillier (1983).
22 On the original initiative from below, Hahn (1971), p. 8.
23 Hahn (1971).
24 Chapelain (1883), p. 502.
25 Depping (1855), no. 1, p. 41; Clément (1868), pp. 237, 281, 293, 346.
26 Jouin (1889); Thuillier (1963).
27 Quoted in Gould (1981), p. 91.
28 Lefebvre de Venise, quoted in Chantelou (1889), p. 105.
29 Dilke (1888), p. 141.
30 Weber (1985), p. 165.
31 Perrault (1909), p. 30; Soriano (1968), pp. 266–93.
32 Couton (1976); Maber (1985).
33 Viala (1985), pp. 69ff; Kettering (1986).
34 Perrault (1909), p. 31.
35 Chapelain (1883), pp. 469, 583.
36 Perrault (1909), pp. 38ff. The historical sketches to be found among Chapelain's manuscripts (Collas, 1912, p. 380) are perhaps part of the project.
37 Jacquiot (1968), p. xx.

V SELF-ASSERTION

1 Wolf (1968), p. 180.
2 *Gazette* (1661), p. 271.
3 Ibid., pp. 332, 403.
4 Longnon (1927), pp. 44, 49–50.
5 Félibien (1703), p. 161.
6 M. G., December 1684, pp. 18–25.
7 Jacquiot (1968), pp. 144ff.
8 *Médailles* (1702).
9 Longnon (1927), p. 34.
10 Chapelain (1883), p. 509n.
11 Pepys (1970–83) 2, p. 187 (30 September 1661): cf. Roosen (1980).
12 Gersprach (1893), pp. 62f; Félibien (1703), pp. 103, 166; M. G., September 1680, p. 297.
13 *Médailles* (1723), nos 69, 78, 79; Menestrier (1689), 2.8, 15, 16, 21; Jacquiot (1968), pp. 158ff.
14 Soriano (1968), p. 101.
15 Magalotti (1968), pp. 157–8.
16 Montaiglon (1875–8) 1, pp. 220–4.
17 A. Coypel, in Jouin (1883) p. 257.
18 Menestrier (1689) does not include medals on these themes; *Medailles* (1702), (1723); Jacquiot (1968), pp. 183ff, 188ff.
19 Perrault (1670a); Longnon (1927) pp. 132ff.
20 Gould (1981), p. 7; contrast Perrault (1909), p. 71, who claims that Bernini's name was suggested by Benedetti.
21 Lavin (1987).
22 Clément (1868), no. 19; cf. nos 20–1; and Perrault (1909), pp. 77f.
23 Menestrier (1689), nos 23, 24, 26 (medals omitted from the 1702 and 1723 collections).
24 Jacquiot (1968), pp. 244ff.
25 Louis XIV (1806), p. 496, May 1672.
26 Clément (1868), no. 24: cf. no. 23.

27 Walton (1986), ch. 5.
28 According to Perrault (1909), p. 120, the plan accepted was his brother's.
29 Gould (1981), pp. 19, 39; cf. Chantelou (1889).
30 Chantelou (1889), p. 104.
31 M. G., January 1684, p. 326.
32 Jammes (1965); Schnapper (1988).
33 Hartle (1957); cf. Grell and Michel (1988).

VI THE YEARS OF VICTORY

1 Chapelain (1883), p. 279; cf. Collas (1912), pp. 433ff.
2 Collas (1912), p. 435.
3 Aubéry (1668).
4 Félibien (1688), pp. 197–270.
5 Maumené and d'Harcourt (1932), nos 237–40; Collas (1912), p. 373.
6 Gersprach (1893), pp. 62ff.
7 *Médailles* (1723), nos 97–107.
8 Chapelain (1883), p. 635.
9 Blondel (1698) 4, 12, 3, p. 608; Brice (1698) 1, pp. 345–6.
10 Perrault (1909), p. 101.
11 Clément (1868) 5, p. 288.
12 Félibien (1680), p. 4; Walton (1986), ch. 6.
13 Collas (1912), pp. 397–8.
14 Dalicourt (1668), p. 43.
15 Corneille (1987), pp. 705–7.
16 Corneille (1987), p. 716.
17 Chapelain (1883), pp. 783, 786–7.
18 Racine (1951–2) 2, pp. 207–38. For a more detached account, Wolf (1968), chs 16–18.
19 Racine (1951–2) 2, p. 207.
20 *Gazette* (1672), pp. 560, 562, 564, 572, 615.
21 Ibid., pp. 684, 849–60.
22 Corneille (1987), pp. 1155–65.
23 Boileau (1969), pp. 45–9; Genest (1672).
24 Jouin (1883), pp. 108–12.
25 Guillou (1963); Néraudau (1986); Walton (1986).
26 M. G., September 1680, pp. 294–5.
27 Dussieux et al. (1854), p. 40; Nivelon (n.d.), f. 327a.
28 Félibien (1703), p. 102.
29 Dussieux (1854) 1, p. 448.
30 Ibid., 2, p. 43.
31 *Médailles* (1723), nos 119–27; Jacquiot (1968), pp. 264f.
32 Desmarets (1673, 1674); Furetière (1674).
33 Félibien (1674), pp. 71f.
34 Petzet (1982).
35 Desmarets (1673), p. 7.
36 Corneille (1987), pp. 1309f, 1317f; *Médailles* (1723), no. 156, pp. 159–62.
37 Wolf (1968), pp. 287f, 304f.
38 Desmarets (1674), p. 2.
39 Corneille (1987), p. 1306.
40 M. G., March 1679, passim; September 1679, pp. 2, 5, 9; November 1682, p. 106.
41 Corneille (1987), p. 1325.

VII THE RECONSTRUCTION OF THE SYSTEM

1 Trout (1967–8).
2 M. G., extraordinary issue, July 1683, p. 188.
3 K. O. Johnson (1981).
4 Autin (1981), pp. 52f.
5 Rainssant (1687); Félibien (1703).
6 Walton (1986), p. 95.
7 M. G., December 1684, p. 7.
8 M. G., December 1684, p. 10.
9 Rainssant (1687), pp. 9–84.
10 Racine (1951–2) 1, p. 68. According to Furetière, however, the original inscriptions were by Tallemant.
11 Jansen (1981).
12 Félibien (1680); M. G., September 1680, pp. 295–310.
13 Saint-Simon (1983–8) 5, p. 607.
14 Ibid., p. 604.
15 Elias (1969).
16 Saint-Simon (1983–8) 5, p. 530.
17 Ibid., 2, pp. 553, 877, 951, etc.
18 Courtin (1671).
19 Cf. Hobsbawm and Ranger (1983), especially the introduction.
20 Saint-Simon (1983–8) 5, pp. 596ff. On him, Coirault (1965).
21 Visconti (1988), p. 61. Cf. the famous account of the duc de Vendôme in a similar posture, Saint-Simon (1983–8) 2, p. 695.

22 Courtin (1671).
23 Saint-Maurice (1910) 1, p. 157.
24 M. G., December 1682, p. 48.
25 Autin (1981).
26 Corvisier (1983), pp. 375–404; cf. Duchene (1985).
27 Perrault (1909), pp. 135–6.
28 Guillet, in Dussieux (1854) 1, p. 67.
29 Mélèse (1936); Mirot (1924); Teyssèdre (1957).
30 Corvisier (1983), p. 390.
31 Josephson (1928); Boislisle (1889); Souchal (1983), who uses the term 'campagne', p. 311; Martin (1986).
32 *Récit* (1685); *Gazette* (1685) p. 560; M. G., October 1685, pp. 13ff.
33 M. G., January 1686, p. 2.
34 Lister (1699), p. 25. Cf. Boislisle (1889), pp. 49ff; *Description* (1686); and M. G., April 1686, pp. 216ff, 224ff, 240–309.
35 Brice (1698), pp. 169ff.
36 Boislisle (1889), pp. 58ff; M. G., April 1686, pp. 250–309.
37 *Relation* (1687).
38 M. G., February 1687, pp. 50, 55, 57, 73.
39 M. G., June 1685, p. 69.
40 M. G., October 1685, p. 13; February 1686, part 2, pp. 49ff.
41 Boislisle (1889), pp. 210ff; Wolf (1968), 465, 787; Souchal (1983), p. 311; Mettam (1988).
42 Rance (1886); N. R. Johnson (1978); Mettam (1988).
43 Mallon (1985); Taton (1985).
44 HARI (1740) 2, pp. 10–13.
45 Rousset (1865) 2, pp. 376, 464.
46 Menestrier (1689), p. 53; *Médailles* (1702), p. 195.
47 *Médailles* (1702), p. 202.
48 On the 'punishment' of Genoa, see the verses in M. G., April 1684, p. 323, and August 1684, pp. 52ff.
49 *Gazette* (1685) pp. 192, 271, 295f, 320; M. G., May 1685, pp. 310ff.
50 Menestrier (1689), p. 51.
51 For a bas-relief, by Coysevox, on the base of a statue of the king for Rennes, Dussieux (1854) 2, p. 36. For medals, Menestrier (1689), p. 66; *Médailles* (1702) p. 216; Lanier (1883), pp. 58ff.
52 M. G., January 1682, p. 10; June 1685, p. 20.
53 M. G., December 1684, pp. 88–9.
54 M. G., October 1685, pp. 324ff.
55 M. G., January 1686, p. 18. Cf. February 1686 (a special issue on the Revocation).
56 Menestrier (1689), pp. 36–7; *Médailles* (1702), pp. 209–11.
57 Perrault (1686), pp. 99–106.
58 Stankiewicz (1960), p. 179.
59 Bossuet (1961), p. 340.
60 Quartier (1681); Jouvancy (1686); Le Jay (1687).
61 Quartier (1681); La Rue (1683).

VIII SUNSET

1 M. G., April 1686, pp. 2–4; November 1686, p. 322.
2 Le Roi (1862), pp. 261, 277.
3 Klaits (1976).
4 Magne (1976).
5 Schnapper (1967).
6 La Bruyère (1960), pp. 452, 454.
7 Mallon (1985); Taton (1985).
8 Herault (1692); Boileau (1969), pp. 123–7; Maumené and d'Harcourt (1932), no. 254.
9 Médailles (1702), pp. 228, 230, 238, 241, 243, 249, 250, 254.
10 *Médailles*, pp. 235, 236, 240, 251, 267; on the Heidelberg medal, Jacquiot (1968), pp. 617ff, p. 110.
11 Wolf (1968), p. 546; *Médailles* (1702), pp. 234, 268.
12 Addison (1890), p. 351.
13 *Médailles* (1723), pp. 303, 309.
14 Ibid., pp. 311, 314.
15 Gaxotte (1930), pp. 126 (Vigo), 136 (Ramillies).
16 Maintenon (1887) 2, p. 30.
17 M. G., August 1704, p. 426, and October 1704, p. 8; Surville quoted Isherwood (1973), p. 281.
18 For the king's private reaction to the defeat at Oudenarde and the loss of Lille, Gaxotte (1930), pp. 143f, 147f.
19 *Gazette* (1708), pp. 118, 360.
20 M. G., July 1708, part 2, preface,

and pp. 141, 167–8.
21 *Médailles* (1723), no. 316.
22 Gaxotte (1930); Klaits (1976), pp. 208f. Torcy confessed to the authorship in his memoirs.
23 Félibien (1703), p. 103.
24 M. G., March 1687, part 1, pp. 7–9, 110ff, and part 2, a special issue on the rejoicings.
25 For the king's reaction to the deaths of the duke and duchess, Gaxotte (1930), p. 158.
26 Painting *c.*1655 in the Jesuit college of Poitiers, in Polleross (1988), fig. 104; statue made for the royal entry into Paris, 1660, Möseneder (1983), pp. 103, 107; statue of 1675 in Guimiliau (Finistère), Polleross (1988), no. 555.
27 *Gazette* (1669), p. 859.
28 Zobermann (1985); cf. M. G., 1679, 1681, 1682, 1689, 1693, 1697.
29 Jacquiot (1968), plate K.
30 Neveu (1988).
31 Menestrier (1699).
32 Jacquiot (1968), p. cxii.
33 Louis XIV (1806) 3, p. 492.
34 N. R. Johnson (1978), p. 100.
35 Hurel (1872), p. xxxixn. Contrast the figure of 35 in N. R. Johnson (1978), p. 78.
36 Mongin (1716), p. 3.
37 Quiqueran (1715), pp. 18, 27.
38 Gaxotte (1930), p. 186.
39 Rave (1957); Le Roy Ladurie (1984).

IX The CRISIS OF REPRESENTATIONS

1 Hatton (1972), p. 42.
2 Jacquiot (1968), p. cviii.
3 Boorstin (1962).
4 Hahn (1971).
5 Gillot (1914a); Jauss (1964); Kortum (1966).
6 Blondel (1698), pp. 167ff, 174; Perrault (1687); Hall (1987).
7 Michel (1987), p. 146.
8 A. Niderst, in Godard (1987), p. 162.
9 Gouhier (1958); Foucault (1966).
10 Borkenau (1934); Hazard (1935); Gusdorf (1969).
11 Simson (1936); Sedlmayr (1954); Bryson (1981).
12 Kantorowicz (1957); Archambault (1967).
13 Schochet (1975).
14 Lévy-Bruhl (1921).
15 Thomas (1971).
16 Cf. Burke (1987), ch. 16; and Burke (1990).
17 Vert (1706–13).
18 Bourdieu and Passeron (1970).
19 Locke (1690) 1, 6, p. 65.
20 Montesquieu (1721), lettre 24.
21 France (1982).
22 Le Roi (1862), pp. 234, 247.
23 Sagnac (1945) 1, p. 87; but note the qualifications in Brockliss (1987), p. 446n.
24 Haueter (1975), p. 250n (correcting Bloch, 1924).
25 Cf. Apostolidès (1981) on 'le passage du système de signes antique au moderne'. However, I cannot agree with his dating of the change to 1674. The date is at once too precise and (as I hope my examples have demonstrated) too early.
26 Cf. Klaits (1976), pp. 293–5 on the shift to more 'reasoned presentations'.
27 *Médailles* (1702), pp. 121, 126, 138, 143, 148, 179, 183, 199, 206, 210, 213, 223, 224, 226, 232, 240, 244, 249, 260, 263, 271, 283.
28 King (1949).
29 Lasswell (1936), p. 31.

X THE REVERSE OF THE MEDAL

1 Raunié (1879) 1, pp. 46–9.
2 For details of hostile pamphlets, most of them anonymous, see Appendix 3.
3 There are a number of monographs on dissenting images of Louis, notably Zwiedeneck-Südenhorst (1888); Schmidt (1907); Gillot (1914b); and Kleyser (1935) on the German material; van Malssen (1936) on the Dutch; and Blum (1913) and Rothkrug (1965) on the French. I know of no monograph on the English material, or any study of the whole.
4 Cf. Burke (1978).

5 *An Historical Romance.*
6 *Nero.*
7 *Present French King.*
8 *French Tyrant.*
9 *French Tyrant*; *Nero.*
10 *Nero*; *Politique Nouvelle.*
11 *Bombardiren*, p. 11; *Französische Ratio Status.*
12 *Nero Gallicanus.*
13 *The French Tyrant.*
14 Ibid.
15 *Soupirs.*
16 *The Most Christian Turk.*
17 Swift (1691).
18 *Remarques.*
19 *Grand Alcandre*, in Bussy (1930), p. 178.
20 Ibid., p. 12.
21 *Nouvelles Amours*, pp. 36, 122.
22 Chevalier (1711).
23 Wolf (1968), p. 261.
24 Cf. ibid., pp. 505f; Köpeczi (1983).
25 Menestrier (1691), p. 39.
26 For mock-inscriptions, see *Der französische Attila* and the epitaphs in Raunié (1879), pp. 58ff.
27 Gillot (1914b) p. 273n; *Solstitium Gallicum.*
28 Swift, 'Ode to the King' (1691), in Swift (1983), pp. 43–6.
29 Medal of 1709, in Chevalier (1711), p. 112. Phaeton had been used officially, but as a symbol of personal rule.
30 *La Peste.*
31 'Louis le Petit', Raunié (1879), p. 58; and *Mars*, p. 108. Great only in ambition, *Bombardiren*, p. 5.
32 *Mars*; *Turk*; *Christianissimus*; *Bombardiren.*
33 *Fragestücke*, p. 11.
34 *Soupirs*, p. 19; *Fragestücke*, p. 14; *Proben*, p. 3.
35 *Turk*, p. 67.
36 Prior (1959) 1, pp. 141, 220.
37 *Soupirs*, p. 19.
38 *Turk*, p. 70.
39 *Politique nouvelle.*
40 Gillot (1914b), pp. 269f.
41 Raunié (1879), p. 27; Chevalier (1711), pp. 30–1, making the message clear with the inscription, AUFERT NON DAT.
42 Clément (1866), pp. 76–7.
43 Janmart (1888).
44 Menestrier (1691), p. 38.
45 Kunzle (1973), pp. 109f.
46 Chevalier (1711).
47 On Werner, Glaesemer (1974).
48 On Larmessin, Grivet (1986), p. 244.
49 On Lisola, Pribram (1894), ch. 15, esp. p. 353n, and Longin (1900).
50 On Becher, Hassinger (1951), p. 210.
51 On Jurieu, Dodge (1947) and Stankiewicz (1970).
52 On Courtilz, Woodbridge (1925).
53 Swift (1983); Prior (1959) 1, pp. 130–51; cf. Legg (1921); Addison (1890), p. 351.

XI THE RECEPTION OF LOUIS XIV

1 Holub (1984); Freedberg (1989).
2 M. G., February 1683, p. 23.
3 Hölscher (1978), p. 448.
4 Furetière (1690).
5 Cf. Habermas (1962).
6 Longnon (1928), p. 32.
7 Quoted in Gould (1981), p. 123.
8 Brice (1698) 2, p. 309; Jacquiot (1968), document 9.
9 Sonnino (1973–4).
10 Auerbach (1933).
11 Loret, quoted Möseneder (1983), p. 13.
12 Boislisle (1889).
13 Locke (1953), p. 150.
14 Storer (1935); Roche (1978) 1, pp. 19–20; Lux (1989).
15 An example from 1693 in Gaxotte (1930), p. 83.
16 M. G. (1678).
17 M. G., August 1682, pp. 224–34.
18 M. G., January 1684, pp. 184ff.
19 M. G. (1687).
20 Vincent (1979); Dotoli (1983).
21 Feyel (1982), p. 33.
22 Stopfel (1964), pp. 63–73.
23 Text in Gaxotte (1930); commentary in Klaits (1976), pp. 209, 213f.
24 Cf. Jones (1982–3), pp. 209ff.
25 M. G., January 1682, p. 53.
26 M. G., May 1684, p. 238.

27 On one occasion in 1654, he touched 2,000 or 3,000 people (Haueter, 1975, p. 251n). The ceremony took place several times a year for just over seventy years, 1654–1715. Hence the figure of 350,000 (70 × 5,000) does not seem exaggerated. For advertisements, Blegny (1692) 1, p. 21.
28 Klaits (1976), p. 219.
29 Corvisier (1964) does not deal with this problem.
30 Locke (1953), p. 150.
31 Charpentier (1683), p. 131.
32 Polleross (1988), no. 556.
33 Mazarin (1906), p. 257, letter of 1659.
34 Jansen (1981), pp. 61ff.
35 Menestrier (1701).
36 On the Turkish envoy, perhaps an impostor, Beaussant (1981). On the Siamese embassy, Lanier (1883), on the Persian, Herbette (1907) and Walton (1986), ch. 1.
37 *Gazette* (1669), p. 1165; M. G., December 1686, part 2, p. 325.
38 Tovar de Teresa (1988), pp. 66–7.
39 Gaxotte (1930), pp. 12f.
40 Bouvet (1697).
41 *Gazette* (1682), pp. 724–39.
42 *Gazette* (1683), pp. 551–672.
43 Leith (1965) p. 22.
44 M. G. (1682).
45 Pastor (1940) 32, p. 396n.
46 Brunot (1917), ch. 2.
47 *Regis Ludovici inauguratio*, ascribed to C. de Hennot; Perrault (1670b).
48 La Chapelle's *Lettres d'un suisse* circulated as *Helvetti ad Gallum epistolae*, and his *Testament politique de Leopold I* as the *Ultima Consilia*. Klaits (1976), pp. 113n, 151, 297.
49 Klaits (1976), pp. 150–1.
50 *Relation* (1660).
51 Félibien (1665, 1667).
52 Klaits (1976), pp. 113, 275.
53 Chapelain (1883), p. 513.
54 Benedetti (1682).
55 Klaits (1976), pp. 151, 174, 199, 275.
56 Ibid., pp. 70n, 106f.
57 Rance (1886) 1, pp. 298f, 340n.
58 Johnson (1978), pp. 50–1.
59 Cf. Roy (1983) and Mettam (1988) pp. 54f, an extreme statement of the view that local elites were thinking only of themselves.
60 Pardailhé-Galabrun (1988), p. 386.
61 Grivet (1986); Rave (1957), p. 4.
62 Bercé (1974), p. 609; Saint-Simon (1983–8) 3, pp. 476ff.
63 Lottin (1968), p. 189.
64 Sohier (1706), f. 13a.
65 Dubois (1965), pp. 70, 175.
66 Evelyn (1697), pp. 78, 81.
67 Northleigh (1702), 2, pp. 7, 54.
68 Verney (1904) 2, p. 447.
69 Kovács (1986), p. 75; Polleross (1987), p. 251.
70 Ellenius (1966), ch. 5; Geffroy (1885), pp. lxxii–lxxiii.
71 Pastor (1940), p. 396n.
72 Bottineau (1962), pp. 154ff, 167ff, 191ff, 258ff; Moran (1990), pp. 15, 46, 50, 62.
73 Josephson (1930), pp. 9ff.
74 Hansmann (1986), pp. 33, 44.
75 Moine (1984), pp. 168f, suggests St Petersburg, Potsdam, Stockholm, Het Loo, Caserta, Racconigi and Washington.
76 Chevalier (1692); cf. Speck (1972); and Schwoerer (1977).
77 D.N.B., s.v. 'Ralph Montagu'; Pevsner (1961), p. 105; Boyer (1703–13) 8, p. 371.
78 HARI, pp. 70, 77.
79 Cracraft (1988), pp. 158, 185.
80 Moraw (1962); Ehalt (1980); Mandlmayr and Vocelka (1985); Kovács (1986); Polleross (1986, 1987); Hawlik (1989).
81 Biach-Schiffmann (1931).
82 Polleross (1987), p. 239.
83 An engraving of the sarcophagus reproduced in Hawlik (1989), p. 39.

XII LOUIS IN PERSPECTIVE

1 Bloch (1924), p. 52.
2 Duchhardt (1981).
3 Möseneder (1983), p. 105; Aubéry (1668).
4 M. G., June 1684, p. 118.
5 Hofmann (1985), p. 23n.

6 Brown and Elliott (1980), ch. 2; Elliott (1977); Elliott (1989), chs 7–8.
7 Brown (1988).
8 Brown and Elliott (1980).
9 Orso (1986).
10 Ibid., ch. 2.
11 Brown and Elliott (1980).
12 Elliott (1989), ch. 9; Elliott (1986), pp. 418ff.
13 Harris (1976).
14 Guillet, in Dussieux (1854) 1, p. 26.
15 Saint-Simon (1983–8) 5, p. 239.
16 Longnon (1928), p. 133.
17 La Rue (1987), p. 716.
18 Mongin (1716), p. 10.
19 M. G., December 1682, pp. 48–50.
20 Mesnard (1857), ch. 1.
21 Thuau (1966), pp. 177ff, 215ff; Church (1972).
22 Solomon (1972), especially pp. 111ff.
23 Ranum (1980), pp. 99, 129f; Dupleix (1635).
24 Valdor (1649).
25 Carew (1749), p. 453.
26 Lecoq (1987), pp. 217ff, 264ff.
27 Lecoq (1986); Boucher (1986), especially pp. 196ff.
28 Bluche (1986), pp. 274, 279.
29 Giesey (1987).
30 Southorn (1988), ch. 2.
31 Campbell (1977), pp. 177ff.
32 Forster (1971).
33 Chapelain (1964), pp. xvff.
34 Strong (1984), pp. 142ff.
35 Menestrier (1684).
36 Perrault (1688–97) 1, pp. 61–3.
37 Edelman (1946); Voss (1972).
38 Schramm (1939).
39 Bossuet (1967).
40 Kantorowicz (1963), p. 165.
41 Treitinger (1938).
42 Bossuet (1961), p. 340; Drake (1976); Warmington (1974); Barnes (1981); McCormick (1986).
43 Perrault (1688–97) 1, p. 80.
44 Hanley (1983), pp. 330ff.
45 Saint-Simon (1983–8) 1, pp. 629–30; Choisy, quoted in Gaiffe (1924), p. 10.
46 Blondel (1698) part 4, books 11–12.
47 Petzet (1982), p. 162.
48 Lectures by G. Marsy, J. van Obstal and M. Anguier, 1667–9.
49 M. G., July 1682, pp. 138–9; Perrault (1688–97) 1, pp. 191–2.
50 M. G., September 1686, part 2, p. 362.
51 Boislisle (1889), p. 118n.
52 M. G., June 1687, part 2, p. 48.
53 Cf. ch. 2, n. 41.
54 M. G., September 1682 p. 52.
55 Charlesworth (1937); Syme (1939); Price (1984); Zanker (1987).
56 Syme (1939), p. 480.
57 Gagé (1955), pp. 499ff.
58 Syme (1939), p. 385.
59 Zanker (1987), pp. 264ff: Syme (1939), p. 519.
60 Zanker (1987), ch. 1.
61 Ibid., pp. 151ff.
62 Perrault (1688–97).
63 Blondel (1698), p. 164.
64 Taylor (1931), pp. 18ff, 74ff.
65 Blondel (1698), p. 164.
66 Herbelot (1697), p. 997.
67 Rotrou (1649).
68 L'Orange (1953); Seux (1967).
69 Sahlins (1985), pp. 18, 19n.
70 Bernays (1928).
71 Boorstin (1962), especially ch. 1.
72 Schwartzenberg (1977).
73 M. G., May 1685, p. 339.
74 Burke (1939–40); Biondi (1967); Melograni (1976); Stern (1975); Kenez (1985); Kershaw (1987).
75 La Bruyère (1693), p. 544.
76 Kostof (1978).
77 Kenez (1985), pp. 153, 237.
78 Kertzer (1988); Kantorowicz (1963).
79 Mickelson (1972), p. 46.
80 Vattel (1758), pp. 42ff.
81 Leith (1965); Ozouf (1976); Schieder and Dipper (1984); Chartier (1990).
82 Heale (1982), p. 51.
83 Perry (1968)
84 McGinniss (1968), p. 27.
85 Kenez (1985), p. 4.
86 Ibid., pp. 62, 91, 109.
87 Bowlt (1978).
88 Schama (1988).
89 Marrinan (1988), pp. 3ff.
90 Tumarkin (1983), p. 63.
91 Ibid., pp. 80, 88, 95f, 107, 131.
92 Pozzi (1990).

BIBLIOGRAPHY

This bibliography contains all publications mentioned in the notes, with the exception of the anonymous attacks on Louis, listed in Appendix 3.

Unless otherwise specified, the place of publication is Paris.

Addison, J. (1890) *Dialogues on Medals*, London.

Adhémar, J. (1983) 'Information gravée au 17e siècle: images au cuivre destinées à un public bourgeois et élegant', *Quaderni del '600 francese* 5, 11–13.

Apostolidès, J. (1981) *Le Roi-machine: spectacle et politique au temps de Louis XIV*.

Archambault, P. (1967) 'The analogy of the body in Renaissance political literature', *Bulletin d'Humanisme & Renaissance* 29, 21–53.

Atkinson, J. M. (1984) *Our Master's Voices: the Language and Body Language of Politics*, London.

Aubéry, A. (1668) *Des justes prétentions du roy sur l'empire*.

Auerbach, E. (1933) 'La cour et la ville', reprinted in his *Vier Untersuchungen zur Geschichte der französischen Bildung*, Bern, 1951; English trans., *Scenes from the Drama of European Literature*, New York, 1959, 133–82.

Autin, J. (1981) *Louis XIV architecte*.

Bardon, F. (1974) *Le Portrait mythologique à la cour de France sous Henri IV et Louis XIII*.

Barnes, T. D. (1981) *Constantine and Eusebius*, Cambridge, MA.

Barozzi, N. and G. Berchet (eds) (1857) *Relazioni degli stati europei dagli ambasciatori veneti*, Venice.

Bayley, P. (1980) *French Pulpit Oratory 1598–1650*, Cambridge.

Beaussant, P. (1981) *Versailles, opéra*.

Benedetti, E. (1682) *Le glorie della virtù nella persona di Luigi il Magno*, Lyons.

Benserade, I. de (1698) *Oeuvres*, 2 vols.

Bercé, Y.-M. (1974) *Histoire des Croquants*, 2 vols. Geneva.

Berger, R. W. (1985) *In the Garden of the Sun King: Studies on the Park of Versailles under Louis XIV*, Washington.

Bernays, E. L. (1928) *Propaganda*, New York.

Bertelli, S. (1990) *Il corpo del Re*, Florence.

Biach-Schiffmann, F. (1931) *Giovanni und Ludovico Burnacini: Theater und Feste am Wiener Hofe*, Vienna and Berlin.

Biondi, D. (1973) *La fabbrica del Duce*, Florence.

[Blegny, N. de] (1692) *Le Livre commode*, rpr. 1878.

Bloch, M. (1924) *The Royal Touch*; English trans. London, 1973.

Bloch, M. (1987) 'The ritual of the royal bath in Madagascar', in Cannadine and Price, 271–97.

Blondel, F. (1698) *Cours d'architecture*, second edn.

Bluche, F. (1986) *Louis XIV*; English trans., London, 1990.

Blum, A. (1913) *Louis XIV et l'image satirique pendant les dernières années du 17e siècle*, Nogent-le-Rotrou.

Blunt, A. (1953) *Art and Architecture in France*, fourth edn, Harmondsworth, 1980.

Boileau, N. (1969) *Oeuvres*, ed. S. Menant, 2 vols.

Boislisle, A. de (1889) 'Notices historiques sur la Place des Victoires et sur la Place Vendôme', *Mémoires de la société de l'histoire de Paris et de l'Ile-de-France*, 15, 1–272.

Boorstin, D. (1962) *The Image*, rpr. Harmondsworth, 1963.

Borkenau, F. (1934) *Der Übergang vom feudalen zum bürgerlichen Weltbild.*

Bosquillon (1688) *Portrait de Louis le Grand.*

Bossuet, J.-B. (1961) *Oraisons funèbres*, ed. J. Truchet.

Bossuet, J.-B. (1967) *Politique tirée des propres paroles de l'écriture sainte* (1709), ed. J. Le Brun, Geneva.

Bottineau, Y. (1962) *L'Art de cour dans l'Espagne de Philippe V, 1700–46*, Bordeaux.

Boucher, J. (1986) *La Cour de Henri III*, La Guerche-de-Bretagne.

Bouhours, D. (1687) *La Manière de bien penser dans les ouvrages de l'esprit.*

Bourdaloue, L. (1707) *Sermons pour le caresme*, 3 vols.

Bourdieu, P. and J.-C. Passeron (1970) *Reproduction in Education, Society and Culture*, English trans., Beverly Hills, CA, 1977.

Bouvet, J. (1699) *L'histoire de l'empereur de la Chine*, The Hague.

Bowlt, J. E. (1978) 'Russian sculpture and Lenin's plan of monumental propaganda', in *Art and Architecture in the Service of Politics*, ed. H. A. Millon and L. Nochlin, Cambridge, MA, 182–93.

Boyer, A. (1703–13) *The History of the Reign of Queen Anne Digested into Annals*, London.

Brice, G. (1698) *Description nouvelle de la ville de Paris*, 2 vols.

Brockliss, L. W. B. (1987) *French Higher Education in the Seventeenth and Eighteenth Centuries*, Oxford.

Brown, J. (1988) 'Enemies of flattery: Velázquez' portraits of Philip IV', in *Art and History*, ed. R. I. Rotberg and T. K. Rabb, Cambridge, 137–54.

Brown, J. and J. H. Elliott (1980) *A Palace for a King*, New Haven, CT and London.

Brunot, F. (1917) *Histoire de la langue française* 5 (rpr. 1966).

Bryant, L. M. (1986) *The King and the City in the Parisian Royal Entry Ceremony*, Geneva.

Bryson, N. (1981) *Word and Image*, Cambridge.

Burke, K. (1939–40) 'The rhetoric of Hitler's battle', reprinted in *Language and Politics*, ed. M. Shapiro, Oxford, 1984, ch. 5.

Burke, P. (1987) *Historical Anthropology of Early Modern Italy*, Cambridge.

Burke, P. (1990) 'Historians, anthropologists and symbols', in *Culture Through Time*, ed. E. Ohnuki Tierney, Stanford, CA, pp. 268–323.

Burke, P. (*c.* 1993) 'The demise of royal mythologies', forthcoming in A. Ellenius (ed.) *Iconography and Ideology.*

Bussy Rabutin, R. (1930) *Histoire amoureuse des Gaules (1665), suivie de La France Galante*, etc., ed. G. Mongrédien, 2 vols.

Campanella, T. (1915) *Poésie*, ed. G. Gentile, Bari.

Campbell, M. (1977) *Pietro da Cortona at the Pitti Palace*, Princeton, NJ.

Cannadine, D. and S. Price, (eds) (1987) *Rituals and Royalty*, Cambridge.

Carew, G. (1749) 'A relation of the state of France', in *An Historical View*, ed. T. Birch, London, 415–528.

Cérémonial français des années 1679, 1680 et 1681, ms B.N., fonds français, 7831.

Chantelou, P. de (1889) *Journal de Voyage du Cavalier Bernin en France*, ed. L. Lalanne, rpr. 1981.

Chapelain, J. (1883) *Lettres*, 2, ed. P. Tamizey de Larroque.

Chapelain, J. (1936) *Opuscules critiques*, ed. A. Hunter.

Chapelain, J. (1964) *Lettere inedite*, ed. P. Ciureanu, Genoa.

Charlesworth, M. P. (1937) 'The virtues of a Roman emperor', *Proceedings of the British Academy* 23, 105–27.

Charpentier, F. (1676) *Defense de la langue françoise pour l'inscription de l'Arc de Triomphe*.

Charpentier, F. (1724) *Carpentariana*.

Chartier, R. (1990) *Les Origines culturelles de la révolution française*.

Châtelain, U. (1905) *Fouquet*.

Chevalier, N. (1692) *Histoire de Guillaume III*, Amsterdam.

Chevalier, N. (1711) *Relation des campagnes de l'année 1708 et 1709*, Utrecht.

Christout, M. F. (1967) *Le Ballet de cour de Louis XIV*, 1643–72.

Church, W. F. (1972) *Richelieu and Reason of State*, Princeton, NJ.

Clément, P. (1866) *La Police sous Louis XIV*.

Clément, P. (ed.) (1868) *Lettres, instructions et mémoires de Colbert*, 5, part 2.

Coirault, Y. (1965) *L'Optique de Saint-Simon*.

Collas, G. (1912) *Jean Chapelain*.

Combes, le sieur de (1681) *Explication historique de ce qu'il y a de plus remarquable dans la maison royale de Versailles*.

Coquault, O. (1875) *Mémoires 1649–68*, ed. C. Loriquet, Reims.

Corneille, P. (1987) *Oeuvres*, 3, ed. G. Couton.

Corvisier, A. (1964) *L'Armée française de la fin du 17e siècle au ministère de Choiseul: le soldat*, 2 vols.

Corvisier, A. (1983) *Louvois*.

Courtin, A. de (1671) *Nouveau traité de la civilité*, Basle.

Couton, G. (1976) 'Effort publicitaire et organisation de la recherche', *Actes du sixième colloque de Marseille*, ed. R. Duchene, Marseilles.

Cracraft, J. (1988) *The Petrine Revolution in Russian Architecture*, Chicago.

Curtius, E. R. (1947) *European Literature and the Latin Middle Ages*, English trans., New York, 1954.

[Dalicourt, P.] (1668) *La Campagne royale*.

Demoris, R. (1978) 'Le corps royal et l'imaginaire au 17e siècle: *Le portrait du roy* par Félibien', *Revue des sciences humaines* 172, 9–30.

Depping, G. P. (ed.) (1855) *Correspondance administrative sous le règne de Louis XIV*, 4, part 4.

Description (1686) du monument érigé à la gloire du roy par M. le Maréchal Duc de la Feuillade.

Desmarets, J. (1673) *Au Roy, sur la prise de Mastrich*.

Desmarets, J. (1674) *Au Roy, sur sa seconde conquête de Franche-Comté*.

Dilke, E. (1888) *Art in the Modern State*, London.

Dipper, C. and W. Schieder (1984) 'Propaganda', in *Geschichtliche Grundbegriffe* 5, Stuttgart, 69–112.

Dodge, G. H. (1947) *The Political Theory of the Huguenots of the Dispersion*, New York.

Dotoli, G. (1983) 'Il *Mercure Galant* di Donneau de Visé', *Quaderni del '600 francese* 5, 219–82.

Drake, H. A. (1976) *In Praise of Constantine*, Berkeley, CA.

Dreyss, C. (1859) *Etude sur la composition des mémoires de Louis XIV*, rpr. Geneva, 1871.

Dreyss, C. (ed.) (1860) *Mémoires de Louis XIV*, 2 vols.

Dubois, A. (1965), *Journal d'un curé de campagne*, ed. H. Platelle.

Du Bos, J.-B. (1709) *Histoire de la Ligue de Cambrai.*

Duchene, R. (ed.) (1985) *De la mort de Colbert à la Revocation de l'Edit de Nantes: un monde nouveau?* Marseilles.

Duchhardt, H. (1981) '*Imperium* und *Regna*', *Historische Zeitschrift* 232, 555–83.

Dupleix, S. (1635) *Histoire de Louis le Juste.*

Dussieux, L. et al. (eds) (1854) *Mémoires inédits de l'Académie Royale de Peinture et de Sculpture.*

Edelman, N. (1946) *Attitudes of Seventeenth-Century French toward the Middle Ages*, New York.

Ehalt, H. C. (1980) *Ausdrucksformen absolutistischer Herrschaft: Der Wiener Hof in 17. und 18. Jht*, Munich.

Eisenstadt, S. N. (1979) 'Communication patterns in centralized empires', in *Propaganda and Communication in World History*, ed. H. Lasswell, D. Lerner and H. Speier, Honolulu, 1, 536–51.

Elias, N. (1969) *The Court Society*, English trans., Oxford, 1983.

Ellenius, A. (1966) *Karolinska bildidéer*, Stockholm.

Elliott, J. H. (1977) 'Philip IV of Spain: prisoner of ceremony', in *The Courts of Europe*, ed. A. G. Dickens, London, 169–90.

Elliott, J. H. (1986) *The Count-Duke of Olivares*, New Haven, CT and London.

Elliott, J. H. (1989) *Spain and its World 1500–1700*, New Haven, CT and London.

Evelyn, J. (1697) *Numismata*, London.

Félibien, A. (1674) *Les Divertissements de Versailles.*

Félibien, A. (1680) 'Le Grand Escalier de Versailles', Appendix to Jansen (1981).

Félibien, A. (1688) *Recueil des descriptions de peintures et d'autres ouvrages faits pour le roi.*

Félibien, J.-F. (1703) *Description sommaire de Versailles.*

Ferrier-Caveriviere, N. (1978) 'Louis XIV et ses symboles dans l'Histoire Metallique', *17e siècle*, 34, 19–30.

Ferrier-Caveriviere, N. (1981) *L'Image de Louis XIV dans la littérature française.*

Feuchtmüller, R. and E. Kovács (eds) (1986) *Welt des Barock*, 2 vols, Vienna.

Feyel, G. (1982) *La Gazette en province à travers ses réimpressions 1631–1752*, Amsterdam and Maarssen.

Finnegan, R. (1970) *Oral Literature in Africa*, Oxford.

Fléchier, E. (1670) *Circus regius.*

Fléchier, E. (1696) *Panegyriques*, 2 vols.

Florisoone, M. (1962) *Charles Le Brun premier directeur de la manufacture royale des Gobelins.*

Forster, K. (1971) 'Metaphors of rule: political ideology and history in the portraits of Cosimo I de'Medici', *Mitteilungen des Kunsthistorischen Institutes in Florenz* 15, 65–104.

Fossier, F. (1985) 'A propos du titre d'historiographe sous l'ancien régime', *Revue d'histoire moderne et contemporaine* 32, 361–417.

Foucault, M. (1966) *The Order of Things*, English trans., London, 1970.

France, P. (1972) *Rhetoric and Truth in France*, Oxford.

France, P. (1982) 'Equilibrium and excess', in *The Equilibrium of Wit*, ed. P. Bayley and D. G. Coleman, Lexington, MA, 249–61.

Freedberg, D. (1989) *The Power of Images*, Chicago.

Furetière, A. (1674) *Ode sur la seconde conquête de Franche-Comté.*

Furetière, A. (1690) *Dictionnaire universel*, 3 vols, The Hague and Rotterdam.

Gagé, J. (1955) *Apollon romain*.

Gaiffe, F. (1924) *L'Envers du grand siècle*.

Gaxotte, P. (ed.) (1930) *Lettres de Louis XIV*.

Gazette [*Recueil des Gazettes, Recueil des Nouvelles*], 1660–1715.

Geertz, C. (1980) *Negara: the Theater State in Nineteenth-Century Bali*, Princeton, NJ.

Geffroy, A. (ed.) (1885) *Recueil des instructions données aux ambassadeurs et ministres de France*.

Genest, C. C. (1672) *Ode pour le roi sur ses conquestes*.

Gersprach, E. (1893) *Repertoire des tapisseries des Gobelins*.

Giesey, R. (1985) 'Models of rulership in French royal ceremonial', in *Rites of Power*, ed. S. Wilentz, Philadelphia, 41–64.

Giesey, R. (1987) 'The King imagined', in *The Political Culture of the Old Regime*, ed. K. M. Baker, Oxford, 41–59.

Gillot, H. (1914a) *La Querelle des anciens et des modernes*, Nancy.

Gillot, H. (1914b) *Le Règne de Louis XIV et l'opinion publique en Allemagne*, Nancy.

Glaesemer, J. (1974) *J. Werner*, Zürich and Munich.

Godard, L. (ed.) (1987) *D'un siècle à l'autre: anciens et modernes*, Marseilles.

Godelier, M. (1982) *The Making of Great Men*, English trans., Cambridge, 1986.

Goffman, E. (1959) *The Presentation of Self in Everyday Life*, New York.

Goubert, P. (1966) *Louis XIV and Twenty Million Frenchmen*, English trans., London, 1970.

Gouhier, H. (1958), 'Le refus du symbolisme dans l'humanisme cartésien', in E. Castelli (ed.) *Umanesimo e simbolismo*, Padua, 65–74.

Gould, C. (1981) *Bernini in France*, London.

Grell, C. and C. Michel (1988) *L'École des Princes ou Alexandre disgracié*.

Grivet, M. (1986) *Le Commerce de l'estampe à Paris au 17e siècle*.

Gros, E. (1926) *Quinault*, Paris and Aix-en-Provence.

Grove, G. (1980) *Dictionary of Music and Musicians*, ed. S. Sadie, 20 vols, London.

Guillet de Saint-Georges, G. (1854) 'Discours sur le portrait du roy', in Dussieux et al. 1, 229–38.

Guillou, E. (1963) *Versailles, le Palais du Soleil*.

Gusdorf, G. (1969) *La Révolution galiléenne*, 2 vols.

Habermas, J. (1962) *The Structural Transformation of the Public Sphere*, English trans., Cambridge, 1989.

Hahn, R. (1971) *The Anatomy of a Scientific Institution: the Paris Academy of Sciences, 1666–1803*, Berkeley, CA.

Hall, G. (1987) 'Le siècle de Louis le Grand: l'évolution d'une idée', in Godard, 43–52.

Hanley, S. (1983) *The* Lit de Justice *of the Kings of France*, Princeton, NJ.

Hansmann, W. (1986) *Balthasar Neumann*, Cologne.

Harris, E. (1976) 'Velázquez' portait of Prince Baltasar Carlos in the Riding School', *Burlington Magazine* 118, 266–75.

Hartle, R. (1957) 'Lebrun's *Histoire d'Alexandre* and Racine's *Alexandre le Grand*', *Romanic Review* 48, 90–103.

Hartung, F. (1949) *'L'état c'est moi'*, *Historische Zeitschrift* 169, 1–30.

Hassinger, E. (1951) *J. J. Becher*, Vienna.

Hatton, R. (1972) *Louis XIV and his World*, London.

Haueter, A. (1975) *Die Krönungen der französischen Könige im Zeitalter des Absolutismus und in der Restauration*, Zurich.

Hautecoeur, L. (1953) *Louis XIV roi soleil.*

Hawlik-van de Water, M. (1989) *Der Schöne Tod: Zeremonialstrukturen des Wiener Hofes bei Tod und Begrabung zwischen 1640 und 1740*, Vienna.

Hazard, P. (1935) *La Crise de la conscience europeénne*; English trans., *The European Mind 1680–1720*, New Haven, CT, 1952.

Heale, M. J. (1982) *The Presidential Quest*, London.

Held, J. S. (1958) 'Le roi à la chasse', *Art Bulletin* 40, 139–49.

l'Herault de Lionniere, T. (1692) *Panegyrique historique de Louis le Grand pour l'Année 1689.*

d'Herbelot, B. (1697) *Bibliothèque orientale.*

Herbette, M. (1907) *Une Ambassade persane sous Louis XIV.*

Himelfarb, H. (1986) 'Versailles, fonctions et légendes', in Nora, 1, 235–92.

Histoire de l'Académie Royale des Inscriptions (1740) 3 vols.

Hobsbawm, E. J. and T. Ranger (eds) (1983) *The Invention of Tradition*, Cambridge.

Hölscher, L. (1978) 'Öffentlichkeit', in *Geschichtliche Grundbegriffe*, ed. O. Brunner, W. Conze and R. Koselleck, 4, Stuttgart, 413–67.

Hofmann, C. (1985) *Das Spanische Hofzeremoniell von 1500–1700*, Frankfurt.

Hofmann, H. (1974) *Repräsentation: Studien zur Wort- und Begriffsgeschichte von der Antike bis ins 19. Jht*, Berlin.

Holub, R. C. (1984) *Reception Theory*, London.

Hurel, A. J. (1872), *Les Orateurs sacrés a la cour de Louis XIV*, rpr. Geneva, 1971.

Hymes, D. (1974) *Foundations in Sociolinguistics*, Philadelphia.

Isherwood, R. (1973) *Music in the Service of the King*, Ithaca, NY and London.

Jackson, R. (1984) *Vive le roi!* Chapel Hill, NC.

Jacquiot, J. (1968) *Médailles et jetons*, 4 vols.

Jammes, A. (1965) 'Louis XIV, sa bibliothèque et le cabinet du roi', *The Library* 20, 1–12.

Janmart, J. (1888) *Histoire de Pierre du Marteau.*

Jansen, B. (1981) *Der Grand Escalier de Versailles*, Bochum, Diss.

Jauss, H.-R. (1964) 'Ästhetischen Normen und geschichtliche Reflexion in der *Querelle des anciens et des modernes*', in Perrault (1688–97), 8–64.

Jenkins, M. (1947) *The State Portrait* (no place of publication).

Johnson, K. O. (1981) *'Il n'y a plus de Pyrénées*: the iconography of the first Versailles of Louis XIV', *Gazette des Beaux-Arts* 98, 29–40.

Johnson, N. R. (1978) *Louis XIV and the Enlightenment.*

Jones, M. (1979a) *Medals of the Sun King*, London.

Jones, M. (1979b) *The Art of the Medal*, London.

Jones, M. (1982–3) 'The medal as an instrument of propaganda in late seventeenth- and early eighteenth-century Europe', *Numismatic Chronicle* 142, 117–25, and 143, 202–13.

Josephson, R. (1928) 'Le monument de Triomphe pour le Louvre', *Revue de l'art ancien et moderne* 32, 21–34.

Josephson, R. (1930) *Nicodème Tessin à la cour de Louis XIV.*

Jouin, H. (ed.) (1883) *Conférences de l'Académie Royale de Peinture.*

Jouin, H. (1889) *Charles Le Brun.*

Jouvancy, J. de (1686) *Clovis.*

Jump, J. D. (1974) *The Ode*, London.

Kantorowicz, E. H. (1957) *The King's Two Bodies*, Princeton, NJ.

Kantorowicz, E. H. (1963) 'Oriens Augusti – Lever du Roi', *Dumbarton Oaks Papers* 17, 117–77.

Kenez, P. (1985) *The Birth of the Propaganda State: 'Mass Mobilisation' in Russia, 1917–29*, Cambridge.

Keohane, N. O. (1980) *Philosophy and the State in France*, Princeton, NJ.

Kershaw, I. (1987) *The 'Hitler Myth': Image and Reality in the Third Reich*, Oxford.

Kertzer, D. (1988) *Ritual, Politics and Power*, New Haven, CT and London.

Kettering, S. (1986) *Patrons, Brokers and Clients in Seventeenth-Century France*, New York.

King, J. E. (1949) *Science and Rationalism in the Government of Louis XIV*, Baltimore, MD.

Klaits, J. (1976) *Printed Propaganda under Louis XIV*, Princeton, NJ.

Kleyser, F. (1935) *Der Flugschriftenkampf gegen Ludwig XIV zur Zeit des pfälzischen Krieges*, Berlin.

Köpeczi, B. (1983) *Staatsräson und christliche Solidarität: Die ungarische Aufstände und Europa in der zweiten Hälfte des 17. Jahrhunderts*, Budapest.

Kortum, H. (1966) *Charles Perrault und Nicolas Boileau*, Berlin.

Kostof, S. (1978) 'The Emperor and the Duce', in *Art and Architecture in the Service of Politics*, ed. H. A. Millon and L. Nochlin, Cambridge, MA, 270–325.

Kovács, E. (1986) 'Die Apotheose des Hauses Österreich', in Feuchtmüller and Kovács, 53–85.

Krüger, R. (1986) *Zwischen Wunder und Wahrscheinlichkeit: Die Krise des französischen Versepos im 17. Jahrhundert*, Marburg.

Kunzle, D. (1973) *The Early Comic Strip*, Berkeley, CA.

Labatut, J. P. (1984) *Louis XIV roi de gloire*.

La Beaune, J. de (1684) *Ludovico Magno Panegyricus*.

La Bruyère, J. (1960) *Les Caractères* (1688), rpr. ed. G. Mongrédien.

La Bruyère, J. (1693) 'Discours de réception à l'Académie Française', ibid., 429–56.

Lacour-Gayet, G. (1898) *L'Éducation politique de Louis XIV*.

La Fontaine, J.(1948) *Oeuvres diverses*, ed. P. Clarac.

Lanier, L. (1883) *Etude historique sur les relations de la France et du royaume de Siam de 1662 à 1703*, Versailles.

La Porte, P. de (1755) *Mémoires*, second edn, Geneva, 1756.

La Rue, C. de (1683) *Ludovicus Pius*.

La Rue, C. de (1987) 'Regi epinicion', trans. P. Corneille as 'Poème sur les victoires du roi en 1667', in Corneille 3, 709–18.

La Rue, C. de (1829) *Sermons*, 2 vols.

Lasswell, H. (1936) *Politics: Who gets what, when, how*, second edn, New York, 1958.

Laurain-Portemer, M. (1968) 'Mazarin, Benedetti et l'escalier de la Trinité des Monts', *Gazette des Beaux-Arts* 110, 273–9.

Lavin, I. (1987) 'Le Bernin et son image du Roi-Soleil' in *Il se rendit en Italie: études offertes à André Chastel*, Rome, 441–65.

Lavisse, E. (1906) *Louis XIV*.

Lecoq, A.-M. (1986) 'La symbolique de l'état', in Nora, 145–92.

Lecoq, A.-M. (1987) *François I imaginaire*.

Lee, R. W. (1940) *Ut Pictura Poesis: the Humanistic Theory of Painting*, rpr. New York, 1967.

Legg, L. G. Wickham (1921) *Matthew Prior*, Cambridge.

Le Goff, J. (1986) 'Reims, ville du Sacre', in *Les Lieux de mémoire*, ed. P. Nora, 2, *La nation*, 1, 89–184.

Leith, J. A. (1965) *The Idea of Art as Propaganda in France 1750–99*, Toronto.

Le Jay, G. (1687) *Le Triomphe de la religion sous Louis le Grand*.

Le Roi, J. A. (ed.) (1862) *Journal de la santé du roi Louis XIV*.

Le Roy Ladurie, E. (1984) 'Réflections sur la Régence', *French Studies* 38, 286–305.

Lévy-Bruhl, L. (1921) *La Mentalité primitive.*

Lister, M. (1699) *A Journey to Paris in the Year 1698*, London.

Locke, J. (1690) *Two Treatises of Government*, ed. P. Laslett, Cambridge, 1960.

Locke, J. (1953) *Journal*, ed. J. Lough, Cambridge.

Loewe, V. (1924) *Ein Diplomat und Gelehrter, Ezechiel Spanheim*, Berlin.

Longin, E. (1900) *François de Lisola*, Dole.

Longnon, J. (ed.) (1927) *Louis XIV, Mémoires*, rpr. 1983.

L'Orange, H. P. (1953) *Studies on the Iconography of Cosmic Kingship in the Ancient World*, Oslo.

Lottin, A. (1968) *Vie et mentalité d'un Lillois sous Louis XIV*, Lille, second edn, Paris.

Lotz, W. (1969) 'Die Spanische Treppe', *Römische Jahrbuch*, rpr. in *Politische Architektur*, ed. M. Warnke, Cologne, 1984, 175–223.

Louis XIV (1806) *Oeuvres*, 6 vols.

Louis XIV, *Lettres*, see Gaxotte (1930).

Louis XIV, *Mémoires*, see Dreyss (1860); Longnon (1927).

Lünig, J. C. (1719–20) *Theatrum Ceremoniale Historico-Politicum*, 2 vols, Leipzig.

Lux, D. S. (1989) *Patronage and Royal Science in Seventeenth-century France*, Ithaca, NY.

Maber, R. (1985) 'Colbert and the Scholars', *17th-Century French Studies* 7, 106–14.

McCormick, M. (1986) *Eternal Victory: Triumphal Rulership in Late Antiquity, Byzantium and the Early Medieval West*, Cambridge.

McGinniss, J. (1968) *The Selling of the President*, New York.

McGowan, M. (1985) *Ideal Forms in the Age of Ronsard*, Berkeley, CA.

Magalotti, L. (1968) *Relazioni di Viaggio*, ed. W. Moretti, Bari.

Magne, B. (1976) *Crise de la littérature française.*

Magne, E. (1909) *Le plaisant abbé de Boisrobert.*

Mai, W. W. E. (1975) *Le Portrait du roi: Staatsporträt und Kunsttheorie in der Epoche Ludwigs XIV*, Bonn.

Maintenon, F. de (1887) *Mme de Maintenon d'après sa correspondance authentique*, ed. A. Geffroy, 2 vols.

Mallon, A. (1985) 'L'Académie des Sciences à Paris (1683–5): une crise de direction?', in Duchene, 17–34.

Malssen, P. J. W. van (1936) *Louis XIV d'après les pamphlets répandus en Hollande*, Amsterdam.

Mandlmayr, M. C. and K. Vocelka (1985) 'Christliche Triumphfreude'. *Südostforschungen* 44, 99–137.

Marder, T. A. (1980) 'Bernini and Benedetti at Trinità dei Monti', *Art Bulletin* 62, 286–9.

Marin, L. (1981) *Portrait of the King*, English trans., London, 1988.

Marrinan, M. (1988) *Painting Politics for Louis-Philippe*, New Haven, CT and London.

Martin, H. J. (1969) *Livre, pouvoir et société à Paris au 17e siècle*, 2 vols.

Martin, M. (1986) *Les Monuments équestres de Louis XIV.*

Massillon, J.-B. (1865) *Oeuvres*, ed. E. A. Blampignon, 2 vols, Bar-le-Duc.

Maumené, C. and L. d'Harcourt (1932) *Iconographie des rois de France*, vol. 2.

Mazarin, G. (1906) *Lettres*, vol. 9, ed. G. D'Avenel.

Médailles (1702) *sur les principaux événements du règne de Louis le Grand* (2 editions, folio and quarto).

Médailles (1723) *sur les principaux événements du règne entier de Louis le Grand.*

Mélèse, P. (1936) *Donneau de Visé.*

Melograni, P. (1976) 'The Cult of the Duce in Mussolini's Italy', *Journal of Contemporary History* 11, 221–37.

Mémoires inédites, see Dussieux et al. (1854).

Menestrier, C.-F. (1681) *Des Représentations en musique anciennes et modernes.*

Menestrier, C.-F. (1684) *L'Art des emblèmes*, rpr. Mittenwald (1981).

Menestrier, C.-F. (1689) *Histoire du roy Louis le Grand par les medailles.*

'Menestrier, C.-F.' (1691) *Histoire du roy Louis le Grand par les medailles* (the counterfeited edition).

Menestrier, C.-F. (1701) *Décorations faites dans la ville de Grenoble*, Grenoble.

Menot, A. (1987) 'Décors pour le Louvre de Louis XIV; le mythologie politique à la fin de la Fronde', in *La Monarchie absolutiste et l'histoire en France*, ed. F. Laplanche and C. Grell, 113–24.

Mercure Galant, 1672–1715.

Mesnard, P. (1857) *Histoire de l'Académie Française.*

Mettam, R. (1988) 'Power, status and precedence: Rivalries among the provincial elites of Louis XIV's France', *Transactions of the Royal Historical Society* 38, 43–62.

Meyer, J. (1981) *Colbert.*

Michel, C. (1987) 'Les enjeux historiographiques de la querelle des anciens et des modernes', in *La Monarchie absolutiste et l'histoire en France*, ed. F. Laplanche and C. Grell, 139–54.

Mickelson, S. (1972) *The Electric Mirror: Politics in an Age of Television*, New York.

Mirot, L. (1924) *Roger de Piles.*

Moine, M.-C. (1984) *Les Fêtes à la cour du roi soleil.*

Molière, J.-B. (1971) *Oeuvres complètes*, ed. G. Couton, 2 vols.

Mongin, E. (1716) *Oraison funèbre de Louis le Grand.*

Montagu, J. (1968) 'The painted enigma and French seventeenth-century art', *Journal of the Warburg and Courtauld Institutes* 31, 307–35.

Montaiglon, A. de (1875–8 edn) *Procès-verbaux de l'Académie Royale de peinture et Sculpture*, 2 vols.

Montesquieu, C.-L. de (1721) *Lettres persanes.*

Montesquieu, C.-L. de (1973) *Oeuvres.*

Moran, M. (1990) *La imagen del rey: Felipe V y el arte*, Madrid.

Moraw, P. (1962) 'Kaiser und Geschichtschreiber um 1700', *Die Welt als Geschichte* 22, 162–203.

Morgan, B. (1929) *Histoire du* Journal des Savants *depuis 1665 jusqu'en 1701.*

Möseneder, K. (1983) *Zeremoniell und monumentale Poesie: Die 'Entrée Solennelle' Ludwigs XIV. 1660 in Paris*, Berlin.

Naudé, G. (1639) *Considérations politiques sur les coups d'état.*

Néraudau, J. P. (1986) *L'Olympe du roi-soleil.*

Neveu, B. (1988) 'Du culte de Saint Louis à la glorification de Louis XIV: la maison royale de Saint-Cyr', *Journal des Savants*, 277–90.

Nivelon, C. (n.d.) *Vie de Charles le Brun*, ms, BN, fonds français 12, 987.

Nora, P. (ed.) (1984–6) *Les Lieux de mémoire*, 4 vols.

Northleigh, J. (1702) *Topographical Descriptions*, London.

Oresko, R. (1989) 'The *Histoire Métallique* of Louis XIV and the Diplomatic Gift', *Médailles et Antiques* I, 49–55.

Orso, S. N. (1986) *Philip IV and the Decoration of the Alcázar of Madrid*, Princeton, NJ.

Ozouf, M. (1976) *Festivals and the French Revolution*, English trans., Cambridge, MA, 1988.

Pardailhé-Galabrun, A. (1988) *La Naissance de l'intime.*

Pastor, L. von (1940) *History of the Popes*, 32, London.

Pellisson, P. (1735) *Oeuvres diverses.*

Pellisson, P. (1749) *Histoire de Louis XIV.*

Pepys, S. (1970–83) *Diary*, ed. R. Latham and W. Matthews, London.

Perrault, C. (1670a) *Courses de testes et bagues.*

Perrault, C. (1670b) *Festiva ad capita annulumque Decursio.*

Perrault, C. (1686) *Saint Paulin evesque de Nole.*

Perrault, C. (1687) *Le Siècle de Louis le Grand.*

Perrault, C. (1688–97) *Parallèle des anciens et des modernes*, rpr. Munich, 1964.

Perrault, C. (1909) *Mémoires*, ed. P. Bonnefon.

Perrault, C. and I. Bensarade (1679) *Labyrinte de Versailles.*

Perry, J. M. (1968) *The New Politics*, New York.

Petzet, M. (1982) 'Das Triumphbogen-monument für Ludwig XIV auf der Place du trône', *Zeitschrift für Kunstgeschichte* 45 (1982), 145–94.

Pevsner, N. (1961) *The Buildings of England: Northamptonshire*, Harmondsworth.

Picard, R. (1956) *La Carrière de Jean Racine.*

Piles, R. de (1699) *Abrégé de la vie des peintres.*

Pincemaille, C. (1985) 'La guerre de Hollande dans la programme iconographique de Versailles', *Histoire Economie et Société* 4, 313–33.

Pitkin, H. F. (1967) *The Concept of Representation*, Berkeley, CA.

Pocock, G. (1980) *Boileau and the Nature of Neo-classicism*, Cambridge.

Podlach, A. (1984) 'Repräsentation', *Geschichtliche Grundbegriffe* 5, 509–47.

Polleross, F. B. (1986) 'Repräsentation der Habsburger in der bildenden Kunst', in Feuchtmüller and Kovács, 87–103.

Polleross, F. B. (1987) 'Sonnenkönig und Österreichische Sonne', *Wiener Jahrbuch für Kunstgeschichte* 40, 239–56.

Polleross, F. B. (1988) *Das sakrale Identifikationsporträt*, 2 vols, Worms.

Pommier, E. (1986) 'Versailles', in Nora, 1, 193–234.

Posner, D. (1959) 'Lebrun's Triumphs of Alexander', *Art Bulletin* 41, 237–48.

Poussin, N. (1964) *Lettres et propos sur l'art*, ed. A. Blunt.

Pozzi, E. (1990) 'Il corpo del Duce', in *Gli occhi di Alessandro*, ed. S. Bertelli, Florence, 170–83.

Pribram, A. F. (1894) *Franz Paul, Freiherr von Lisola*, Leipzig.

Price, S. (1984) *Rituals and Power*, Cambridge.

Prior, M. (1959) *The Literary Works*, ed. H. B. Wright and M. K. Spears, 2 vols, Oxford.

Quartier, P. (1681) *Constantin ou le triomphe de la religion.*

Quinault, P. (1739) *Théâtre*, 5 vols.

Quiqueran de Beaujeu, H. de (1715) *Oraison funèbre de Louis XIV.*

Racine, J. (1951–2) *Oeuvres complètes*, ed. R. Picard, 2 vols.

Rainssant, P. (1687) *Explication des tableaux de la galerie de Versailles.*

Rance, A.-J. (1886) *L'Académie d'Arles au 17e siècle*, 3 vols.

Ranum, O. (1980) *Artisans of Glory*, Chapel Hill, NC.

Rapin, R. (1677) *Instructions pour l'histoire.*

Raunié, E. (ed.) (1879) *Chansonnier historique du 18e siècle*, 10 vols.

Rave, P. O. (1957) *Das Ladenschild des Kunsthändlers Gersaint*, Stuttgart.

Récit (1685) *de ce qu'est fait à Caen*, Caen.

Reinach, S. (1905) *Cultes, mythes et religions.*

Relation (1660) *was für Ceremonien, Magnificentz . . . bey Vollziehung des königl. Heyraths zwischen Lodovico XIV . . . und Maria Teresia* (no place of publication).

Relations (1687) *de l'erection de la statue à Poitiers*, Poitiers.

Roche, D. (1978) *Le siecle des lumieres en province*, Paris/The Hague.

Römer, P. (1967) *Molières Amphitryon und sein gesellschaftlicher Hintergrund*, Bonn.

Roosen, W. (1980) 'Early modern diplomatic ceremonial: a systems approach', *Journal of Modern History* 52, 452–76.

Rosasco, B. (1989) 'Masquerade and enigma at the court of Louis XIV', *Art Journal* 48, 144–9.

Rosenfield, L. C. (1974) 'Glory and antiglory in France's age of glory', *Renaissance Studies in Honor of I. Silver*, Lexington, MA, 283–307.

Rothkrug, L. (1965) *The Opposition to Louis XIV*, Princeton, NJ.

Rothschild, J. de (ed.) (1881) *Lettres en vers*, 2 vols.

Rotrou, J. (1950) *Cosroès*, ed. J. Scherer, Paris.

Rousset, C. (1865) *Histoire de Louvois*, 2 vols.

Roy, A. (1983) 'Pouvoir municipal et prestige monarchique: les entrées royales', in *Pouvoir ville et société*, ed. G. Livet and B. Vogler, 317–22.

Sabatier, G. (1984) 'Le roi immobile', *Silex* 27–8, 86–101.

Sabatier, G. (1985) 'Versailles, un imaginaire politique', *Culture et idéologie dans la genèse de l'état moderne*, Rome, 295–324.

Sabatier, G. (1988) 'Le parti figuratif dans les appartements, l'escalier et la galerie de Versailles', *17e siècle* 161, 401–26.

Sagnac, P. (1945) *Formation de la société française moderne*, 2 vols.

Sahlins, M. (1985) *Islands of History*, Chicago.

Saint-Maurice, T. F. de (1910) *Lettres sur la cour de Louis XIV 1667–73*, ed. J. Lemoine, 2 vols.

Saint-Simon, L. de (1983–8) *Mémoires*, ed. Y. Coirault, 8 vols.

Schama, S. (1988) 'The domestication of majesty: royal family portraiture 1500–1850', in *Art and History*, ed. R. I. Rotberg and T. K. Rabb, Cambridge, 155–83.

Schieder, W. and C. Dipper (1984) 'Propaganda', *Geschichtliche Grundbegriffe*, Stuttgart, 5, 69–112.

Schmidt, P. (1907) 'Deutsche Publizistik in den Jahren 1667–71', *Mitteilungen des Instituts für Österreichische Geschichtsforschung* 28, 577–630.

Schnapper, A. (1967) *Tableaux pour le Trianon de marbre, 1688–1714.*

Schnapper, A. (1988) 'The king of France as collector in the seventeenth century', in *Art and History*, ed. R. I. Rotberg and T. K. Rabb, Cambridge, 185–202.

Schochet, G. (1975) *Patriarchalism in Political Thought*, Oxford.

Schramm, P. (1939) *Der König von Frankreich*, 2 vols, Weimar.

Schramm, W. (1963) 'Communications research in the United States', in *The Science of Human Communication*, ed. Schramm, New York, 1–15.

Schwartzenberg, A. (1977) *L'État-spectacle.*

Schwoerer, L. G. (1977) 'Propaganda in the revolution of 1688–9', *American Historical Review* 82, 843–74.

Scudéry, M. de (1654–61) *Clélie.*

Scudéry, M. de (1669) *La Promenade de Versailles*, rpr. 1920.

Scudéry, M. de (1671) *Discours de la gloire.*

Sedlmayr, H. (1954) 'Allegorie und Architektur', rpr. in *Politische Architektur in Europa*, ed. M. Warnke, Cologne, 1984, 157–74.

Seux, M.-J. (1967) *Epithètes royales akkadiennes et sumériennes.*

Shils, E. (1975) *Center and Periphery*, Chicago.

Silin, C. I. (1940) *Bensarade and his Ballet de Cour*, Baltimore, MD.

Simson, O. von (1936) *Zur Genealogie der weltliche Apotheose in Barock*, Leipzig.

Sohier, J. (1706) *Gallerie . . . dédiée a la gloire de Louis le Grand*, ms, B.N., fonds français 6997.

Solomon, H. (1972) *Public Welfare, Science and Propaganda in Seventeenth-Century France*, Princeton, NJ.

Sonnino P. (1964) 'The dating and authorship of Louis XIV's memoirs', *French Historical Studies* 3, 303–37.

Sonnino, P. (1973–4) 'Louis XIV's *Mémoire pour l'histoire de la guerre de Hollande*', *French Historical Studies* 8, 29–50.

Soriano, M. (1968) *Les Contes de Perrault*, second edn 1977.

Soriano, M. (1972) *Le Dossier Perrault*.

Souchal, F. (1983) 'Des statues équestres sous le règne de Louis XIV', in *Pouvoir ville et société*, ed. G. Livet and B. Vogler, 309–16.

Southorn, J. (1988) *Power and Display*, Cambridge.

Spanheim, E. (1900) *Relation de la cour de France*, ed. E. Bourgeois.

Speck, W. A. (1972) 'Political propaganda in Augustan England', *Transactions of the Royal Historical Society* 22, 17–32.

Spitzer, L. (1931) 'St-Simon's portrait of Louis XIV', English trans. in his *Essays on Seventeenth-Century French Literature*, ed. D. Bellos, Cambridge, 1983, Chapter 2.

Ssymank, P. (1898) *Ludwig XIV in seinen eigenen Schriften und im Spiegel der zeitverwandten Dichtung*, Leipzig, Diss.

Stankiewicz, W. J. (1960) *Politics and Religion in Seventeenth-Century France*, Berkeley, CA.

Stern, J. P. (1975) *Hitler: the Führer and the People*, London.

Stopfel, W. E. (1964) *Triumphbogen in der Architektur des Barock in Frankreich und Deutschland*, Freiburg, Diss.

Storer, M. E. (1935) 'Information furnished by the *Mercure Galant* on the French Provincial Academies in the Seventeenth Century', *Publications of the Modern Language Society of America* 50, 444–68.

Strong, R. (1984) *Art and Power*, Woodbridge.

Swift, J. (1983) *Complete Poems*, ed. P. Rogers, New Haven, CT and London.

Syme, R. (1939) *The Roman Revolution*, Oxford.

Tambiah, S. J. (1985) 'A reformulation of Geertz's conception of the theatre state', in his *Culture, Thought and Social Action*, Cambridge, MA, 316–38.

Tamse, C. A. (1975) 'The political myth', in J. S. Bromley and E. H. Kossman, *Some Political Mythologies*, The Hague, 1–18.

Taton, R. (1985) 'Espoirs et incertitudes de la science française', in Duchene, 9–17.

Taylor, L. R. (1931) *The Divinity of the Roman Emperor*, Middletown, CT.

Teyssèdre, B. (1957) *Roger de Piles et les débats sur les coloris au siècle de Louis XIV*.

Teyssèdre, B. (1967) *L'Art au siècle de Louis XIV*.

Thireau, J.-L. (1973) *Les Idées politiques de Louis XIV*.

Thomas, K. V. (1971) *Religion and the Decline of Magic*, London.

Thompson, J. (1987) 'Language and ideology', *The Sociological Review* 35, 516–36.

Thuau, E. (1966) *Raison d'état et pensée politique à l'époque de Richelieu*.

Thuillier, J. (1963) *Exposition Lebrun*, catalogue and introduction.

Thuillier, J. (1967) 'The birth of the Beaux-Arts', in *The Academy*, ed. T. B. Hess and J. Ashbery, New York, 29–37.

Thuillier, J. (1983) 'Félibien' *17e siècle* 138, 67–90.

Tovar de Teresa, G. (1988) *Bibliografía novohispana de arte* 2, Mexico City.

Treitinger, O. (1938) *Die Oströmische Kaiser- und Reichsidee*, rpr. Darmstadt, 1956.

Trilling, L. (1972) *Sincerity and Authenticity*, London.

Tronçon, J. (1662) *L'Entrée triomphante de leurs majestés dans la ville de Paris*, rpr. Möseneder (1983), 259–322.

Trout, A. P. (1967–8) 'The proclamation of the peace of Nijmegen', *French Historical Studies* 5, 477–81.

Truchet, J. (1960) *La Prédication de Bossuet*, 2 vols.

Tumarkin, N. (1983) *Lenin Lives! The Lenin Cult in Soviet Russia*, Cambridge, MA.

Tyvaert, M. (1974) 'L'image du Roi', *Revue d'histoire moderne et contemporaine* 21, 521–47.

Valdor, J. (1649) *Les Triomphes de Louis le Juste*.

Vattel, E. de (1758) *La Droit des gens*, rpr. Washington, 1916.

Verlet, P. (1985) *Le Château de Versailles*.

Verney, F. P. and M. M. Verney (eds) (1904) *Memoirs of the Verney Family*, London.

Vert, C. de (1706–13) *Explication simple, littérale et historique des cérémonies de l'Eglise*, 4 vols.

Vertron, C.-G. de (1686) *Le nouveau panthéon*.

Veyne, P. (1988) 'Conduct without belief and works of art without viewers', *Diogenes* 143, 1–22.

Viala, A. (1985) *Naissance de l'écrivain: sociologie de la littérature à l'âge classique*.

Viguerie, J. de (1985) 'Les serments du sacre des rois de France', *Le sacre*, 205–16

Vincent, M. (1979) 'Le *Mercure Galant* et son public féminin', *Romanische Zeitschrift für Literaturgeschichte* 3, 76–85.

Visconti, P. (1988) *Mémoires sur la cour de Louis XIV, 1673–81*, ed. J.-F. Solnon.

Vocelka, K. (1981) *Die politische Propaganda Kaiser Rudolfs II*, Vienna.

Voss, J. (1972) *Das Mittelalter im historischen Denken Frankreichs*, Munich.

Vries, P. de (1947) *Het beeld van Lodewijk XIV in de Franse geschiedschrijving*, Amsterdam.

Walton, G. (1986) *Louis XIV's Versailles*, New York.

Warmington, B. H. (1974) 'Aspects of Constantinian Propaganda', *Transactions of the American Philological Association* 104, 371–84.

Weber, G. (1985) *Brunnen und Wasserkünste in Frankreich im Zeitalter von Louis XIV*, Worms.

Whitman, N. (1969) 'Myth and politics, Versailles and the Fountain of Latona', in J. Rule (ed.), *Louis XIV and the Craft of Kingship*, Ohio, 286–301.

Wittkower, R. (1961) 'Vicissitudes of a dynastic monument', rpr. in his *Studies in the Italian Baroque*, London, 1975, 83–102.

Wolf, J. (1968) *Louis XIV*, second edn, London 1970.

Woodbridge, B. M. (1925) *Gatien de Courtilz*, Baltimore.

Zanker, P. (1987) *The Power of Images in the Age of Augustus*, English trans. Ann Arbor 1988.

Zobermann, P. (1985) 'Généalogie d'une image', *17e siècle* 37, 79–91

Zwiedineck-Südenhorst, H. von (1888) *Die öffentliche Meinung in Deutschland im Zeitalter Ludwigs XIV*, Stuttgart.

INDEX

Note: Plate numbers are italicized.